Why People Obey the Law

Why People Obey the Law

TOM R. TYLER

YALE UNIVERSITY PRESS

New Haven and London

Designed by Sonia L. Scanlon
and set in Bodoni Book type by The Composing Room of
Michigan, Inc.
Printed in the United States of America by BookCrafters,
Inc., Chelsea, Michigan.

Library of Congress Cataloging-in-Publication Data
Tyler, Tom R.   Why people obey the law.
    Includes bibliographical references.
        1. Law—Philosophy—Public opinion.   2. Justice,
    Administration of—Public opinion.   2. Punishment—
Public opinion.   4. Public opinion—Illinois—Chicago.
I. Title.
K250.T95 1990   340'.1   89-16699
ISBN 0-300-04403-8

The paper in this book meets the guidelines for permanence
and durability of the Committee on Production Guidelines
for Book Longevity of the Council on Library Resources.

10   9   8   7   6   5   4   3   2   1

Contents

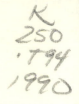

Acknowledgments

Support for the initial collection and analysis of the data discussed in this book was provided by the Law and Social Science Program of the National Science Foundation (SES-8310199). I would like to thank the director of the program, Felice Levine, for her encouragement and support of this project, as well as of all my work on procedural justice. Additional funding was provided by the American Bar Foundation. John Heinz, its former director, arranged for this support and also helped me place the psychological issues in a legal perspective. William Felstiner, the current director of the American Bar Foundation, has continued to support this project both financially and intellectually. Finally, I would like to thank the Center for Urban Affairs and Policy Research for supporting my research, especially its former director Margaret Gordon, and the Survey Research Center of Northwestern University for collecting the data used in this book. I have received very helpful comments on the manuscript from Susie Allen, Jeanne Ferris, Lee Hamilton, Reid Hastie, Larry Heuer, Herbert Jacob, Fred Kameny, E. Allan Lind, Jane Mansbridge, Robert Nelson, Sharon Peelor, Susan Scott, Neil Vidmar, and Ellen Wright. I would especially like to thank Jane Mansbridge for her encouragement and support at several key points in my writing.

PART ONE

Introduction

CHAPTER 1

Procedural Justice, Legitimacy, and Compliance

Americans are typically law-abiding people. Compliance is never complete, however. Everyone breaks the law sometimes, and some people break it often. In recent years, for example, many people have refused to pay their taxes, used illegal drugs, engaged in illegal sexual practices, and driven when drunk. This book explores the everyday behavior of citizens toward the law and examines why people obey or disobey it.

Legal authorities know that the key to their effectiveness is their ability to make laws and decisions that will be followed by the public, so they try to act in ways that will promote public compliance with the law. On the other hand, social critics opposed to existing authority may try to promote noncompliance. An understanding of why people obey or disobey the law is therefore of interest to both legal authorities and their critics.

The first goal of this book is to contrast the instrumental and normative perspectives on why people follow the law. The instrumental perspective on the citizen underlies what is known as the deterrence literature: people are viewed as shaping their behavior to respond to changes in the tangible, immediate incentives and penalties associated with following the law—to judgments about the personal gains and losses resulting from different kinds of behavior. For example, increasing the severity and certainty of punishment for committing a crime has frequently been viewed as an effective way of reducing the rate at which the crime is committed. When policymakers think about how to obtain compliance, they often adopt implicitly an instrumental perspective.

Although the instrumental perspective has dominated recent examinations of citizens' reactions to the law and legal authorities, this study explores compliance from a normative perspective. It is concerned with the influence of what people regard as just and moral as opposed to what is in their self-interest. It also examines the connection between normative commitment to legal authorities and law-abiding behavior.

If people view compliance with the law as appropriate because of their attitudes about how they should behave, they will voluntarily assume the obligation to follow legal rules. They will feel personally committed to obeying the law, irrespective of whether they risk punishment for breaking the law. This normative commitment can involve personal morality or legitimacy. Normative commitment through personal morality means obeying a law because one feels the law is just; normative commitment through legitimacy means obeying a law because one feels that the authority enforcing the law has the right to dictate behavior.

According to a normative perspective, people who respond to the moral appropriateness of different laws may (for example) use drugs or engage in illegal sexual practices, feeling that these crimes are not immoral, but at the same time will refrain from stealing. Similarly, if they regard legal authorities as more legitimate, they are less likely to break any laws, for they will believe that they ought to follow all of them, regardless of the potential for punishment. On the other hand, people who make instrumental decisions about complying with various laws will have their degree of compliance dictated by their estimate of the likelihood that they will be punished if they do not comply. They may exceed the speed limit, thinking that the likelihood of being caught for speeding is low, but not rob a bank, thinking that the likelihood of being caught is higher.

From the perspective of the authorities, voluntary compliance with the law has a number of advantages. If police officers and judges need to compel the public to obey by threatening or using force, they are required to expend enormous amounts of resources. Voluntary compliance costs much less and is, as a result, especially highly valued by legal authorities.

A normative perspective leads to a focus on people's internalized norms of justice and obligation. It suggests the need to explore what citizens think and to understand their values. By contrast, an instrumental perspective regards compliance as a form of behavior occurring in response to external factors. It leads to a focus on the extent and nature of the resources that authorities have for shaping public behavior.

Although both morality and legitimacy are normative, they are not identical. Leaders are especially interested in having legitimacy in the eyes of their followers, because legitimacy most effectively provides them with discretionary authority that they can use in governing. Morality can lead to compliance with laws, but it can also work against it. For example, during the war in Vietnam those who believed in the legitimacy of the government fought in the war regardless of their personal feelings about its wisdom. For others the perceived immorality of the war was a factor leading them to oppose and violate the law. With drunk driving, on the other hand, legitimacy and morality typically work together to prevent illegal behavior.

In this book I examine the extent to which normative factors influence compliance with the law independently of deterrence judgments. Data collected in a longitudinal study of randomly selected citizens in Chicago are used to examine the role of normative factors. In the first wave of the study 1,575 citizens were interviewed about their normative and instrumental views concerning the law, as well as their behavior toward the law. A subset of 804 respondents were reinterviewed about the same topics one year later (this procedure is the basic characteristic of a panel study).

The Evaluation of Personal Experience

The second goal of this book is to explore how people react to their personal experiences with legal authorities. Of particular importance is the impact of these experiences on views of the legitimacy of legal authorities, because legitimacy in the eyes of the public is a key precondition to the effectiveness of authorities. Changes in legitimacy will affect the degree to which people comply with laws in their everyday lives.

I focus in this book on the judgments people make about their personal experience; I identify those aspects of experience that people consider important and I examine the influence of these aspects on their reactions to the experience as a whole. For example, do people distinguish between procedures (how decisions are made) and outcomes (what the decisions are)? Do they distinguish between winning and being fairly treated? To the extent that they do, which of these judgments influences their reactions to their experience?

As before, I contrast a normative perspective with an instrumental one. According to a normative perspective, people will be concerned with whether they receive fair outcomes, arrived at through a fair procedure, rather than with the favorability of the outcomes. A normative perspective is supported to the extent that people want justice from police officers and judges, and evaluate those authorities according to whether they get it. If people have such a normative perspective, police officers and judges can maintain their authority by acting in ways that will be viewed as fair.

The recent literature on citizens' dealings with legal authorities has been dominated by the view that citizens are concerned with winning—that is, with receiving favorable outcomes when dealing with police officers and judges. An alternative, normative perspective is represented by psychological theories of justice, which hold that people care about the justice of outcomes (distributive justice) and of the procedures by which they are arrived at (procedural justice). These justice concerns are seen as acting independently of the influence of an outcome's favorability.

Imagine a person going to traffic court after getting a traffic citation. An instrumental perspective suggests that the person's reaction to the experience is based on the favorability of the outcome: if the ticket is dismissed, the person will feel positive about the experience; if the person receives a fine or is required to attend traffic school, the reaction will be more negative. Theories of distributive justice suggest that people would like things to come out fairly—that they would like to receive the level of punishment they feel they deserve. Finally, theories of procedural justice suggest that people focus on court procedures, not on the outcomes of their experiences. If the judge treats them fairly by listening to their arguments and considering them, by being neutral, and by stating good reasons for his or her decision, people will react positively to their experience, whether or not they receive a favorable outcome.

In both waves of the Chicago study respondents who had had a recent experience with police officers or judges were asked about it, and their responses were used to identify the normative and instrumental aspects of their experience. The first wave of the study identified 652 respondents who had recently had personal experiences with legal authorities, whereas 291 of the panel respondents had experiences with legal authorities during the year between the two interviews.

It may appear to stretch the definition of the term *normative* to have it refer on the one hand to justice-based reactions to experience and on the other to issues of the legitimacy of legal authorities and the immorality of law breaking. What unites the two uses is that in both cases the reactions of people are determined by their attitudes about what is ethically appropriate, rather than by their assessments of costs and benefits.

The two normative questions raised here—whether legitimacy affects compliance, and whether judgments about the justice or injustice of experiences influence their impact—are not independent of each other. The effect of people's ethical attitudes on their behavior would be especially striking if there were a two-stage process, with people's judgments about the justice or injustice of their experience affecting their views about the legitimacy of the authorities, and these views in turn shaping compliance with the law. This two-stage model will also be explored in this book.

The Meaning of Procedural Justice

The final goal of this book is to explore the meaning of procedural justice by contrasting the normative and instrumental approaches. The instrumental view of procedural justice contained in the control theory of Thibaut and Walker (1975, 1978) suggests that people do not focus directly on the favorability of the outcomes they receive from third parties. Instead, they focus on the degree to which they are able to exert influence over third-party decisions. People recognize that to the extent they have it, control over decisions leads to favorable outcomes. This control therefore represents indirect control over the favorability of outcomes. Thibaut and Walker suggest that people react to their experiences in terms of the favorability of outcomes, which is the key characteristic of an instrumental model (Tyler 1986b).

The instrumental perspective on procedure suggests that assessments of procedural fairness are based on the favorability of the outcomes received: where people feel that they have control over decisions they believe that the procedure is fair; where they feel they lack control they believe it is unfair.[1] If judgments about procedural fairness do simply reflect the favorability of outcomes, then aspects of procedure not linked to outcomes will contribute little to an understanding of whether people feel fairly treated, beyond what would already be learned by knowing the degree to which they control decisions.[2]

The normative perspective on procedural justice views people as being concerned with aspects of their experience not linked only to outcomes. Normative aspects of experience include neutrality, lack of bias, honesty, efforts to be fair, politeness, and respect for citizens' rights. All these potential features of a procedure are conceptually distinct from its outcome and therefore represent values that may be used to define procedural fairness in terms not related to outcome. The extent to which people define the fairness of a procedure by using aspects of the procedure that are related and unrelated to its outcome reflects the influence of instrumental and normative aspects of experience on their judgments of whether they have received a fair procedure.

The meaning of procedural justice is examined in the same interviews about recent personal experience that are used to explore the impact of experience on legitimacy. Those interviewed were asked a series of questions about different aspects of their experience. These aspects of experience corresponded to elements of procedural justice related and unrelated to outcome.

CHAPTER 2

Design of the Chicago Study

This book draws on the results of a study of the experiences, attitudes, and behavior of a random sample of citizens in Chicago. In spring 1984 interviews were held by telephone with 1,575 respondents for about twenty-five minutes each. A randomly selected subset of 804 respondents was reinterviewed one year later. The data are analyzed in two ways. Cross-sectional analysis looks at the relationship between attitudes and behavior measured at one point in time. Panel analysis uses the data collected at both points in time to examine the relationship between changes in attitudes and changes in behavior. Cross-sectional analyses were conducted using all 1,575 respondents; longitudinal analyses were conducted using the 804 people interviewed twice.

Sociologists have made most of the major recent efforts to understand the attitudinal antecedents of compliance with the law (see for example Eiser 1976; Grasmick and Green 1980; Jacob 1980; Meier and Johnson 1977; Paternoster et al. 1984; Schwartz and Orleans 1967; Silberman 1976). Their research has examined the role of three factors in shaping compliance: the threat of sanctions, the opinions of peers, and personal morality.

In addition to these recent efforts by sociologists, there is a long history of concern among political psychologists about the role of political factors in shaping obedience to the law. Their efforts explore the interactions of citizens' evaluations of the performance of legal authorities, their assessments of the legitimacy of the law and legal authorities, and their compliance with the law. Studies in this area have viewed legitimacy in two different ways: as a perceived obligation to obey the law, and as support or allegiance to political and legal authorities.

In this analysis I use the sociological approach to compliance as a framework for exploring the influence of legitimacy on compliance: the approach of political psychologists is integrated into the sociological framework. Within the context of this combined approach I examine which factors have an independent influence on compliant behavior. In addition, I compare the relative strengths of different influences.

Legal authorities with whom citizens have contact include the police and the courts. Rather than focus on trials, I consider the natural range of citizens' contacts with legal authorities. Although trials are a highly visible legal institution in our society that matter a great deal to those involved in them, few citizens ever are. Most contacts with legal authorities are more informal. For example, a person may call the police for help with a problem or be stopped by the police for a traffic violation.

Although the study was designed to be inclusive, not all self-reported contacts are used in the analysis. Two criteria were used to define suitable personal experiences: (1) the individual must have had direct, personal contact with the authorities; and (2) the individual must have had a personal stake in the situation. The first criterion excluded citizens who called the police but did not know what happened in response to their call.[1] Based on the second criterion, being a witness or juror was not considered a personal experience. Although such experiences were personal they did not involve a personal stake in the outcome.

Analysis

Two approaches may be used to measure the effects of experience: (1) studying a random sample of the general population, identified through some random selection process; or (2) studying people identified as having had experiences with the police or courts, by using court and police records or interviews in police stations, courtrooms, and prisons. In one study that used the first approach (Tyler, Rasinski, and McGraw 1985), a random sample of citizens was telephoned and interviewed about the fairness of government policies. An example of the latter approach is a study in which litigants were approached as they left misdemeanor court and interviewed in person about their experience (Tyler 1984).

This study used random sampling, for several reasons. Most important, the goal of this research is to investigate the broad range of experiences that people have with legal authorities. The most effective approach is to use a random sample of people, who have presumably had a wide range of experiences, rather than to select subjects from a few segments of the population.[2] Choosing subjects from police and court records also has the problem of ignoring contacts that may be important to citizens but may not appear in formal records. Random sampling increases the possibility of including all contacts among police, courts, and citizens. Finally, random sampling allows a clear separation of the survey from government agencies. Although respondents can always be promised anonymity, this promise is more likely to be believed if there is a clear separation between the authorities and the researcher.

Contact with authorities at two levels might potentially be studied. Earlier research on citizen contact with government authorities has considered agencies of both the local and national governments. This study is concerned with the police and courts and as a result focuses on local government.

Many legal problems or disputes are resolved through informal mechanisms (Best and Andreasen 1977; Felstiner, Abel, and Sarat 1980–81; Ladinsky and Susmilch 1982) or consultation with lawyers (Curran 1977). Thus the Chicago study does not deal with the full range of social mechanisms through which people solve their problems or disputes: it examines only contact with formal legal authorities, such as the police and courts.

The design of the Chicago study presumes that mundane, everyday experiences with the police and courts influence citizens. There is considerable evidence that they do (Bayley and Mendelsohn 1969; Jacob 1971; Sarat 1977; Tyler 1984; Tyler and Folger 1980; Walker et al. 1972). In addition, a similar effect has been found in ordinary encounters between citizens and federal agencies (Katz et al. 1975). It therefore seems likely that the experiences studied will influence attitudes.

The focus on experiences also presumes that respondents have the ability to recall their past experiences accurately. The studies cited above suggest that respondents do recall at least some of their experiences; others are forgotten. The key issue is whether there are biases associated with recall—that is, whether certain types of experience are more likely than others to be forgotten. This question has been extensively studied by the Department of Justice in connection with the National Crime Surveys. Several studies suggest that within one year after a crime has been committed forgetting is essentially random (it is unrelated to the characteristics of victim or incident; see Gottfredson and Hindelang 1977; Lehnen and Skogan 1981; Schneider 1977).

In addition to the question of whether people recall an incident is that of whether the accuracy of recall changes as time passes. Gutek (1978) examined this issue by using the data of another study (Katz et al. 1975) on encounters with the federal bureaucracy and found that recall did not become substantially less accurate over time, at least not within one year.

These results suggest that respondents' reports of incidents are not systematically biased. All incidents may not be recalled, but reported incidents will reflect the population of total incidents. Further, if an incident is recalled, the memory of the incident will not substantially differ according to the time elapsed since it occurred.

There are two reasons for reinterviewing members of the initial group of respondents. First, doing so strengthens the researcher's inferences about what factors influenced compliance with the law. For example, respondents in the Chicago study were asked how often they broke the law during the year preceding the first interview: the attitudes they expressed during the interview were used in cross-sectional analyses to deduce their behavior during the one year preceding the interview. In a follow-up interview the attitudes expressed at one point in time (the first interview) were used to predict what behavior had occurred by a second point in time (the second interview).

The second advantage of the panel design is that it enables the researcher to study experiential effects. For example, citizens judge the fairness of the procedures to which they are subject and of the outcome they receive. It must be shown that these judgments reflect the nature of citizens' actual experiences and not their prior views about the agency involved. In other words, it is important to show that all actions taken by the police are not viewed as fair by those who have positive attitudes about the police to begin with. By using panel data it is possible to examine experiences while controlling for prior expectations and evaluations.

Using a panel design raises the potential problem of losing respondents. Ideally every respondent from the first wave of interviews could be reinterviewed one year later. But some respondents cannot be found one year later, or will not agree to be reinterviewed. The key concern is the possibility that those who were not available for second interviews had attitudes or experiences different from those of the people who were available.

Previous research suggests that victims do move more than nonvictims (Reiss 1978), delinquents more than nondelinquents (Polk and Ruby 1978), and young people more than old people (Lansing, Withey, and Wolfe 1971). The Chicago study sought to lessen this problem by tracking respondents who had moved. Fortunately, it is possible to measure any biases due to the inability to reinterview respondents by comparing the panel respondents with the larger group of respondents interviewed during the first wave of interviews.

A list of all operating telephone prefixes in Chicago was used to select respondents. It was based on a list used earlier in the Reactions to Crime Project of the Center for Urban Affairs and Policy Research at Northwestern University (Skogan 1978). A computer program was then used to generate telephone numbers randomly by matching a working telephone prefix with four randomly chosen digits. Once a home was reached, standard procedures were used to select a respondent randomly within the home (according to the modification in Bryant 1975 of the approach used in Troldahl and Carter 1964).[3] The Survey Research Center at Northwestern University conducted interviews lasting twenty to twenty-five minutes (in English or Spanish, depending on the language of the person interviewed). The overall response rate for the first wave of interviews was 63 percent.[4]

The use of telephone interviews raises two potential problems. First, a less random sample of residents may be located by telephone than in person. Second, respondents may be less willing to discuss over the telephone their experiences

with the police and courts. Several studies have compared interviews by telephone with personal interviews and found that they yield similar types of samples
(Groves and Kahn 1979; Tuchfarber and Klecka 1976). Research has also found
that respondents will discuss sensitive material over the telephone (see Quinn,
Gutek, and Walsh 1980 for a review of twenty-three studies). In addition, evidence suggests that accuracy is not lower in the reporting over the telephone of
sensitive behavior (Rogers 1976), and may even be increased by the heightened
sense of social distance in telephone surveys (Colombotos 1965; Groves, Miller,
and Cannell 1981).

The Questionnaire in the First Wave

Those interviewed were asked about their views of the police and
courts in Chicago and about their level of behavioral compliance with the law.
Each respondent was also asked whether he or she had had any personal experience with the police or courts during the twelve months preceding the interview.
In the first wave 47 percent of those interviewed (n = 733) said they had had at
least one such experience. Respondents who had had more than one experience
with legal authorities (n = 311) were asked which was the "most important," and
they were questioned about that experience.[5] The resulting interviews included
384 situations involving calls to the police (52 percent); 202 of being stopped by
the police (28 percent); and 147 of going to court (20 percent).

Of those 733 respondents with prior experience with the police or courts, the
experiences of 81 respondents were considered too superficial for detailed analysis. Those experiences all involved calls to the police. For example, on some
occasions citizens called the police to report a traffic accident or suspicious
activity in the neighborhood, and had no knowledge of the consequences of their
call. On other occasions they called the police and were told to call another
agency to handle their problem. These respondents were treated as if they had
had no personal experience with the police, resulting in an actual sample size of
652 (89 percent of those with any kind of experience). Of this final group of
respondents 47 percent had called the police for help, 31 percent had been
stopped by the police, and 23 percent had been to court.[6]

At the conclusion of the first wave of interviews respondents were asked to
provide personal identifying information (their name, nickname, or initials), so
that they could be identified when called for the second wave of interviews; 76
percent of respondents agreed to do so. For the call-sheets used during the second
wave of interviews, this information was combined with demographic informa-

tion, such as age, sex, education, and position in the household (for example, youngest woman). During the second wave of interviews this information was used to identify the correct respondent.

All respondents randomly chosen for the panel were called again, whether or not they had given their names. If the interviewer had no name for the respondent, he or she used the demographic information to identify the correct respondent, and in any case verified that it was the correct respondent by asking the respondent if he or she had been interviewed before.

In the first wave 43 percent of the sample was male, 52 percent was white, and 77 percent had at least a high school education. The mean age of the sample was forty-two. Annual income was below fifteen thousand dollars for 44 percent of the respondents, below thirty thousand dollars for 78 percent. When asked to describe their politics 29 percent called themselves liberal, 28 percent called themselves conservative, and 42 percent called themselves moderate. As would be expected of a random sample of the residents of Chicago, the sample contains many nonwhite respondents, as well as a large group of poorer ones.[7]

The Second Wave

Of those panel respondents who were reached again, complete reinterviews were obtained from 60 percent.[8] Within the second wave's sample, 329 respondents (41 percent) indicated having had experience with the police or courts during the year following the first interview. As before, those respondents with several experiences (n = 120, or 36 percent of those with any experience) were interviewed about their "most important" experience. Of respondents with experience, 192 (58 percent) had called the police, 64 (19 percent) had been stopped by the police, and 73 (22 percent) had gone to court.

As in the first wave's sample, some respondents had had superficial experiences with the police and courts and were excluded from the analysis. The criteria of exclusion used in the first wave were also used in the second. The remaining sample included 291 respondents with experience, of whom 53 percent had called the police, 22 percent had been stopped by the police, and 25 percent had gone to court.

In the second wave 45 percent of the sample was male, 60 percent was white, and 79 percent had at least a high school education. The mean age of the sample was forty-three. Annual income was below fifteen thousand dollars for 35 percent of the respondents, and below thirty thousand dollars for 74 percent. As for political leanings, 29 percent described themselves as liberal, 30 percent as conservative, and 41 percent as moderate. Those in the panel were more likely to be white and to have high incomes, because less mobile respondents were more likely to be reached after one year had passed.[9]

It is also possible to identify differences between the samples of the two waves by correlating characteristics of respondents in the first wave with their presence or absence in the sample of the second wave. If the subset of respondents interviewed the second time is a true random sample of the larger population in the first wave of interviews, such correlations should be zero. Correlational analysis confirms that the second wave's sample was more likely to be white, well educated, and of a higher income than the first wave's sample.[10] With each of these three demographic characteristics—race, education, and income—there is a significant nonzero correlation with the likelihood of being reinterviewed. In no case, however, is the relationship very strong.

Another way to compare the two waves' respondents is by examining whether the attitudinal variables dealt with in this study (legitimacy, evaluation, and so on) predicted a second interview. If respondents more favorably disposed toward the law were more likely to be reinterviewed, this could introduce bias into the results of the study. But an examination reveals no significant relationship between the likelihood of being reinterviewed and judgments of one's obligation to obey the law, support for the police and courts, the likelihood of seeking help from legal authorities, any of the sociological factors predicting compliance, or evaluations of how well legal authorities performed. In addition, there is no relationship between self-reported compliance with the law and the likelihood of being reinterviewed.

The most striking difference between the two samples is the lower proportion of respondents in the second who reported having had experience with the police or courts (41 percent as opposed to 47 percent). There are several possible explanations for this finding. One is that the first wave of interviews involved some telescoping (respondents included, incorrectly, experiences that occurred more than a year before). Such telescoping is less likely to have occurred during the second interview, because respondents had the first interview as a reference point.

One can test for telescoping by seeing whether respondents reported a larger number of experiences as having occurred late in the year preceding the first interview. If respondents included many experiences that occurred thirteen to twenty-four months before the interview in their reports of experiences occurring "in the year prior to the interview," this should be reflected in a large number of experiences reported as having occurred ten to twelve months before the interview. No such effect is observed: 24 percent of respondents reported that their experience occurred one to three months before the interview, 23 percent said four to six months before, 28 percent said seven to nine months before, and 25 percent said nine to twelve months before.

A second possibility is that the second wave of interviews was more likely to find less mobile respondents (who tend to be wealthier, white, and upper-class), and that these respondents were less likely to be involved with the police. The demographic analysis of panel respondents discussed above suggests that less mobile respondents were more likely to be reinterviewed. They are also less likely to deal with the police and courts. There is also a greater proportion of calls to the police among respondents from the second wave (58 percent as opposed to 52 percent). The panel respondents were more likely to have had contact with the police because they initiated the contact by calling them. This is also consistent with the observation that panel respondents are more likely to be white and to have high incomes.

The data examined offer evidence of some bias connected with the second interviews. It is however clear that this bias was unrelated to the attitudes addressed in this study. For example, it is not respondents who support the police and courts who are willing to be reinterviewed. Difficulties in finding and reinterviewing respondents were essentially unrelated to their views about the police, the courts, and the law. Instead these difficulties were related to the nature of the respondents' life-styles. Although an examination of the data collected reveals some biases, the biases are small and do not influence the key variables in this study. The assumptions made in designing the Chicago study are essentially supported by the data, and the study consequently provides data of a high quality for addressing the issues at hand.

PART TWO

Legitimacy and Compliance

CHAPTER 3

Legitimacy as a Theoretical Issue

Judges, lawyers, legal scholars, and social scientists interested in the exercise of legal authority all know how important it is to secure public compliance with the law and with the decisions of legal authorities like police officers and judges. To be authoritative, legal rules and decisions must affect the actions of those toward whom they are directed. A judge's ruling means little if the parties to the dispute feel they can ignore it. Similarly, passing a law prohibiting some behavior is not useful if it does not affect how often the behavior occurs. To be able to act as an authority, "The lawgiver must be able to anticipate that the citizenry as a whole will . . . generally observe the body of rules he has promulgated" (Fuller 1971, 201),[1] because "the ability to exert influence is the major operational quality of authority" (Hollander 1978, 45). Effective leadership requires compliance with the leaders' decisions from "the bulk of the members [of society] . . . most of the time" (Easton 1975, 185).

Because they are interested in securing compliance with the law, legal authorities want to establish and maintain conditions that lead the public generally to accept their decisions and policies. This is not easy. Anecdotal evidence suggests many types of behavior that police officers and judges have been unable to stop, ranging from tax evasion to drunk driving and drug abuse. On the national level, when Supreme Court justices make controversial decisions about school prayer or desegregation, they cannot take public compliance for granted (Dolbeare and Hammond 1970).[2]

This book is not about noncompliance with particular controversial laws or decisions. It examines the general level of noncompliance with everyday laws regulating behavior. Its concern is with the degree to which people generally follow the law in their daily lives. Why is securing compliance difficult? The nature of the behavior for which compliance is needed makes compliance with legal decisions problematic. Laws are passed and enforced to mandate behavior that people would prefer to avoid, such as paying damages to an injured party, or to discourage people from doing certain things that might benefit them, such as stealing.

Although securing compliance with legal restrictions is difficult, it is important. It is often argued that a society cannot function effectively unless citizens' desires are curbed to some extent (Cohen 1966; Gamson 1968). It is a basic tenet

19

of political theory that any society restricts some behavior and fails to provide its citizens with some things they want and feel they deserve (Gamson 1968). For this reason societies develop the governmental and legal institutions needed to formulate rules of acceptable conduct. They also organize and support the legal authorities needed to interpret and enforce these rules. Effective societal functioning requires that citizens obey the decisions of the legal authorities.[3]

Recent research on solutions to social dilemmas provides an example of the positive value of regulatory authorities. In a social dilemma a society must prevent citizens from engaging in actions that are individually beneficial in the short term but that hurt society in the long term. Studies suggest that one solution that groups voluntarily adopt when faced with social dilemmas is to designate formal leaders who are empowered to control the behavior of the group's members (Messick et al. 1983; Samuelson et al. 1984). Similarly, groups develop rules governing members' conduct to preserve valuable social relationships (Thibaut and Faucheux 1965). These informal rules are the precursors of formalized law (Fuller 1971).[4]

It is also important to recognize the potential dangers of giving authorities the power to affect public behavior. Authorities may use that power to advance their own interest, or the interest of a particular group or individual, over the interest of others. It cannot be assumed that authorities will be benevolently motivated and will use their power and legitimacy to promote the positive objectives outlined above. Although they can facilitate the productive exchange of resources to the benefit of all members of society, it is not inherent in the nature of authority that it will function in this way. The effects of authority depend on the motives of those exercising it.

Legal authorities are among the most visible agents functioning to restrict citizens. For example, a major role of the police is to enforce rules that restrict citizens' behavior, often through the use of negative sanctions. The civil and criminal courts also function in this manner. In addition, civil courts must settle disputes arising between citizens through misunderstandings or incompatible desires and goals. In each case, legal authorities must often deliver negative outcomes to parties that the parties may feel are not fair.

Given the importance attached by the legal system to securing citizens' compliance with the law, it is not surprising that social scientists interested in the law should have tried to understand why people comply. Answering this question involves exploring the psychological nature of the citizen—that is, understanding the factors that motivate the citizen's behavior.

Much traditional social theory is built on the assumption that behavior is motivated by rewards and punishments in the external environment. This instrumental perspective is often referred to as the study of social control (Krislov et al.

1972; Wood 1974). It assumes that the nature of the immediate environment influences people's actions (Fishbein and Ajzen 1975; Friedman 1975; Muller 1979; Wrong 1980).

Social control refers specifically to altering citizens' behavior by manipulating access to valued social resources or by delivering or threatening to deliver sanctions. Such social control has been viewed as achieving influence by "changing the nature of the situation" (Parsons 1963, 1967), and as effecting change by securing compliance (Kelman 1958). In either case, legal authorities attempt to modify behavior by rewarding compliance with the rules and punishing or threatening to punish the violation of rules.

Recently the social control approach to compliance has received strong impetus from the emergence of the public choice perspective in policy studies. The public choice perspective represents the extension into the legal arena of economic models of the person. It assumes that the behavior of people in relation to the law is governed by the same types of instrumental judgments that shape behavior in relation to decisions in their private lives.[5]

Like models of social control a public choice perspective suggests that people are intrinsically motivated to maximize their personal gain in their behavior toward the law. Public choice theory has been refined, however, by more complex approaches to modeling judgments of gain and loss, and to combining such judgments with personal utilities recently developed in the field of economics (Laver 1981; Mueller 1979; Tyler 1986b).[6]

The social control and public choice perspectives have led those concerned with securing compliance with the law to focus on the ability of authorities to influence the personal costs of rule breaking. This focus has brought about a large literature on deterrence (Blumstein, Cohen, and Nagin 1978; Gibbs 1975; Tittle 1980; Zimring and Hawkins 1973), which has established that variations in deterrence (primarily variations in the likelihood of punishment) do affect citizens' compliance with the law.[7]

If rewards and punishments alone produced sufficient compliance for society to function effectively, the authorities would find their task simple and straightforward. They would need only to control societal resources and could focus their attention on how best to deploy them. Such a deterrence-based strategy for securing public compliance is very appealing to political and legal authorities. Social control requires very little effort to communicate with the public or be responsive to it; it focuses on the rewards and punishments associated with obeying and disobeying the law, and allows the authorities to control their own agenda. In contrast, a normative focus on compliance emphasizes the voluntary aspects of compliance, placing a considerable power over the effectiveness of authorities in the hands of those they lead. Of course, in both models people are ultimately the key to successful leadership: it is they who decide whether or not to comply.[8]

The dominance of the social control and public choice perspectives can be seen in the selection of issues considered important enough to study, and in the way these issues are examined. In studying general compliance with the law, attention has been directed to instances where compliance cannot be easily explained using a simple deterrence perspective. Citizens have been found to obey the law when the probability of punishment for noncompliance is almost nil and to break laws in cases involving substantial risks. Neither form of behavior makes sense from a strictly instrumental perspective. An example of an effort to examine such an issue is that of Ross (1981) to explain why publicity campaigns against drunk driving decrease law breaking, even though they have little or no influence on the likelihood that a person will be punished.

In the public policy arena the economic perspective has directed study toward behavior that appears paradoxical or problematic when viewed from an economic perspective (Tyler 1986b). One such area is the problem of noncompliance with laws that place on citizens such burdens as taxes. The probability of being severely punished for avoiding taxes is low, making equally low the negative utility to inhibit nonreporting of income. From an instrumental perspective people should frequently avoid paying their taxes. In reality, the rate of nonreporting of income is relatively low.[9] This has been called the "free rider" problem, and it appears particularly likely to be a serious social problem if citizens are viewed as motivated solely by personal gain (Barry and Hardin 1982).

In addition to shaping the issues considered important enough to study, public choice perspectives have shaped the way these issues are thought about. People have been viewed as seeking favorable outcomes from the legal and political system and behaving toward it in a manner designed to obtain such outcomes. This perspective suggests that people will break rules when they feel that the likelihood that they will gain from doing so outweighs the potential costs of being caught and punished.

Normative Issues and Compliance

Although the idea of exercising authority through social control is attractively simple, it has been widely suggested that in democratic societies the legal system cannot function if it can influence people only by manipulating rewards and costs (Easton 1965, 1968, 1975; Engstrom and Giles 1972; Gamson 1968; Kelman 1969; Parsons 1963, 1967; Sarat 1977; Scheingold 1974). This type of leadership is impractical because government is obliged to produce benefits or exercise coercion every time it seeks to influence citizens' behavior. These strategies consume large amounts of public resources and such societies would be "in constant peril of disequilibrium and instability" (Saphire 1978, 189).[10]

The problem of the drunk driver (Ross 1981) illustrates the difficulties of altering public behavior through incentives and the threat of punishment. Policymakers concerned with combating the problem have used various strategies of deterrence. Ross examines these and shows that an extremely high investment of societal resources is needed to have any noticeable effect on citizens' assessments of their likelihood of being caught and punished for driving while drunk.

Ross finds that massive public campaigns have been successful in the past in temporarily decreasing the rate of drunk driving. He however suggests that such effects occur because the high visibility of public education campaigns leads citizens to overestimate the actual probability of being caught and punished. As the massive publicity declines and citizens' experiences lead them to estimate their risks more accurately, the rate of law breaking increases.

Ross's treatment of drunk driving illustrates the practical difficulties of implementing a policy based only on the increased use of threatened or delivered punishment. This is especially true in democratic societies, which minimize governmental intrusiveness into people's lives. For example, the public has resisted the random stopping of motorists at roadblocks to detect drunk drivers. Although control through reward and punishment may be theoretically possible, the government cannot afford to undertake many such expensive efforts to shape how citizens behave.

Given that the regulation of behavior through social control is inefficient and may not be effective enough to allow a complex democratic society to survive, it is encouraging that social theorists have recognized other potential bases for securing public compliance with the law. Two such bases are commonly noted: social relations (friends, family, and peers) and normative values. Concerns about social relations reflect the influence of other people's judgments; normative values reflects a person's own ethical views.

These two influences on behavior have been widely recognized by social scientists. They have emerged in studies by social psychologists on attitudes (Ajzen and Fishbein 1980; Fishbein and Ajzen 1975) and on the changing of attitudes (Kelman 1958), by sociologists on power (Wrong 1980), by political scientists on discontent (Muller 1979), and by psychologists on moral development (Hoffman 1977).

Influence by the social group can be instrumental. Like authorities, social groups reward and punish their members (Wrong 1980), either by withholding or conferring signs of group status and respect, or more directly by channeling material resources toward or away from particular members. Such variations in rewards and costs are not under the control of public authorities, but they function in the same manner as do public incentives and disincentives. In focusing on peer group pressures, the deterrence literature has recently documented that law breaking is strongly related to people's judgments about the sanctions or rewards their behavior elicits from members of their social group. People are reluctant to commit criminal acts for which their family and friends would sanction them.

Group influence may also exert normative pressure on people, because individuals look to their social groups for information about appropriate conduct. Such normative influences are similar to the influence of personal morality (see below). People's behavior is strongly affected by the normative climate created by others.

The final influence on social behavior is the person's own set of normative values—the sense of what is right or appropriate. Normative influences respond to factors different from those affected by considerations of reward and punishment. People focus not on personal gain or loss within a given situation but on the relationship between various kinds of potential behavior and their assessments of what behavior is appropriate.

The key feature of normative factors that differentiates them from considerations of reward and punishment is that the citizen voluntarily complies with rules rather than respond to the external situation. Because of this, normative influences are often referred to by psychologists as "internalized obligations," that is, obligations for which the citizen has taken personal responsibility. This sense of the internalized quality of moral norms is captured by Hoffman: "The legacy of both Sigmund Freud and Emile Durkheim is the agreement among social scientists that most people do not go through life viewing society's moral norms as external, coercively imposed pressures to which they must submit. Though the norms are initially external to the individual and often in conflict with his desires, the norms eventually become part of his internal motive system and guide his behavior even in the absence of external authority" (1977, 85).

Voluntary compliance is of course important only to the extent that compliant behavior is different from behavior derived from self-interest. Moral influences would be substantially less important if people typically viewed the behavior that most benefited them as normatively appropriate. The suggestion that citizens will voluntarily act against their self-interest is the key to the social value of normative influences. Given this assumption, leaders can gain voluntary compliance with their actions if the actions are consistent with people's views about right and wrong, even if not personally beneficial.

If the effectiveness of legal authorities ultimately depends on voluntary acceptance of their actions, then authorities are placed in the position of balancing public support against the effective regulation of public behavior. Legal authorities of course recognize their partial dependence on public goodwill, and are concerned with making allocations and resolving conflicts in a way that will both maximize compliance with the decision at hand and minimize citizens' hostility toward the authorities and institutions making the decision (Murphy and Tanenhaus 1969; Scheingold 1974; Wahlke 1971).

The dilemma faced by legal authorities is not unique to law. All leaders need discretionary authority to function effectively in their roles. Industrial managers must direct and restrict those who work under them. They also require support and cooperation from those they manage. When managers lack the legitimacy they need to secure the cooperation of workers, inefficiencies such as those caused by slowdowns and sabotage occur. Similar problems of authority are encountered by teachers, political leaders, army sergeants, and any other authorities who need legitimacy to function.

The compliance literature has recognized two important types of internalized obligation. First, citizens may comply with the law because they view the legal authority they are dealing with as having a legitimate right to dictate their behavior; this represents an acceptance by people of the need to bring their behavior into line with the dictates of an external authority (Friedman 1975; Gerstein 1970). Easton makes this the essential component of his definition of authority, suggesting that legitimacy exists when the members of a society see adequate reason for feeling that they should voluntarily obey the commands of authorities (Easton 1958).

A second type of internalized obligation is derived from a person's desire to behave in a way that accords with his or her own sense of personal morality. Like views that accord legitimacy to authorities, personal morality is an internalized sense of obligation characterized by voluntary compliance. It differs from legitimacy in content, however. Personal morality is not a feeling of obligation to an external political or legal authority. It is instead an internalized obligation to follow one's personal sense of what is morally right or wrong.

Consider a specific illegal activity such as using cocaine. What is a person's motivation for complying with the law prohibiting its use? If people refrain from using drugs because they think laws ought to be obeyed, then legitimate authority is influencing their behavior. If they do so because drug abuse violates their convictions, then personal morality is influencing their behavior. If they fear being caught and sent to prison, deterrence is influencing their behavior. And if they do not use drugs because they fear the disapproval of their friends, the social group is exerting its influence.

From the perspective of the authorities in a political or legal system, legitimacy is a far more stable base on which to rest compliance than personal or group morality, for the scope of legitimate authority is much more flexible. It rests on a conception of obligation to obey any commands an authority issues so long as that authority is acting within appropriate limits. Leaders with legitimate authority have open-ended, discretionary authority within a particular range of behavior. They may act in ways that will most effectively advance their objectives, expecting to receive public support for their actions.

Unlike legitimacy, personal morality is double-edged. It may accord with the dictates of authorities and as a result help to promote compliance with the law, but on the other hand it may lead to resisting the law and legal authorities. The distinction between personal morality and legitimacy suggests that two dimensions underlie the different motivations that can influence compliance. The first is whether the motivation is instrumental or normative; the second is whether the normative motivation is linked to a political authority. (Legitimacy is linked to a political authority, but personal morality may or may not be.)

Because of its value as a normative base for authorities, legitimacy has been an important concern among social scientists. It has been prominent in treatments of law by sociologists beginning with Weber (see Weber 1947), and by psychologists (French and Raven 1959), political scientists (Easton 1965, 1968, 1975; Gamson 1968), and anthropologists (Fried 1967). In each case citizens who accept the legitimacy of the legal system and its officials are expected to comply with their dictates even when the dictates conflict with their self-interest. Legitimacy is regarded as a reservoir of loyalty on which leaders can draw, giving them the discretionary authority they require to govern effectively.

Because they are concerned with securing compliance, legal authorities are interested in public evaluations of the legitimacy of police officers, judges, lawyers, and the like. Interest in these issues is reflected in Roscoe Pound's famous address of 1906 on public dissatisfaction with the courts, as well as in more recent efforts to understand this dissatisfaction (Fetter 1978). Efforts to explore public opinion about the police, the courts, and the law reflect the belief among judges and legal scholars that public confidence in the legal system and public support for it—the legitimacy accorded legal officials by members of the public—is an important precursor to public acceptance of legal rules and decisions. To the extent that the public fails to support the law, obedience is less likely.[11]

This focus on public views of the law and legal authorities has heightened concerns about the extent of public support. A number of social scientists and social commentators have noted the low levels of public support in recent public opinion polls for legal and political authorities. Studies of the public's evaluation of political leadership, of such institutions as the Supreme Court and the presidency, suggest that large segments of the public have little confidence in their legal and political authorities (Lipset and Schneider 1983; Miller 1979; Wright 1981). [12] There is an implicit belief that these low levels of confidence in authority will lessen compliance with the law.

More recently, researchers in political science, sociology, and policy studies have shifted their attention away from theories of the state and issues of legitimacy and toward citizens' assessments of the benefits and burdens of participation in society. The assumption that legitimacy is an important element in the exercise of authority has however remained an essential element in theories of the relationship between citizens and legal authorities.

Legitimacy as an Empirical Issue

Although the assumption that legitimacy enhances compliance has traditionally been accepted by lawyers and social scientists, it has been pointed out that the assumption is not supported by convincing data. Instead of testing the role of legitimacy in compliance, scholars have simply assumed that it is important, and as a result the value of the concept of legitimate authority has not been established. Boulding, for example, suggests that "the nature and underpinnings of legitimacy are among the most neglected aspects of the dynamics of society. . . . We all tend to take legitimacy for granted" (1970, 509). Similarly, Schwartz argues that the view that the impact of law is "deeply affected by the legitimacy accorded to [it] . . . has not yet been subjected to rigorous test" (1978, 588). As McEwen and Maiman (1986) aptly summarize, "The virtual absence of empirical examination of legitimacy leaves us vulnerable to the charge that the concept is a magical one to be invoked when our power of explanation otherwise fails us" (p. 258).

Legal scholars have also recognized the lack of clear empirical support for the value of legitimacy. Hyde (1983) has challenged social scientists to demonstrate convincingly that legitimacy can be distinguished from other factors that may influence compliance, and that it has an independent effect on law-abiding behavior.

To examine whether legitimacy influences behavioral compliance with the law one must first develop indicators for each of the variables to be analyzed. The most direct way in which legitimacy has been measured is as the perceived obligation to comply with the directives of an authority, irrespective of the personal gains or losses associated with doing so. This concept of legitimacy is central to the original work of Weber, which emphasizes the perceived obligation to obey (see Weber 1947). Easton focuses on the belief held by members of a society that they should obey their leaders: "In a political system in which the governing group bases its activity on a principle which the members of the system consider to be adequate grounds for obeying their rulers, the power is said to be legitimate" (1958, 180). In such a context citizens feel that the rules ought to be obeyed. This concept of legitimate authority has also been important in definitions of legitimacy by social psychologists (French and Raven 1959).

Typically, studies of perceived obligation pose such questions as the following: "If a policeman asks you to do something that you think is wrong, should you do it anyway?" These questions presume a conflict between self-interest or personal morality and the legitimacy of the authority making a request. The central question is whether people will allow their external obligations to authority to override their personal self-interest or their moral views. A second approach to assessing legitimacy is to measure the extent to which authorities enjoy the public's support, allegiance, and confidence (in political science often subsumed under the heading "trust in government"). Citizens are asked to indicate their affective orientation toward government leaders and institutions or to respond to general evaluations, such as "Government leaders can usually be trusted to do what is right," or "Most police officers are honest."

The essential concept in definitions of support is a "favorable affective orientation" toward an authority, an orientation that prepares a citizen to act as directed by the authority (Easton 1965, 1968, 1975; Easton and Dennis 1969; Gamson 1968; Parsons 1963, 1967). A favorable orientation has variously been called support, attachment, loyalty, and allegiance to the political or legal system.

Most empirical work examining legitimacy has focused on issues of allegiance or attachment to the political and legal systems, rather than studied directly the perceived obligation to obey the law. This is due in large part to the influence of Easton's approach on political scientists, who have done most of the empirical work in this area. Although he discussed legitimacy in terms of perceived obligation to obey, Easton measured legitimacy by measuring support (see Easton and Dennis 1969). In addition, the scale of "trust in government" developed for the national election studies provided an index of support suitable for use in political surveys.

The fundamental difference between obligation and support lies in the clarity of the motivation underlying compliance. Theories that measure legitimacy by measuring support assume that support for the government leads to the type of discretionary authority directly tapped by measuring the perceived obligation to obey. Support is therefore a less direct means of examining the role of legitimacy. If a relationship between support and compliance is found, it must be inferred that citizens comply because they feel an obligation to obey.[13]

In addition to the question of whether legitimacy matters is the question of what the object of legitimacy is. Three potential objects of legitimacy have been distinguished by political scientists: authorities, the regime, and the community. The legitimacy of authorities involves support for those in positions of power, such as judges and police officers, for elected representatives, and for the policies and actions of the authorities. The legitimacy of the regime involves support for the offices and institutions that officials occupy and for the procedural rules that guide their conduct. Finally, views about the social groups that make up the political community may also be important. [14] This final type of influence represents the possible overlap of legal and political authorities with members of one's social groups. For example, if members of a society have a common ethnic or religious heritage, they may think of their leaders as members of their own social group as well as formal authorities.

The basic distinction for our purposes is between the legitimacy of particular authorities and the legitimacy of the institutions or procedures of government. Easton refers to the latter type of legitimacy as "diffuse" support for the system, that is, support accorded the procedures and institutions of government. He distinguishes it from support for particular incumbent authorities and their decisions and policies, which he calls "specific" support. [15]

Legitimacy can reside either in a person who occupies a position of authority or in an institution. Political and legal theories of legitimacy have emphasized that using legitimate institutions and rules when making decisions enhances the likelihood that members of the public will comply, even if they do not agree with the decisions or support those who have made them.

Hyde's challenge to social scientists to distinguish legitimacy from self-interest is based on the premise that a theory of legitimacy is not needed to explain why citizens obey rules that they view as personally beneficial. If legitimacy is an important concept, it should lead citizens to behave in ways not always consistent with their short-term self-interest. Unfortunately, Easton's theory of system persistence does not distinguish clearly between the object of legitimacy and its motivation. It assumes that evaluations of incumbent authorities are based in self-interest, whereas evaluations of institutions and processes are at least partly normative. [16] To test the importance of self-interest one must differentiate the legitimacy of authorities and legal institutions from the degree to which their legitimacy is linked to self-interest or normative judgments. If these are separated then the influence of legitimacy on compliance can be examined.

Why might normative influences be expected to be distinct from issues of short-term self-interest? According to one model, normative judgments are enduring values that develop early in a person's life, during the political socialization process (Sears 1983). Although potentially responsive to later events, such dispositions are distinct from short-term judgments of self-interest in any given situation.

Of course, normative judgments could be distinct from judgments of short-term self-interest without representing enduring values. They may simply be contemporaneous judgments formed on a different basis. (The discussion of procedural justice in later chapters, for example, considers a normative judgment that may or may not be rooted in enduring values.) The distinction between normative and self-interested judgments is illustrated in Easton's theory of system persistence, which divides legitimacy into two components: diffuse system support is viewed as including a strong residue of the socialization process; specific system support is based on short-term calculations of self-interest.[17] If enduring values are the residue of socialization, behavior will be guided by underlying normative values and will have a consistency from one situation to the next: it will not change as the immediate environment changes.[18]

The separation of support for institutions and procedures from support for incumbent authorities and their actions is clear conceptually but in practice is not likely to be absolute. In the long term the legitimacy of legal and political procedures and institutions, as well as of legal authorities, may be linked to the outcomes they produce. As Kelman suggests, "Ultimately the political system is a way of meeting the needs and interests of the population and unless it accomplishes this, at least to a moderate degree, it cannot maintain its legitimacy in the long run" (1969, 283). In other words, people may accord legitimacy to social systems because of long-term self-interest rather than short-term self-interest.[19]

Studies typically find that those who disagree with the decisions of legal authorities consider these authorities less legitimate (Murphy and Tanenhaus 1969; Wasby 1970). The "cushion of support" provided by diffuse support is therefore not an absolute protection for authorities; it may, however, be an important element in their ability to function effectively as leaders in most situations.

Empirical Issues

There are two ways to examine the relationship between legitimacy and compliance. One is to focus on specific acts of compliance. For example, if a judge makes a decision, do the parties to the dispute obey it? If a policeman tells a person to do something, does he or she do it? Another approach examines overall levels of legitimacy and their relationship to obedience with the law. It examines whether those who view the law and legal authorities as more legitimate are more likely to obey them.

Because this book is concerned with the role of law throughout the everyday life of citizens, I examine general compliance with the law as well as general views about the legitimacy of legal authority. This approach is drawn from studies by sociologists and political scientists on compliance with legal and political authority, which have focused on overall judgments about legitimacy, morality, and deterrence and their influence on behavior.

Both adults and children feel a strong obligation to obey the law. In Sarat's study, for example, 70 percent of adults said a law "must always be obeyed"; in Iowa, 93 percent of 1,001 adults said a law should always be obeyed regardless of personal feelings (Boynton, Patterson, and Hedlund 1968). Similar feelings are expressed by children and adolescents. In Engstrom's sample of children in the fourth to eighth grades only 4 percent of whites and 8 percent of blacks said they might disobey a policeman if he were "wrong in what he tells you to do" (Engstrom 1970). In a survey of high school students, 77 percent of whites and 72 percent of blacks agreed that "people should always obey the law" (Rodgers and Lewis 1974).

The six studies summarized in table 3.1 address the question of whether feelings of legitimacy lead to behavioral compliance with the law and legal authorities, regardless of whether these feelings are expressed as support for the authorities or as an obligation to obey. Four of the studies examine the relationship between obligation and behavior, three the relationship between support and behavior.

These studies suggest that those who view authority as legitimate are more likely to comply with legal authority, whether the legitimacy is expressed as obligation or as support.[20] They also suggest that the link between legitimacy and compliance is only moderately strong. In Brown's study, which reports the strongest correlations, only 14 percent to 21 percent of the variance in willingness to comply with the law is explained by variations in views about its legitimacy.

What the studies show most strikingly is the lack of research on the relationship between legitimacy and compliance. There are few studies; most involve children or adolescents, examine only a hypothetical willingness to comply with the law, and make little or no effort to control for potential confounding factors like social disapproval and concerns about reward and punishment. Suggestions that the enhancing effect of legitimacy on compliance has not been adequately demonstrated empirically are well founded. Nonetheless, the current literature suggests that it does exist.

The influence of legitimacy on behavior can also be examined in studies of the

Table 3.1
Legitimacy of legal authorities and compliance with the law

Study	Sample	Results
Support		
Gibson (1967)	94 precollege students in England	Support for the police related to low self-reported delinquency ($r = .41$)
Jaros and Roper (1980)	600 college students in Kentucky	Diffuse support for the Supreme Court related to hypothetical willingness to comply with Supreme Court decisions (gamma = .16)
Obligation		
Rodgers and Lewis (1974)	651 students (tenth grade to twelfth grade)	Perceived obligation to obey the law related to general willingness to comply (gamma = .25), but not to willingness to comply in specific instances
Sarat (1975)	220 residents of Madison	Perceived obligation to obey related to self-report of past law-abiding behavior ($r = .33$)
Tittle (1980)	1,993 adults	Views about legitimacy related to self-reported law breaking
Support and Obligation		
Brown (1974)	261 adolescents (seventh grade to twelfth grade)	Self-report of compliance related to support ($r = .44$ for the police; $r = .37$ for the courts) and to obligation ($r = .46$)

willingness of citizens to take part in illegal protests. These are peripheral to the issue of general everyday compliance with law, for they involve a violation of the system of law and government itself rather than simple acts of self-interest that contradict existing rules of conduct. Stealing a car is not typically a political statement (although it could be one), nor is running a red light. In addition, in these studies legitimacy is usually expressed as allegiance to the authorities or support for the authorities, rather than as the obligation to obey.

Table 3.2 outlines sixteen studies that examine the behavioral impact of supportive attitudes on social and political protest. Even though less directly relevant, these studies provide a more extensive test of the possible behavioral impact of legitimacy: there are a large number of studies, they examine adult behavior, and they rely less on hypothetical statements about what one would do in a particular situation.[21]

The results of these studies support the hypothesis that behavior is strongly influenced by legitimacy (in this case viewed primarily as support or trust). Citizens with higher levels of support for the authorities are less likely to engage in behavior against the system. Thirteen of the studies found support for the hypothesis, two found mixed support, and one found no support. Further, the relationship is reasonably strong. The average variance explained by the studies that report correlations is 18 percent ($r = .42$).[22] This level of correlation is quite high. In addition, there are suggestions in several of the studies that the level might be higher still if additional controlling factors were taken into account.

Several authors have noted that the correlation between supportive attitudes and behavior increases when factors of political context are taken into account. Useem and Useem find that nonsupportive attitudes are more strongly expressed in behavior when there are viable political groups for a citizen to join (Useem and Useem 1979). Similarly, Muller finds that nonsupportive attitudes are enacted into behavior when people feel they can effect beneficial change (Muller 1970a, 1970b). Craig (1980) has also suggested that nonsupport is more likely to be expressed in the form of behavior against the system when those involved have a sense that their behavior will be effective—a position supported by several studies (Balch 1974; Flaming 1968; Paige 1971).

That political disaffection promotes unconventional political behavior is consistent with the conclusions reached by two recent reviews of the literature on political behavior (Kinder and Sears 1985; Rasinski and Tyler 1986) and by a review of factors leading to civil disorder (McPhail 1971). Wright (1981), however, finds little relationship between support and unconventional political behavior. (Because Wright deals with many of the studies examined here and in the other reviews cited, his contrary conclusion reflects a different threshold of importance.) Although studies do find a consistent, statistically significant rela-

Table 3.2

Support for authorities and willingness to participate in political protest

Study	Sample	Results
Aberbach (1969); Aberbach and Walker (1970)	855 residents of Detroit	Political distrust leads among blacks to a willingness to riot (gamma = .40); among whites to a willingness to vote for extremists (gamma = .33)
Citrin (1977); Citrin et al. (1975)	963 residents of Bay area	Political alienation leads to a willingness to participate in unconventional political activity (r = .36)
Craig and Wald (1985)	1,500 college students	Diffuse support significantly related to willingness to employ violence for political ends
Farah, Barnes, and Heunks (1979)	Citizens in the United States (1,719), United Kingdom (1,719), Germany (2,307), Austria (1,534), and Netherlands (1,201)	Evaluations of the regime consistently related to potential for protest
Muller (1970a, 1970b)	296 college students	Low support for government procedures leads to a willingness to engage in protests (r = .47)
Muller (1972)	500 residents of Iowa	Low support for political institutions leads to a willingness to riot among those who feel that rioting is in

Table 3.2 *(Continued)*

Study	Sample	Results
		their self-interest (r = .32)
Muller (1977); Muller and Jukam (1977); Muller (1979)	2,663 German adults	Lack of support for basic values of the system leads to aggressive political behavior (r = .50)
Muller, Jukam, and Seligson (1982)	1,018 residents of New York City	Lack of support for basic values of the system leads to a willingness to engage in aggressive political behavior (r = .44)
Olsen (1968)	154 residents of Ann Arbor	Political disenchantment leads to tolerance for protest activity (eta = .38)
Paige (1971)	237 black males in Newark	Low trust in government related to self-report of having rioted
Schwartz (1973)	500 college students; 67 blacks of low socioeconomic status	Political alienation correlated with self-reported support for revolutionary behavior (r = .47 for students; r = .43 for blacks)
Seligson (1980)	531 Costa Rican peasants	Low trust in government related to participation in strikes (gamma = .19) and land invasions (gamma = .26)

(continued)

Table 3.2   *(Continued)*

Study	Sample	Results
Useem and Useem (1979); Useem (1982)	1,352 adults	Overall trust in government moderately related to support for political protest
Wesbrook (1980)	425 soldiers	Cynicism about government lessened responsiveness to military discipline (tau = .21); lowered reliability (tau = .42); and increased the likelihood of military discharge (tau = .26)
Worchel, Hester, and Kopala (1974)	148 college students	Low legitimacy of authority scores related to willingness to engage in violent protest (r = .39)
	22 members of Young Socialist Alliance	Legitimacy scores significantly lower than for conventional groups
Wright (1976)	1,200 adults	Low trust in government not related to endorsement of civil disobedience or disruption of government

tionship between support and unconventional political behavior, considerable variance remains to be explained.

Evidence for the role of normative concerns in securing compliance can be gathered by examining not only legitimacy but also the effects of personal morality. In studies of these effects, people are asked to what extent a law or rule accords with their own judgments of right and wrong, and these judgments are correlated to whether they obey the law. Five studies of this kind found that personal assessments of the morality of the law typically have a strong influence on whether citizens say that they break the law (see table 3.3). The average correlation across the studies is .45, suggesting that about 20 percent of variance in obedience to the law can be explained by differences in judgments about the morality of law.

The influence of moral assessment on behavior toward the law is also examined in the large literature on moral judgment and juvenile delinquency. Studies in this area are typically based on the assumption that children who are influenced by instrumental considerations of reward and punishment are more likely to break laws than are children who are influenced by issues of obligation to obey the law. This assumption has been generally supported. Blasi (1980) reviewed fifteen studies and found that ten showed significant behavioral differences of the type predicted by developmental theory. As with legitimacy, studies of personal morality support the suggestion that normative concerns influence compliance.

Although the studies examined differ in many ways, such as in their topics, methods, and subjects, they all reinforce the conclusion that normative support

Table 3.3
Judgments about morality of a law and willingness to obey it

Study	Sample	Results
Grasmick and Green (1980)	400 adults	Those who view a law as moral more likely to say that they have obeyed it (r = .42) and will do so in the future (r = .55)
Jacob (1980)	176 adults	Those who view a law as moral more likely to say they obey it (r = .47)
Meier and Johnson (1977)	632 adults	Those who view using marijuana as immoral less likely to report using it (r = .21)
Silberman (1976)	174 students	Those who view laws as immoral less likely to report that they obey them (r = .56)
Tittle (1980)	1,993 adults	Those who view laws as immoral significantly less likely to report obeying them

for the system leads to compliant behavior.[23] Whether legitimacy operates as obligation or as support, the studies reviewed suggest a moderately strong positive relationship between the legitimacy of legal and political authorities and behavioral compliance.

At the same time, there is merit to the concerns that research has failed to demonstrate compellingly the value of the concept of legitimacy. Given the important theoretical role that legitimacy plays in social science treatments of the law, the weakness of the evidence reviewed is disappointing. The lack of strong studies is especially striking with studies of the obligation to obey the law, the most direct measure of citizens' assessments of legitimacy. The evidence that does exist is positive, but it has clear limits.

The Chicago study tests the hypothesis that legitimacy has a positive influence on compliance. The data collected are used to examine the extent to which legitimate authorities can rely on voluntary acceptance of the law by members of the public. To the extent that they can, authorities have discretionary authority. Assuming that the study confirms that legitimacy is important, the question remains of where the legitimacy of authority resides. Is the attitudinal mechanism through which legitimacy functions the perceived obligation to obey, affective support for authorities, or both? Typically studies have viewed legitimacy in only one of these two ways, and as a result little evidence is available for a direct comparison. The research does suggest, however, that both types of legitimacy have some relationship to compliance. The Chicago study addresses this question by comparing the roles of obligation and support in promoting compliance.

The Chicago study also distinguishes between support for authorities and support for rules and institutions. When other studies have done so they have consistently found the legitimacy of institutions to be most clearly linked to political behavior (Craig 1980; Muller and Jukam 1977). The Chicago study differentiates personal legitimacy of the type that Easton called specific (based in performance) from that which he called diffuse (represented by obligation to obey and generalized affective support). In the case of citizens' dealings with the police and the courts, specific system support refers to citizens' views of how well these legal authorities perform; diffuse support refers to underlying feelings of obligation toward the law, the police, and the courts, or to underlying attachment to them.

The question of whether legitimacy influences compliance has been stated as one demanding an answer either wholly affirmative or wholly negative, but it is likely that the degree to which legitimacy influences compliance depends on the circumstances. Such a conclusion is suggested by the literature on political behavior, which has identified several moderating variables affecting the strength of the relationship between support for the authorities and compliance.

The Chicago study explores in several ways the circumstances in which legitimacy matters. It deals first with the extent to which the relationship between legitimacy and compliance changes when other behavioral factors change. Four such factors are considered: deterrence, peer opinion, personal morality, and the evaluation of authorities. These factors are examined in works on compliance by political scientists and sociologists, and reflect plausible alternative factors which might be affecting compliance. Suppose for example that people thought they could break the law without being caught. In such circumstances, would their degree of compliance be more likely to depend on whether they viewed the law as legitimate? What if they felt that the police and courts performed poorly, or saw law breaking as conflicting with their personal morality? Each analysis poses the question of whether legitimacy is more strongly related to compliance in some circumstances than in others. The question of when legitimacy influences compliance is also extended to the examination of demographic subgroups, to see for example whether the behavior of those who are well educated or have higher incomes is more strongly related to issues of legitimacy than is the behavior of other groups. Finally, the Chicago study explores the impact of past experience on the relationship between legitimacy and compliance—that is, the question of whether poor or unfair outcomes from the legal authorities, or poor or unfair treatment, leads citizens later to base their compliance with the law less on legitimacy and more on other factors.

CHAPTER 4

Measuring Legitimacy and Compliance

The Chicago study focuses on six laws chosen to represent the range of laws people deal with in their everyday lives. The laws examined differ in their severity. The forms of behavior they prohibit are as follows: making enough noise to disturb neighbors, littering, driving a car while intoxicated, driving faster than fifty-five miles an hour, taking inexpensive items from stores without paying, and parking illegally. In each case citizens were asked whether they had often, sometimes, seldom, or never violated the law during the year preceding the interview.

Like most earlier research on compliance, the Chicago study relies on self-reporting of compliant behavior. Its results must therefore be viewed with caution: citizens may not be reporting accurately how often they break the law. On the other hand, self-reporting is the most frequently used method of assessing law breaking (Hirschi, Hindelang, and Weis 1980) and has been found to be related to police records of law breaking (Erickson 1972; Farrington 1973; Kulik, Stein, and Sarbin 1968), to behavioral reports by teachers and friends (Gold 1970), and to unobtrusive assessments of lawbreaking (Erickson and Smith 1974).

An additional potential problem in measuring compliance with the law is the time frame used. In the first wave of interviews respondents were asked about their behavior during the preceding year. Such a broad time frame was chosen so that respondents would be more likely to indicate that they had engaged in at least some illegal behavior. But even with an extended time frame, self-reporting of some forms of behavior was low.[1]

A consequence of the approach used to assess behavior in the Chicago study is that the behavior examined occurred before the interviews, whereas the attitudes reflected the views of people at the time of the interviews. This casts some doubt on the causal order assumed in this study—that attitudes cause behavior; it may in fact be behavior that causes attitudes. The extent to which this is a problem cannot be determined by using cross-sectional data; panel analysis is required.

Respondents' self-reporting on how often they broke the law is shown in table 4.1. People were most likely to say that they had committed less serious offenses, such as parking illegally (51 percent) and speeding (62 percent). Very few respondents said they had stolen items from a store (3 percent). For each of the other offenses, the proportion fell somewhere in between: for making noise, 27 percent; for littering, 25 percent; for drunk driving, 19 percent.

Table 4.1
Frequency of law breaking: first wave (in percentages)

	Mean (standard deviation)	Often	Sometimes	Seldom	Never
Drove over 55 miles per hour on the highways	3.6 (.74)	16	28	18	38
Parked car in violation of the law	3.6 (.69)	6	22	23	49
Made enough noise to disturb neighbors	3.7 (.63)	2	8	17	73
Littered in violation of the law	2.8 (1.1)	2	8	15	75
Drove a car while intoxicated	4.0 (.27)	1	7	12	81
Took inexpensive items from stores without paying for them	3.1 (1.0)	0	1	2	97

n = 1,575

Because of rounding, percentages may not add to 100.

The various indices of law breaking were found to have a moderately strong positive relationship (mean r = .23).[2] As would be expected given the proportions shown in table 4.1, the overall scale of compliance with the law is skewed, with most respondents indicating little law breaking (see appendix C). In all, 22 percent of the respondents said they had never broken any of the six laws during the year preceding the interview.

Because many of the respondents in the first wave of interviews said they never broke the law, the questionnaire used in the second wave was designed to differentiate more finely among members of this "law-abiding" group, by using a more complex scale that included five frequencies of behavior: often, sometimes, seldom, almost never, and never. It was believed that the additional category, almost never, would be chosen by many respondents who had said in the first interview that they never broke the law.

A more differentiated scale was needed in the second wave especially because the period being asked about was shorter: instead of being asked whether they had broken the law "in the past year," respondents were asked about "the last several months." This abbreviated period was adopted because of concerns about the problem of causal order. Unfortunately, the use of this shorter period also increased the likelihood that respondents would say they never broke the law.

The results of the second wave of interviews suggest that the greater differentiation of the scale of behavior more than counteracted the effects of the shorter time period. Overall, there was slightly more variance in the second wave in self-reported law breaking. The proportions of respondents who acknowledged having broken the law were as follows: for making excessive noise, 35 percent; for littering, 34 percent; for driving while intoxicated, 19 percent; for speeding, 65 percent; for shoplifting, 3 percent; for parking illegally, 53 percent (see table 4.2).

As in the first wave of the study, the six items studied were found to have a low but positive correlation (mean r = .20). The expanded set of categories produced greater variance in responses and as a result a less skewed scale of compliance (see appendix C).

Given differences in compliance among the people interviewed, the first question to be considered is who complies with the law. One way to address the question is by examining demographic correlates of compliance with the law.[3] In this study demographic characteristics explain a substantial proportion of the variance in compliance (24 percent). Age and sex are the major influences: the old and women are more likely to say they comply with the law. Similar findings were obtained in the second wave of interviews.

Influences on Compliance

The sociological framework focuses on three factors that influence compliance: deterrence, peer opinion, and personal morality. Judgments based on deterrence involve assessments of the likelihood of being caught, the likelihood of being punished, the expected severity of punishment, or some combination of these factors. Because research suggests that certainty of apprehension and punishment most strongly influences behavior, this is the factor that was used in this study. As in other recent studies (for example Paternoster et al. 1984), the expected severity of punishment was not assessed.

Table 4.2
Frequency of law breaking: second wave (in percent)

	Mean (standard deviation)	Often	Sometimes	Seldom	Almost never	Never
Made enough noise to disturb neighbors	4.4 (.96)	1	6	10	18	65
Littered in violation of the law	4.4 (.98)	1	7	9	17	66
Drove a car while intoxicated	4.7 (.79)	0	4	6	9	81
Drove over 55 miles per hour on the highways	3.2 (1.5)	17	28	13	8	35
Took inexpensive items from stores without paying for them	5.0 (.27)	0	0	1	2	97
Parked car in violation of the law	3.7 (1.4)	5	22	15	11	47

n = 804

Because of rounding, percentages may not add to 100.

To establish the strength of concerns about deterrence, citizens were asked how likely they thought it was that they would be "arrested or issued a citation by the police" if they committed each of the six offenses: very likely, somewhat likely, somewhat unlikely, or very unlikely.

Citizens generally thought that the likelihood of being arrested or cited for law breaking was high. In the first wave of the survey 35 percent said this was very likely or somewhat likely for making too much noise; 31 percent said the same for littering; 83 percent said so for drunk driving; 72 percent said so for speeding; 78 percent said so for shoplifting; and 78 percent said so for violating parking rules.

A second factor considered was peer disapproval. Respondents were asked to what degree the "five adults they know best" would "disapprove or feel that [they] had done something wrong" if they were arrested for committing one of the six offenses. [4] For four offenses about half of those interviewed said their peers would disapprove "a great deal" or "somewhat": for making too much noise, 53 percent; for littering, 51 percent; for speeding, 52 percent; for parking illegally, 44 percent. In two cases disapproval was higher: for drunk driving it was 86 percent and for shoplifting 89 percent.

Finally, citizens were asked whether breaking each law was morally "very wrong," "somewhat wrong," "not very wrong," or "not wrong at all." In each case breaking the law was considered very wrong or somewhat wrong by a large proportion of the respondents: 96 percent in the case of disturbing neighbors (very wrong by 61 percent); 96 percent for littering (very wrong by 63 percent); 100 percent for drunk driving (very wrong by 95 percent); 84 percent for speeding (very wrong by 39 percent); 99 percent for shoplifting (very wrong by 92 percent); and 86 percent for parking illegally (very wrong by 37 percent).

Citizens seem to view breaking laws as a violation of their personal morality. Almost all the respondents felt it wrong to break any of the six laws studied. Most also thought that the likelihood of being caught for breaking the laws was high (70 percent to 80 percent felt this way, except for the minor offenses of littering and making too much noise, for which around 30 percent did). But respondents were not likely to feel that their friends or family would disapprove of their breaking the law (except for shoplifting and drunk driving). [5] Peer disapproval therefore seems an unlikely source of pressure to obey the law.

One possibility is that people's views about each of the six laws studied are unrelated. But an examination of the correlations measuring reactions to the six laws suggests that this is not the case. Some viewed the likelihood of being arrested for breaking the laws as higher than did other citizens: the mean correlation between estimates during the first wave was .34. Similarly, the mean correlation of the peer items at the second wave was .39, suggesting a generalized view about peer feelings. Views about the immorality of breaking the various laws were also moderately related (mean r = .31 at the first wave).

An examination of the various sociological factors shows that they also are all related. Those who view law breaking as immoral are more likely to see it as being disapproved of by their peers (r = .46); they are also more likely to think that it will lead to arrest (r = .41), as are those who think that peers will disapprove (r = .41). Finally, all three factors are correlated with self-reported behavioral compliance with the law (for morality, r = .42; for peer disapproval, r = .34; for certainty of punishment, r = .28).

Legitimacy

Legitimacy was examined in two ways: as the perceived obligation to obey the law and as support for legal authorities. This parallels earlier studies. In examining obligation to obey the law, the researchers asked the respondents to what degree they felt they should comply with directives from police officers or judges, irrespective of their personal feelings (see table 4.3).

The extent to which respondents endorsed the obligation to obey is striking. For example, 82 percent agreed that "a person should obey the law even if it goes against what they think is right."[6] This uniformity of responses poses a problem, because without variance in responses it is not possible to identify the antecedents or consequences of views about obligation. To increase variance,

Table 4.3
Perceived obligation to obey the law

	Percentage agreeing
People should obey the law even if it goes against what they think is right.	82
I always try to follow the law even if I think that it is wrong.	82
Disobeying the law is seldom justified.	79
It is difficult to break the law and keep one's self-respect.	69
If a person is doing something and a police officer tells them to stop, they should stop even if they feel that what they are doing is legal.	84
If a person goes to court because of a dispute with another person, and the judge orders them to pay the other person money, they should pay that person money, even if they think that the judge is wrong.	74

n = 1,575

the perceived obligation to obey was examined differently in the second wave: for each statement, respondents could agree strongly, agree, disagree, or disagree strongly.

The results of the first wave of interviews also suggested that some respondents had difficulty understanding the last two items of the obligation scale, which dealt with compliance in specific instances. To clarify the obligation scale in the second wave, the first four items of the original scale were combined with two new ones: "A person who refuses to obey the law is a menace to society," and "Obedience and respect for authority are the most important virtues children should learn." This elaborated scale seems to have been more effective in capturing variance in the perceived obligation to obey the law (table 4.4).[7]

It is interesting to compare responses to the items on obligation with those to the items on personal morality. Just as respondents almost universally feel that breaking the law is immoral, they feel a strong obligation to obey the law: both personal morality and the legitimacy of legal authorities encourage citizens to be law-abiding. Although these two forces could be in conflict, in this study they support each other.

Table 4.4
Perceived obligation to obey the law: second wave (in percent)

	Agree strongly	Agree	Disagree	Disagree strongly
People should obey the law even if it goes against what they think is right.	33	52	13	2
I always try to follow the law even if I think that it is wrong.	27	58	15	1
Disobeying the law is seldom justified.	25	57	16	2
It is difficult to break the law and keep one's self-respect.	22	49	25	3
A person who refuses to obey the law is a menace to society.	24	50	23	3
Obedience and respect for authority are the most important virtues children should learn.	31	51	15	3

n = 804

Legitimacy was also examined as a general affective orientation toward authorities, that is, as "allegiance" or "support" for the authorities involved. Support was measured separately for the police (table 4.5) and the courts (table 4.6). In each case the respondent was given a series of general statements about the authority with which to agree strongly, agree, disagree, or disagree strongly.

The respondents were much more evenly split on support than on obligation. Only a narrow majority of citizens agreed with positive statements about the police and the courts. For example, in the first wave 42 percent of the sample disagreed with the statement that police officers in Chicago are generally honest, and 43 percent disagreed with the statement that judges are.[8]

Although support and the perceived obligation to obey represent two aspects of the same underlying construct of legitimacy, the correlation between the two indices was only moderately strong (in the first wave r = .26, p < .001). This suggests that respondents differentiated between their generally positive affect toward the courts and police and their judgments about their personal obligation to obey the law. The revised obligation scale used in the second wave of the study had a higher interitem correlation, indicating that it is a stronger scale. It nevertheless continued to show only a moderately strong correlation to support (r = .25). Thus in the second wave, as in the first, the two ways of expressing legitimacy proved quite distinct.

Given the existence of two distinct indicators of legitimacy, two approaches can be taken: one is to create a single indicator that combines them; the other is to treat them separately. A preliminary analysis using zero-order correlations suggested that both obligation and support influenced compliance with the law. The major effect was of obligation, but support also had one.[9] Because both conceptualizations of legitimacy influenced compliance, this study compromised by first using a combined indicator and then analyzing separately the two indicators of legitimacy. One consequence of combining into a single indicator obligation, which is skewed, and support, which is not, is that the combined legitimacy scale is less skewed than the obligation scale.[10] Analyzing legitimacy effects with regression and correlation techniques is therefore more reasonable if a combined scale is used.

Who feels obligated to obey the law and who indicates support? An analysis of demographic correlates suggests a weak relationship between the two groups. Demographic characteristics explain 24 percent of the variance in behavioral compliance with the law, but only 10 percent of the variance in legitimacy.[11] As is true with compliance, the major demographic correlate of legitimacy is age. Older respondents view the law as more legitimate, according to each of the indicators of legitimacy. Education also is related to legitimacy, with highly educated respondents less likely to evince high levels of legitimacy. This accords with the earlier association by Sarat (1975) of knowledge with lower support.

Table 4.5
Support for the police (in percent)

	Agree strongly		Agree		Disagree		Disagree strongly	
	First wave	Second wave	First wave	Second wave	First wave	Second wave	First wave	Second wave
I have a great deal of respect for the Chicago police.	19	21	57	61	20	15	4	3
On the whole Chicago police officers are honest.	7	10	51	54	34	31	8	5
I feel proud of the Chicago police.	12	14	54	61	29	22	5	3
I feel that I should support the Chicago police.	20	25	68	66	10	7	3	2

First wave: n = 1,575
Second wave: n = 804
Because of rounding, percentages may not add to 100.

Table 4.6
Support for the courts (in percent)

	Agree strongly		Agree		Disagree		Disagree strongly	
	First wave	Second wave	First wave	Second wave	First wave	Second wave	First wave	Second wave
The courts in Chicago generally guarantee everyone a fair trial.	6	7	53	55	35	33	6	5
The basic rights of citizens are well protected in the Chicago courts.	4	5	53	57	37	34	6	5
On the whole Chicago judges are honest.	4	5	53	57	34	31	9	7
Court decisions in Chicago are almost always fair.	3	3	53	56	39	36	5	5

First wave: n = 1,575
Second wave: n = 804
Because of rounding, percentages may not add to 100.

Correlations reveal that views about the personal morality of law breaking, judgments about peer disapproval, and judgments about deterrence are all related to support and to feelings of obligation to obey the law.[12] These correlations are however small (mean r = .15): the two factors are largely distinct, although not totally so.

Other Influences on Compliance

Another potentially important influence on compliance is the respondents' evaluation of the quality of service received from the authorities. Obviously, less feeling of obligation is required for one to support authorities viewed as solving problems well: if people feel that their interests are being furthered by the authorities, they will support the authorities for reasons of short-term gain. Evaluations of performance should therefore be distinguished from legitimacy, which is a perceived obligation to obey based on motivations other than short-term self-interest. In the Chicago study performance was evaluated separately for the police and the courts. In the case of the police the scale had fourteen items, assessing overall performance and the perceived likelihood of good performance in the future.

Satisfaction with performance was established by asking respondents how good a job the police (or courts) were doing, how well the police (or courts) solved problems and helped those who dealt with them, and how satisfied the respondents were with the fairness of outcomes when they dealt with the police (or courts). The results show general but far from universal satisfaction with legal authorities (table 4.7). In addition, they suggest that satisfaction is higher with the police than with the courts.

Satisfaction with the performance of legal authorities also involves assessing the quality of their work. Quality of performance was measured by asking respondents how frequently the police (or courts) provided satisfactory service, how often they handled problems satisfactorily, and whether they treated citizens fairly and dispensed fair outcomes. Similar questions were asked about those who went to court (table 4.8). The police and courts seem to be viewed as often failing to resolve problems satisfactorily and often as being unfair. Again the courts were viewed more negatively than the police.

Finally, respondents were asked whether they would receive satisfactory and fair outcomes and treatment if they called the police in the future (table 4.9). The answers were affirmative, even though citizens expressed the view that unsatisfactory and unfair treatment of citizens by the police and courts is widespread. They almost universally believe that their future dealings with these authorities will be satisfactory and fair.

Table 4.7
Satisfaction with legal authorities (in percent)

	First wave		Second wave	
	Police	Courts	Police	Courts
How good a job are they doing?				
Very good	10	4	11	5
Good	44	22	48	25
Fair	38	47	36	45
Poor	6	18	5	21
Very poor	2	9	1	4
How satisfied are you with the way they solve problems?				
Very satisfied	17	7	16	7
Somewhat satisfied	55	48	64	52
Neutral (volunteered)	2	1	1	1
Somewhat dissatisfied	21	32	16	32
Very dissatisfied	6	13	3	9
How satisfied are you with the fairness of the outcomes people receive?				
Very satisfied	13	7	12	8
Somewhat satisfied	52	49	65	57
Neutral (volunteered)	2	1	1	1
Somewhat dissatisfied	26	30	18	28
Very dissatisfied	8	12	4	7
How satisfied are you with the fairness of the way that people are treated?				
Very satisfied	14	9	15	8
Somewhat satisfied	56	53	66	59
Neutral (volunteered)	0	0	0	0
Somewhat dissatisfied	24	30	17	28
Very dissatisfied	7	9	2	6

First wave: n = 1,575
Second wave: n = 804
Because of rounding, percentages may not add to 100.

Table 4.8
Perceived quality of legal authorities (in percent)

| | First wave | | | | Second wave | | | |
| | Police | | | Courts | Police | | | Courts |
	Called police	Stopped by police	All police		Called police	Stopped by police	All police	
Handle the problem satisfactorily?								
Always	12	12		5	11	10		4
Usually	45	43		29	50	52		38
Sometimes	34	35		49	34	31		48
Seldom	10	10		18	5	7		11

Provide people with
fair outcomes?

Always	7	5	9	5
Usually	43	34	48	42
Sometimes	40	49	38	45
Seldom	10	13	5	8
Treat people fairly?				
Always	9	6	9	6
Usually	47	38	53	45
Sometimes	36	45	34	42
Seldom	8	11	4	8

First wave: n = 1,575
Second wave: n = 804
Because of rounding, percentages may not add to 100.

Table 4.9
Expected future behavior toward the respondent (in percent)

	First wave			Second wave		
	Police		Courts	Police		Courts
	Called police	Stopped by police		Called police	Stopped by police	
How satisfied would you be with the outcome?						
Very satisfied	25	20	14	24	19	15
Somewhat satisfied	61	58	67	65	63	71
Somewhat dissatisfied	11	16	16	9	15	12
Very dissatisfied	3	6	3	2	4	3
How fair would the outcome probably be?						

Very fair	24	23	16	24	20	15
Somewhat fair	67	64	70	70	69	73
Somewhat unfair	7	11	11	5	10	9
Very unfair	3	3	3	2	2	3
How fairly would you probably be treated?						
Very fairly	33	27	24	35	30	25
Somewhat fairly	59	63	65	61	64	66
Somewhat unfairly	6	9	9	4	7	7
Very unfairly	2	2	2	1	1	2

First wave: n = 1,575

Second wave: n = 804

Because of rounding, percentages may not add to 100.

A similar distinction between general judgments and feelings about the self can be found in responses to questions about discrimination. When respondents were asked whether the police treated citizens equally or favored some citizens over others, 74 percent said there was favoritism; 72 percent made the same statement about the courts. When asked whether people like themselves were discriminated against, however, most respondents said no (75 percent for the police, 77 percent for the courts). People see widespread unfairness, yet do not see themselves as being discriminated against.[13]

Because the various judgments about the police were found to be highly related,[14] a single scale of performance was used. The ten items concerning the courts also were found to be highly correlated, so for these a single scale was used as well. These two scales for evaluating performance were found to be highly related, and performance evaluations were also related to assessments of legitimacy.

As with legitimacy, the correlation of evaluations of the police and courts with demographic variables was low (mean r = .08). Police evaluations were influenced strongly by race (nonwhites gave more negative evaluations) and by age (older respondents gave more positive ones). Evaluations of the courts were influenced by sex (men gave more positive evaluations), by education (those with less education were more positive), and by income (those with high income were more negative).

The Chicago study's examination of legitimacy and compliance suggests several reasons why people obey the law. One is their instrumental concern with being caught and punished: people typically think it quite likely that this will happen if they commit serious crimes. Deterrence may be exerting an influence on their behavior. Obedience to the law is also strongly linked to people's personal morality. The data suggest a general feeling among respondents that law breaking is morally wrong. A similarly strong feeling emerges in the case of the perceived obligation to obey the law. Most of the respondents interviewed felt obliged to obey the law and the directives of legal authorities. In contrast to the strong normative commitment found in studying personal morality and perceived obligation to obey the law, support for the police and courts was not particularly high, and neither were evaluations of their performance. This does not mean, however, that dissatisfaction with the police or the courts is widespread.

The lack of a strong feeling of peer disapproval toward law breaking is also noteworthy. Although respondents thought that their friends and family would disapprove of some violations of the law, this perceived disapproval applied only to such serious crimes as drunk driving. In more mundane cases respondents thought their peers would not disapprove very strongly of illegal behavior.

CHAPTER 5

Does Legitimacy Contribute
Independently to Compliance?

Normative factors are widely held to have an important role in facilitating compliance with the law. Legitimacy is a particularly important normative factor, for it is believed to be the key to the success of legal authorities. If authorities have legitimacy they can function effectively; if they lack it it is difficult and perhaps impossible for them to regulate public behavior. As a result, those interested in understanding how to maintain the social system have been concerned with identifying the conditions that promote legitimacy; those seeking social change have sought to understand how to undermine it.

A review of the literature on legitimacy reveals no compelling evidence that legitimacy in practice has the important role given it in theory in facilitating compliance. The first concern of the Chicago study was to test whether legitimacy in fact makes an independent contribution to compliance. Does the extent to which people view legal authorities as having legitimate power influence their compliance with the law?

First Wave: Cross-Sectional Analysis

The zero-order relationship between legitimacy and compliance is significant, suggesting that legitimacy is related to compliance.[1] Those who regard legal authorities as having greater legitimacy are more likely to obey the law in their everyday lives. If legitimacy is used alone in a regression analysis to predict compliance, the analysis explains 5 percent of the variance in compliance.[2] Respondents were divided into ten groups of about equal size based on their legitimacy scores, and the average level of compliance was then computed for each of the groups. The relationship between legitimacy and compliance was found to be linear:[3] as legitimacy increases, so does compliance (fig. 5.1).

Although the significant correlation between legitimacy and compliance shows the two concepts to be related, it does not show causality: a correlational analysis ignores the possibility of spurious influences by third variables. Such influences occur when two measured variables are both related to a common, unmeasured

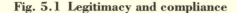

Fig. 5.1 Legitimacy and compliance

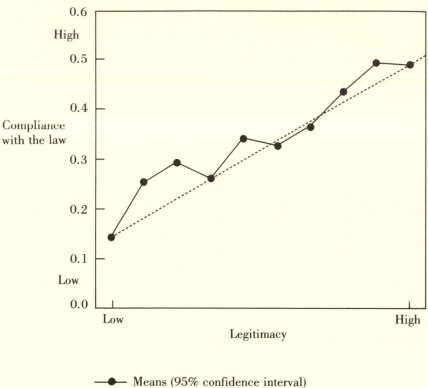

——●—— Means (95% confidence interval)

------- Regression line

one. The correlation between the two measured variables will therefore not represent the true relationship between the variables.

Regression analysis was used to test the independent contribution of legitimacy to compliance when the influence of such third variables as demographic and sociological factors is controlled for. Such a regression analysis allows the independent impact of each factor in an equation to be assessed. In this case two types of regression analysis were used: simple and reliability-adjusted. Simple multiple regression assumes that all variables in the equation are measured with equal reliability; reliability-adjusted multiple regression controls for differences in the reliability with which the various constructs are measured. The analysis was performed using the LISREL-VI structural equation program (Joreskog and Sorbom 1986a).[4]

The results of the regressions suggest that legitimacy has a significant independent effect on compliance, even when other potential causal factors are controlled for (see table 5.1). This effect is even stronger in the reliability-adjusted regression.[5] The increase in the relative importance of legitimacy when adjustments are made for reliability of measurement reflects the relatively poorer quality of its measurement. The results also suggest that other factors influence compliance. As has been previously noted, sex and age exert a strong influence on compliance. In addition, judgments of personal morality were found to have an important independent influence.[6] Interestingly, evaluations of performance did not influence compliance.[7]

Because regression analysis looks at independent influences, controlling for other factors in an equation, the results of the regression analysis support the premise that legitimacy has an independent influence on compliance. This premise can also be tested by means of a "usefulness" analysis, in which first one

Table 5.1
Influences on compliance with the law, first wave

	Zero-order correlation	Beta	Beta with reliability adjustment
Legitimacy	.22***	.06*	.11**
Sociological factors			
Deterrence	.28***	.05	.02
Peer disapproval	.34***	.11***	.08*
Personal morality	.42***	.23***	.33***
Political factors			
Evaluation	.09**	.03	.01
Background factors			
Sex	.28***	.18***	.26***
Race	−.11***	.00	−.02
Age	.38***	.25***	.24***
Income	−.24***	−.05	−.15**
Education	−.26***	−.03	−.06*
Conservatism	.11***	−.04	−.03
R-squared		.32***	

n = 1,575

NOTE. High scores indicate the belief that lawbreakers are likely to be caught and punished, the belief that peers would disapprove of law breaking, the belief that law breaking is immoral, evaluating the authorities positively, believing that the authorities are legitimate, being female, being white, being old, being well educated, having a high income, being conservative, and complying with the law.

group of variables is added to an equation, and then a relevant cluster of other variables is added. The aim of the analysis is to test whether the cluster of variables added second explains variance beyond that explained by the addition of the first set of variables.[8] An analysis of this type was performed by testing the ability of each of the attitudinal factors—deterrence, peer opinion, morality, evaluation, and legitimacy—to predict variance in compliance beyond what could be explained by the other factors.[9]

The usefulness analysis showed that four of the five factors contributed significantly to this ability to predict. Legitimacy makes an incremental contribution of 2 percent ($F(1, 1486) = 40.16$, $p < .001$). Deterrence and peer opinion each make an incremental contribution of 1 percent (for deterrence, $F(1, 1287) = 17.39$, $p < .001$; for peer opinion, $F(1, 1308) = 17.68$, $p < .001$). The most important incremental contribution is made by personal morality, which explains 8 percent of the variance beyond that which can be explained by other factors ($F(1, 1418) = 153.30$, $p < .001$). Performance evaluation makes no contribution.

The usefulness analysis confirms what the regression equations suggested: that legitimacy makes an independent contribution to the prediction of compliance. It also suggests, however, that this ability to explain is shared by other factors in the equation, in particular peer opinion and deterrence. None of these three factors explains a large amount of variance that cannot be explained by other factors.

The Use of Panel Respondents

The finding that legitimacy influences compliance can also be replicated by analyzing the second wave of interviews. As before, legitimacy emerges as a significant predictor of compliance with or without adjustments for the reliability of measurement.[10] Also as before, personal morality, sex, and age are important influences on compliance.

One potential problem with regression analysis based on cross-sectional data is that the dependent variable, behavioral compliance, measures behavior occurring before the interview, whereas the independent variables measure judgments made at the time of the interview. It is therefore possible that the dependent variable of compliance causes the independent variables, not the other way around. Panel analysis can test whether legitimacy continues to contribute to behavioral compliance once this problem is corrected. In the panel analysis that was designed the independent variables were the attitudinal and demographic variables from the first wave of interviews and the dependent variable was compliance at the second wave. When the measure of behavioral compliance from the second wave is substituted as the dependent variable in the regression equation and the independent variables from the first wave are kept, the level of the coefficients generally decreases,[11] but a significant legitimacy effect remains. When panel data are used to ensure that the behavioral compliance follows the assessment of legitimacy, the significant influence of legitimacy on compliance remains as well.

The panel analysis considered simultaneously attitudes and behavior from the two waves of interviews. The goal of the panel analysis was to strengthen the validity of the causal inferences already made using the data from the first wave. If legitimacy emerged as a significant predictor of behavioral compliance with the law in a panel analysis, this would strengthen the basic validity of the legitimacy hypothesis.[12] According to the panel analysis, legitimacy has a significant influence on compliance at both times.[13] As in the cross-sectional analyses, other factors also emerge as important predictors of compliance: sex and age influence compliance at both times, as does personal morality. On the other hand, deterrence does not significantly influence behavior at either time, nor does peer influence or performance evaluation.

The coefficients for the influences on compliance measured in the second wave are generally smaller than the coefficients for the same influences in the first wave. This occurs because the influences from the first wave are controlled for in the second wave. The first analysis does not control for the influence of the same variables at an earlier point in time, because no earlier measurements are available. In the case of legitimacy this tendency is counterbalanced by the better measurement of legitimacy in the second interviews, leading to similar coefficients for both points in time.

The various types of analysis employed are similar in many respects but differ in the variables they consider, the respondents they include, and the assumptions they make about causality. As might be expected, methodological variations lead to some changes in the findings. In particular, weak but statistically significant effects found in some forms of analysis are not statistically significant in others. Despite methodological variations, however, legitimacy effects always emerge as significant: the finding that legitimacy influences compliance is robust across a variety of changes in methodology.

Given that the summary measure of legitimacy confirms its effect, one may explore whether the effect is due to obligation or to support. It has already been noted that both types of legitimacy have a significant zero-order correlation with compliance.[14] A more appropriate means of analysis is multiple regression. In this case a series of multiple regression analyses were conducted using compliance as a dependent variable and each index of legitimacy as an independent variable, and using as controls the other factors in the previous equations (demographic and sociological factors). In these regressions a significant effect was found for obligation but not for support.[15]

Support can be further divided into support for the police and support for the courts. A separate analysis for the two subscales found that support for the police significantly influenced compliance and that support for the courts did not,[16] although both effects were weak.

The analysis of the components of legitimacy can be extended by using panel data. In this case a causal model was created using each means of evaluating legitimacy as a predictor of compliance at each point in time. Support for the police and support for the courts were treated separately. As in the other such models presented, adjustments were made for differences in the reliability with which each variable was measured. In both waves of the survey, obligation and support for the police were found to influence compliance.[17] In addition, in the first wave support for the courts was found to influence compliance.

An analysis of the panel data and cross-sectional data suggests that people's feelings about the extent of their obligation to obey the law are the major aspect of legitimacy influencing their obedience to the law. Support is less influential, although support for the police produces a statistically significant effect in both waves, and support for the courts produces such an effect in the first, larger sample when adjustments are made for differences in the reliability of measurement. The strong effect of perceived obligation is especially striking given the highly skewed nature of the obligation scale. As noted earlier, people are very likely to say that they feel obligated to obey the law, just as they are very likely to say that they do obey it.

When Does Legitimacy Most Strongly Influence Compliance?

Citizens who view legal authority as legitimate are generally more likely to comply with the law. It seems plausible that the strength of the influence of legitimacy on behavior will vary depending on other factors. This possibility raises the question of when legitimacy affects compliance.

To test for variations in the influence of legitimacy on compliance, the first sample was divided into subgroups along various dimensions, and the correlation between legitimacy and compliance was examined within each subgroup. In each case the division was made so as to divide the subgroups as closely as possible to the median score.

The first set of factors that may influence the relation of compliance to legitimacy are the other attitudinal factors included in the compliance model: deterrence, peer opinion, feelings that breaking the law is morally wrong, and evaluations of how well the authorities perform. Respondents were divided into two groups based on their attitudes. In the case of deterrence, for example, people were divided into groups based on their judgments of the likelihood that they would be caught and punished if they broke the law. The strength of the relationship between legitimacy and compliance is not different in these two subgroups.[18] Peer disapproval and moral judgments about law breaking were also used to create attitudinal subgroups. In each case there was no significant difference between the subgroups. Finally, division into subgroups according to evaluations of the quality of performance of the police and courts did indicate a significant difference between groups. Those who viewed performance favorably showed a significantly higher relationship between legitimacy and compliance.[19] The results suggest that the influence of legitimacy on compliance is lessened when performance evaluations are low. Respondents who feel that the authorities perform poorly are still significantly more likely to comply with the law if they view the authorities as more legitimate, but the strength of the influence of legitimacy on compliance is diminished.

The analysis by subgroup using attitudinal factors showed that the relationship between legitimacy and compliance is at best weakly affected by sociological factors. Respondents are almost equally likely to comply with the law because they view it as legitimate whether they think the likelihood of their being caught is high or low, whether or not they think their peers would disapprove of law breaking, and whether or not they think law breaking is morally wrong.

The degree to which legitimacy influences compliance may also be affected by the nature of the respondent's past experience with legal authorities. An analysis of 652 respondents from the first wave of the study who had recently had experience with the law defined the experience in five ways, according to the absolute favorability of the outcome, the favorability of the outcome relative to people's expectations, the favorability of treatment relative to people's expectations, the fairness of the outcome, and the fairness of the procedures used by the police or courts.[20] The results showed that experience influences the extent to which citizens base their compliance with the law on their assessments of legitimacy.[21] Of the five aspects of experience examined, one is the key to how the citizen will behave: the citizen's assessment of the fairness of procedures used by the police and courts. If citizens feel they have been treated unfairly, their behavior is less strongly influenced by their judgments about the legitimacy of legal authorities.

When compliance is not being shaped by legitimacy, what takes its place? The answer is peer disapproval, both when people evaluate negatively the performance of the authorities and when they have had an experience where they felt unfairly treated. In contrast, the importance of personal morality and the threat of sanction do not increase as the influence of legitimacy diminishes.

Finally, the demographic characteristics of the respondents may influence the degree to which compliance is linked to legitimacy. But a subgroup analysis using demographic factors did not find this influence to be significant. No differences were found for sex, age, race, income, or education. The only difference found was that between liberals and moderates: the correlation between legitimacy and compliance is significantly stronger for liberals.[22]

A key assumption of theories about legal authority is that legitimacy enhances the effectiveness of legal authorities by increasing public compliance with the law. The results of the Chicago study strongly support this assumption. People who regard legal authorities as legitimate are found to comply with the law more frequently. This relationship holds across a variety of types of analysis and is robust across changes in methodology.

Implications of the Chicago Study

Compliance is the basis for the effective operation of legal authorities. Widespread noncompliance leads to an unstable system. Despite the value that authorities place on obtaining compliance with the law, they can never take it for granted. Legal authorities often find that they must tolerate occasional noncompliance with laws that are generally followed, and at some times they are faced with noncompliance so widespread that it threatens their ability to govern effectively. What determines the extent to which people will or will not follow the law in their daily lives? The Chicago study suggests that normative concerns are an important determinant of law-abiding behavior, in contrast to the instrumental concerns that have dominated the recent literature on compliance.

The most important normative influence on compliance with the law is the person's assessment that following the law accords with his or her sense of right and wrong; a second factor is the person's feeling of obligation to obey the law and allegiance to legal authorities. According to the Chicago study, those who feel that they "ought" to follow the dictates of authorities are more likely to do so. One important and striking finding of the study is the high level of normative commitment found among the public to abiding by the law. People generally feel that law breaking is morally wrong, and that they have a strong obligation to obey laws even if they disagree with them. Further, within the range of everyday laws studied, these two sources of commitment to law-abiding behavior reinforce each other. Law breaking is viewed both as morally wrong and as a violation of an obligation owed to authorities. This high level of normative commitment to obeying the law offers an important basis for the effective exercise of authority by legal officials. People clearly have a strong predisposition toward following the law. If authorities can tap into such feelings, their decisions will be more widely followed.

Although normative commitment is obviously desirable, if only for the money it saves, it may also be difficult to obtain. Unlike deterrence, the success of which depends primarily on the willingness of the authorities to spend money on enforcement, normative commitment requires intensive education and socialization, and these take time. Despite such problems authorities are not free to ignore the need for normative support. Democratic societies require normative commitment to function effectively. Authorities cannot induce through deterrence alone a level of compliance sufficient for effective social functioning. Society's resources are inadequate to such a task and some base of normative commitment to follow the law is needed.

Although the Chicago study found that people endorse the obligation to obey legal authorities, it did not disclose how people decide how much they ought to obey. It remains unclear why people endorse the obligation to obey so strongly. Their endorsement clearly reflects widely held views about the function of laws and authorities, but it is not known what people think would happen if they ignored legitimate authorities more often. What do people think would be the consequences, for example, if they behaved according to personal morality or the pressures of peer groups, and ignored legal authorities and the law?

An interesting effort to explore public conceptions of law and authority is the work of Tapp and Kohlberg (1977), which explores developmental changes in people's views about the functions of legal rules. Although their work is directed primarily at children's views, it does illustrate that efforts to explore public conceptions of authority and rules may prove fruitful. It is also important to recognize the dangers of obedience based on legitimacy. Many have behaved questionably while professing to follow "legitimate" orders or have even committed atrocities, such as Adolf Eichmann and, during the war in Vietnam, William Calley. In a series of studies on obedience to authority, Milgram (1974) has shown the potentially powerful destructive effects of following "legitimate" authorities (see also Kelman and Hamilton 1989).

Because legitimacy is under the control of legal authorities, it is the primary focus of attention in my discussion of normative forces promoting compliance. The Chicago study was aimed at finding out what political and legal authorities can do to shape public behavior. Authorities cannot plan based on the assumption that personal morality will support compliance with their actions, but they can rely on their legitimacy.

Personal morality is especially problematic for legal authorities in a pluralistic society such as the United States, which lacks a commonly accepted moral code. For example, the United States has no state church but instead accepts the idea that different moral values can coexist in a single society. In such a setting authorities are likely to confront a wide range of moral values, none of which is the clearly appropriate standard for resolving policy issues or judging conduct. Against this pluralistic background the high levels of normative commitment to law-abiding behavior are striking.

Authorities draw on legitimacy because it is easier to influence behavior by so doing than through deterrence. Similarly, legitimacy is the main focus of the social critic, who seeks to promote a questioning of existing social rules that ultimately leads to disobedience. Because it is the key to discretionary authority, legitimacy is the natural focus of such efforts at reeducation. The social critic asks why the legitimacy was accorded in the first place and urges people to withhold it unless it is earned.

Several questions are left unanswered by the Chicago study. Although the study confirms the influence of legitimacy on compliance, it does not directly examine the nature of the perceived obligation to obey the law that brings about this influence. It does establish that the obligation to obey the law is a widely held value among those studied. It is also unclear what the boundaries of legitimacy are. To which authorities and to which of their actions is it granted? In the case of behavior that falls outside the range of what is appropriate, such as police brutality, the public becomes sharply divided about whether such behavior should be accorded legitimacy (see for example Kelman and Lawrence 1972). Further, the basis of legitimacy is unexplored. What are the characteristics of authorities that lead them to be viewed as legitimate by those with whom they deal? To what extent is it the social position occupied by a third party (a police officer or judge), and to what extent is it an inference that the person being dealt with has particular characteristics, such as competence or trustworthiness?

Several questions raised by the Chicago study are worthy of further investigation. The first is the question of how legitimacy is built and maintained across the life cycle. Easton and Dennis (1969) found that children develop attachments to authorities during the socialization process. They view socialization as the key to the development of attachment; this is consistent with their view of legitimacy as affective—as support rather than as a perceived obligation. They regard this affective attachment to authority as one needed to cushion people against the many disappointments that occur during adulthood.

It is also possible to imagine legitimacy developing and being maintained in a more cognitive manner. In the literature on social dilemmas, for example, the development of authorities is one response of social groups to the need to regulate the allocation of resources under conditions of scarcity. That literature suggests that people may regard the establishment of authorities and rules as a rational response to the need to resolve social problems: they may grant legitimacy to authorities because they understand why groups need to have authorities. If granting legitimacy to authorities is reasonable on cognitive grounds, it could develop during adulthood as a response to social needs, as well as developing as part of the socialization process of childhood. Clearly it is important to understand how values related to legitimacy develop during childhood and are enhanced or diminished during adulthood, just as it is important to understand people's reasons for granting legitimacy to authorities, laws, and institutions.

If legitimacy is a belief that develops during socialization and is then maintained as an affective residue, this will have important implications for legal authorities; support for legal authorities will be developed and dissipated only over the long term. If such a cushion of support does not exist, leaders in need of discretionary authority will be unable to generate it quickly. On the other hand beliefs in the legitimacy of authority, once developed, will be stable over long periods.

The Chicago study finds leaders to be less helpless than would a model of legitimacy oriented completely toward socialization. As will be discussed in the second part of this book, adult experience does influence legitimacy. Authorities can influence the extent to which they have discretion to act as they choose.

The legitimacy effects are especially striking given that legitimacy is not the best-measured construct in this study. The scale measuring obligation to obey was weak, with low interitem correlations, and those measuring obligation to obey and support are correlated with each other only moderately strongly. Nonetheless, legitimacy emerged as important both in analyses that did control for differences in the reliability of measurement and in analyses that did not. Corrections for reliability enhanced the effects of legitimacy, for it is more poorly measured than other concepts used in the Chicago study. Because of the weaknesses of the measurement of legitimacy in the study, legitimacy may emerge as a more important construct when more extensive efforts are made to study how it operates. For this reason the conclusions reached here probably understate the importance of normative factors on compliance. The better we understand legitimacy, the better we are likely to understand behavioral compliance in general.

The findings of the Chicago study also support the suggestion that the influence of deterrence on compliance may be overrated (Paternoster et al. 1984). The Chicago study used an approach to measurement patterned after that of Paternoster and a similarly designed panel study, and found little evidence of deterrence effects. Although the study does not question the assumption that deterrence works, other studies may well.

Finally, personal views about the morality of law breaking are important in shaping compliance with the law. Although the Chicago study deals with legitimacy, personal morality is clearly a more important influence on compliance than legitimacy. This finding suggests a second type of normative support for the law, one not necessarily linked to views about the legal system. If the people interviewed in the study were to lose their sense that legal authorities are legitimate, many would still comply with the law, because of their moral belief that they should. The strength of this influence demonstrates that such moral influences on compliance are an important area for future research.

PART THREE

Citizens' Concerns When Dealing with Legal Authorities

CHAPTER 6

What Do People Want from Legal Authorities?

This discussion of legitimacy has been framed by the perspective of legal authorities, highlighting the balance that they must strike between controlling the public and being sensitive to the public's views. Legal authorities must restrict the activities of those over whom they exercise power, but at the same time their effectiveness depends ultimately on their ability to secure voluntary public compliance with their directives. That voluntary behavior by citizens is an important precursor to effectiveness demonstrates the need to explore a second perspective on the relationship between authorities and those they lead: what people consider when they are evaluating the legitimacy of authorities. In other words, issues of legitimacy need to be explored from the public's perspective. This means asking what people want from authorities.

Doing so focuses attention on the psychology of the person (Tyler, Rasinski, and Griffin 1986). The image of the person that has dominated recent discussions in the literature on law and social science has been drawn from the field of economics and extended to the legal arena in theories of social control and public choice. It has already been noted that models of social control have traditionally been central to the study of compliance, and this emphasis has grown as models of public choice have increasingly dominated legal scholarship. As a consequence of this dominance, the authorities' perspective on compliance has focused heavily on issues of social control.

It is equally true that discussions of citizens' concerns in their dealings with the authorities have been dominated by instrumental issues. It has been widely believed that people evaluate legal authorities in terms of the favorability of the outcomes provided by the authorities. Models of public choice offer a straightforward basis on which citizens may support these authorities: the authorities provide positive, desired outcomes. This is true whether people are evaluating a police officer with whom they have just dealt or making a general assessment of their support for the courts. In either case people are concerned with how the past and future behavior of officials will benefit their short-term self-interest. If they call the police, for example, people will evaluate them according to whether they solve the problem at hand.

Both adherents of theories of public choice (Downs 1957; Laver 1981; Shapiro

1969; Tyler 1986b) and some adherents of psychological theories of leadership (Hollander 1978; Hollander and Julian 1970) have argued that support for legal authorities is linked to the ability of the authorities to provide favorable outcomes, that citizens obey and view as legitimate those authorities and institutions that produce positive outcomes for them.

Studies of personal experiences with the police and courts have also assumed typically that the level of citizens' satisfaction with legal authorities is determined largely by instrumental concerns, such as the favorability of outcomes. Some studies have examined the relationship between satisfaction with the police and other factors, such as whether the person interviewed was the victim of a crime, the time it took the police to respond to a call, and whether the police solved the problem (Kelling et al. 1974; Parks 1976; Skogan 1975). Similarly, studies of citizens' experiences in court have related their reactions to the favorability of verdicts (Jacob 1969).

The public choice perspective has also directed attention toward aspects of citizens' dealings with the police and courts that appear puzzling from an economic perspective. For example, given that the police can do little to influence such social problems as crime, why are evaluations of the police generally positive? To take one concrete instance, if a person's home is burglarized, the likelihood that the police can recover the stolen property is almost nil. Yet people typically report satisfaction with how the police handle such situations, even when nothing is recovered (Parks 1976). From a perspective oriented toward outcomes this seems paradoxical.[1]

One alternative to evaluating the authorities from a perspective based entirely on outcomes is to view evaluations as resulting from the level of outcomes people receive relative to their expectations. This is the basis of theories of adaptation level (Helson 1964), which hold that a feeling of psychological equilibrium develops at the level of resources to which people become accustomed. Outcomes that exceed or fall short of this level violate expectations, producing an aversive psychological state.[2] Theories of adaptation level focus on violations in expected outcomes; it is also possible that people react to violations in expected procedures.

An example from the political and legal arena of a theory of violated expectations is the J-curve model of relative deprivation used by Davies (1962, 1969). Davies finds that societal dissatisfaction results from violated expectations, and that citizens riot when they do not receive the level of resource that they expect based upon past allocations of resources. This perspective uses the psychological concept of expectancies in that no reference is made to concepts of fairness or deservedness (Lawler 1977). People may become upset if they do not get what they expected, without thinking that it is unfair that they did not get what they expected.[3]

An alternative to these perspectives based on the favorability of outcomes is psychological models that emphasize people's concerns for fairness in their dealings with legal and political authorities.[4] Like the normative theories discussed earlier, these models view people as concerned with their ethical judgments about what is right or proper. The first of these models is built on the concept of distributive fairness, according to which citizens evaluate public policies by examining the extent to which they distribute government benefits and burdens fairly. This view is represented in psychology by theories of relative deprivation (Crosby 1976) and by the literature on equity (Walster, Walster, and Berscheid 1978).

The role of distributive injustice in stimulating discontent has been supported by research in both political science (Gurr 1970; Moore 1978; Sarat 1977) and organizational theory (Crosby 1982; Martin 1981). For example, Sarat's review of the literature on citizens' contacts with the police and courts concludes that it is "the perception of unequal treatment [which] is the single most important source of popular dissatisfaction with the American legal system" (p. 434). Similarly, Muller (1980) found that feelings of distributive unfairness more effectively predicted political behavior against the system than did judgments about the favorability of outcomes.

Citizens' reactions to government decisions and allocations have also been linked to the fairness of the procedures used to distribute outcomes (Lind 1982; Lind and Tyler 1988; Thibaut and Walker 1975; Walker and Lind 1984), rather than to either the outcomes themselves or to aspects of procedures unrelated to fairness, such as efficiency or expectedness. According to theories of procedural justice, citizens are not only sensitive to what they receive from the police and courts but also responsive to their own judgments about the fairness of the way police officers and judges make decisions (Lind and Tyler 1988; Tyler 1984, 1986c; Tyler and Caine 1981).

A number of legal scholars and political scientists have also noted the potential importance of procedural issues to citizens: "People may believe specific decisions are wrong, even wrongheaded, and individual judges unworthy of their offices and still continue to support the court if they respect it as an institution that is generally impartial, just and competent" (Murphy and Tanenhaus 1969, 275). Similarly, "Tenants, consumers, and welfare recipients often regard the way in which they are treated by governmental institutions as at least as important as the extent to which they achieve their substantive goals" (Saphire 1978, 124–125).

Recent research confirms that people evaluate their experience in procedural terms. Such procedural effects have been found in trials (Lind et al. 1980) as well as in other procedures used to resolve disputes, including plea bargaining (Houlden 1980; Casper, Tyler, and Fisher 1988; Landis and Goodstein 1986), mediation (Adler, Hensler, and Nelson 1983), and decision making by police officers (Tyler and Folger 1980). Similar effects have also been found in the workplace (Greenberg and Folger 1983; Folger and Greenberg 1985), in politics (Tyler and Caine 1981; Tyler, Rasinski, and McGraw 1985), in schools (Tyler and Caine 1981), and in interpersonal relations (Barrett-Howard and Tyler 1986). Wherever procedural issues have been studied they have emerged as an important concern to those affected by the decisions (for a review see Lind and Tyler 1988).

Each of these theories of justice emphasizes that citizens evaluate the actions of legal and political authorities based on how fair the outcomes are for themselves and others, rather than on the personal benefit or harm resulting from the decisions. Theories of distributive justice, for example, emphasize people's assessments that their outcome was fair, rather than whether they won their case. This is even clearer in the case of procedural justice.

Empirical Issues

The theories reviewed suggest four types of judgment that may influence people's reactions to their experiences (see fig. 6.1). The first differentiation is between issues of outcome and issues of procedure. Judgments of outcomes and those of procedures can be further distinguished according to whether they are based on fairness. The framework shown in fig. 6.1 reflects the difference among psychological theories about which aspects of experience influence people's reactions. Another differentiation is that between judgments that involve issues of justice and those that do not.

This framework is similar to the one previously outlined in that it discusses the antecedents of behavioral compliance. There too instrumental and normative factors were distinguished. In this case such judgments are not viewed as directly driving behavior. Instead, they are seen as shaping attitudinal reactions to experiences, in particular the impact on people's views about the legitimacy of legal authorities. The recognition that there are several potential determinants of evaluation is an important contribution of recent research on justice. In the past it had been assumed that citizens wanted favorable outcomes from legal authorities and evaluated the legal system in terms of its ability to provide them. It is now

Fig. 6.1 Potential bases of evaluation and behavior

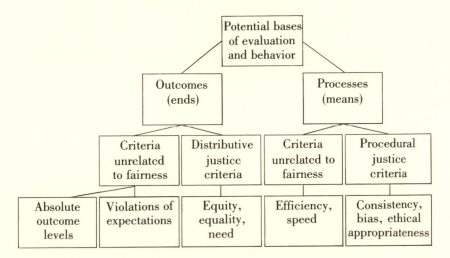

clear that there are many potential effects on citizens' evaluations of legal authority. As a result, identifying what it is that actually drives citizens' support is an important issue for empirical research.

It is important to distinguish not only different aspects of experience that may shape people's reactions to their encounters with legal authorities, but also various attitudes that may be affected by experience. One level of reaction is the citizen's personal satisfaction or dissatisfaction with the experience, its outcome, and the procedures used. Related to this assessment are citizens' emotional or affective reactions to the particular authorities with whom they deal: whether they feel anger at the authorities they encountered. Most psychological research on justice has focused heavily on such personal reactions to experiences.

Reactions to a particular decision or authority are crucial if compliance with the decision made by the authority is the focus of attention. If a judge issues an order to resolve a dispute between two parties, both parties must be willing to accept and obey the judgment. Such compliance might be strongly related to feelings about the judge and satisfaction with his or her decision. A second level of reaction to an experience is more important to those concerned with the viability of the legal system. That concern is with how people's experiences with particular authorities shape their overall orientation toward authorities and institutions. It focuses on citizens' generalizations from their personal experiences to their views about the legitimacy of legal authority. Here citizens use information about particular authorities—the police officers and judges they deal with—

to modify their overall assessments about the legitimacy of groups of authorities. Such views about legitimacy in turn influence citizens' general level of compliance with the law.

Of the four categories of reaction to experience that have been outlined, three are considered in the Chicago study. The one that is not is compliance with specific decisions made by the legal authorities. In the case of police officers this would mean complying with a police order or citation (for example, paying a parking ticket). With judges it would mean abiding by their decision in a case.

Because generalization to citizens' overall attitudes about the legitimacy of legal authorities is the issue, one would expect the impact of experience to be smaller. Citizens will not lose all their faith in legal authorities owing to one bad experience with a police officer or judge, nor would the feeling that legal authorities are not legitimate be overcome by a single favorable experience. What ultimately matters is the sum of one's experiences.

Both the differentiation among factors shaping reactions to experiences and the differentiation among various possible reactions are conceptual frameworks; they identify factors and reactions distinguished on theoretical grounds. It is not necessarily true that the people studied make these distinctions. They may not think about some of the factors identified, and their reactions to experiences may influence only some of the attitudes noted in the study.

Two empirical questions are raised by the existence of alternative models of the citizen. The first is whether the dimensions of experience that theoretical models identify are really viewed by people as different from one another. Although concerns with the favorability of outcomes, the fairness of outcomes, and procedural fairness are distinct theoretically, it is not clear that citizens actually differentiate between these various aspects of experience in their daily lives. An alternative possibility is that judgments about justice are simply rationalizations arrived at by subjects after the fact to justify favorable outcomes. If this is so, judgments about fairness should be strongly related to judgments about the personal gain or loss resulting from a decision.

If citizens distinguish between the favorability of outcomes and distributive or procedural fairness, the role of each judgment in their reactions to experience should be explored. In particular, it is possible that citizens distinguish what is fair from what helps or hurts them, but evaluate authorities in terms of the favorability of outcomes. In this case judgments about fairness may be of interest to psychologists, but they will play little role in maintaining the legitimacy of authorities.

Of course, the conflict between the approach that stresses favorability and that which stresses fairness should not be presented as a struggle to determine which of the two approaches is always correct. Undoubtedly each approach is correct in some circumstances. What is ultimately needed is a typology of factors that predispose individuals toward considering fairness instead of personal gains and losses. A number of studies have examined whether the factors noted have any influence on satisfaction, evaluation, or support. For several reasons it is difficult to use these studies to assess the role of perceived injustice in reactions to authorities. First, none of the studies adequately assesses relative outcome judgments, that is, assessments of the relationship of the outcome received to what was expected before the experience. This failure to measure judgments of relative outcome is particularly troubling because relative outcomes have been found to be much more important than absolute outcomes as predictors of dissatisfaction in the areas of job satisfaction (Lawler 1977) and political discontent (Muller 1980). In addition, many of the studies do not distinguish between distributive and procedural fairness.

The key problem with studies that assess only some of the various potential determinants of evaluation is that they do not form fully specified models (models that include all likely causal factors). If a causal factor is not included, it exists as a plausibly influential third variable. The relationship observed between two measured variables may actually be due to their joint association to a third, unmeasured one. The best method for guarding against such errors is to assess all potentially relevant variables, so that all can be included in any analysis of influence. Because the studies outlined have not typically used this approach, confidence in their conclusions is less warranted.

Several efforts have been made to compare the importance to the evaluation of authorities of the favorability of outcomes and assessments of fairness.[5] Both outcomes and judgments of procedural fairness have been found to influence citizens' evaluations of their experiences with the police (Tyler and Folger 1980), a finding replicated in a study using students' evaluations of teachers and citizens' evaluations of political leaders (Tyler and Caine 1981).

Two recent studies have compared the influence of outcome levels and judgments of fairness in the more general context of encounters with government authorities. A general study of bureaucratic encounters found that both absolute outcomes and judgments of fairness influenced the impact of the experience on trust in government (Katz et al. 1979). This dual influence was also found by Michener and Lawler (1975), who constructed groups of three persons each (one of whom was the group's leader) and varied the character of the groups' interaction. Both the absolute level of outcomes and the fairness of the distribution of outcomes were varied and both had independent effects on the evaluation of each group's leader. Although neither study deals specifically with the police or courts, both show evaluations of leadership to be influenced by both justice and concerns related to outcome. A study of general evaluations of the police obtained similar results. A study of attitudes toward the police in four Midwestern cities found that evaluations were related both to feelings that if called the police would be effective in solving complaints, and to feelings that the police treat all citizens equally (Baker et al. 1979).

All the studies found that both outcomes and issues of justice are important. They are however limited by their failure to specify fully a model of potential effects on evaluation. Several recent studies have used a more complete range of potential variables to explore their effect on the evaluation of authorities; these include measures of absolute outcomes, outcomes relative to expectations, judgments of distributive justice, and judgments of procedural justice. These studies allow the influence of each type of factor to be examined within the context of a fully specified model. One study (Tyler 1984) explored the influence of citizens' experiences in court on their views about their judges and the legal system. The respondents in the study, 121 citizens who had been defendants in traffic or misdemeanor court, were interviewed by telephone. In the interviews they were asked about the disposition of their cases (their absolute outcomes), their outcomes relative to their expectations and to the outcomes of others, and the fairness of their outcomes; they were also asked about the fairness of the trial procedure. The impact of these judgments on satisfaction with outcomes, evaluations of the judge, and evaluations of the overall court system was then examined. The most important dependent variables were evaluations of the judge and of the overall court system. Overall assessments are especially so because they represent the respondents' generalization from their personal experience to broader evaluations of the court system itself. The favorability of outcomes received and fairness judgments were found to be distinguishable, but not totally independent (mean r = .39). Respondents differentiated between the favorability of outcomes and distributive and procedural fairness, but those who received favorable outcomes also regarded their experience as fairer.

The influence of the favorability of outcome and distributive and procedural fairness on views about the judge and the legal system was also examined, using regression analysis. This showed that judgments about the justice or injustice of the respondents' experience had an independent impact on views about the judge, as well as on overall views about the court system.[6] Judgments on justice explained 40 percent of the variance in evaluations of the judge beyond what could be explained by judgments of outcomes, and 15 percent of the variance in evaluations of the court system.

Although the disposition of cases and relative judgments of outcome influenced satisfaction with outcomes (explaining 4 percent of the variance in satisfaction beyond that explained by judgments of fairness), these did not independently influence the impact of the courtroom experience on evaluations of the judge or views about the court system. Only judgments of fairness uniquely influenced views about the judge and the court. Within the overall construct of fairness, both distributive and procedural justice had significant independent influences on evaluations of the judge (Tyler 1984). In contrast, views about the court system were independently influenced only by judgments about the justice of the procedures used to handle the case.

Although no direct influence of outcomes on attitudes toward the judge or court system is found, it is possible that outcomes indirectly influence views about the judge or the courts, by influencing assessments of fairness. The possibility of such an indirect influence is clear, because the favorability of outcomes and judgments of fairness are correlated. A path analysis was conducted to detect such indirect influences.

The path analysis showed that outcome does have indirect influences. Both favorability of outcome (as reflected by how favorably each defendant's case was disposed) and violations of expectancy influence evaluations indirectly, through their effect on judgments of fairness.[7] As a result, the outcomes people receive in court are indirectly related to their evaluations of the judge or the court, although the direct effect of judgments of fairness is greater.

Ideally one would be able to compare the magnitude of two effects on reactions to experience: that of the favorability of outcome, and that of factors unrelated to outcome. Unfortunately, the study (Tyler 1984) did not examine the influence of factors unrelated to outcome that might lead people to feel fairly or unfairly treated (see part III, which deals with the relative impact on perceived fairness of factors related and unrelated to outcome).

Two other studies focused on defendants charged with felonies. They used interviews with 411 felony defendants who either pleaded guilty or were found guilty in trials to examine the basis of the defendants' satisfaction with the process used to settle their cases (Casper, Tyler, and Fisher 1988), and the effect of the disposition of their cases on their views about law and government (Tyler, Casper, and Fisher 1989). The first question examined in these studies was how indices of the favorability of outcomes related to judgments of distributive and procedural justice (as in Tyler 1984). The favorability of outcomes was indexed by the amount of time defendants were sentenced to serve in jail or prison (0 to 360 months), distributive justice was indexed by judgments of the fairness of the sentence received, and procedural justice was indexed by defendants' assessment of the fairness of the process used to settle their cases. Outcome was found to be only weakly related to judgments of distributive justice ($r = .14$) and judgments that the procedure was fair or unfair ($r = .20$). The two types of judgment of justice also were only weakly related ($r = .29$).

The second question was that of the impact of different judgments about experience on defendants' satisfaction with the trial, and the influence of the trial experience on generalizations about legal authorities, law, and government. These influences were explored using a causal model. When the defendant's satisfaction with the disposition of his or her case was the dependent variable, procedural justice was found to have a significant influence on satisfaction, as was distributive justice. In the case of defendants' generalizations from their experiences to broader views about legal authorities, law, and government, a more complex causal analysis was performed that took advantage of the nature of panel data (that is, the defendants were interviewed both before and after their legal experience). In the analysis the judgments based on experience (assessed after the trial) were supplemented with the measure of attitudes made before the trial. The regression analysis examined change in views about legal authorities, law, and government resulting from the experience of having one's case settled. The results of that analysis showed that procedural issues dominate generalization. In fact, the justice of the procedure of settling a case is the only factor with a significant influence on generalizations from experiences to attitudes toward legal authorities, law, and government.

Both studies examined people's reactions to particular experiences with legal authorities. It is also possible to examine the effect on evaluations of general judgments about authorities. For example, if people feel that they generally receive good treatment from the police or that the police typically solve problems effectively, do these general judgments affect their views of the police? Unfortunately, no general study has explored views about legal authorities. One study, however, has conducted such an exploration using political authorities.

Another study examined political views among a random sample of 300 residents of the Chicago area interviewed by telephone during spring 1983 (Tyler, Rasinski, and McGraw 1985). The study looked at factors affecting evaluations of President Reagan and of the political system in general. The two dependent variables were similar to those used to distinguish between evaluation of the formal leader and evaluation of the overall system; the difference is that general views rather than the results of a specific experience were evaluated. In addition, the antecedents of political evaluations are more complex: people were asked about their satisfaction with government benefits, with the level of taxes they paid, and with government policies.

To measure respondents' judgments about the level of benefits they received from the federal government and the level of federal taxes they paid, respondents were asked for each issue both to indicate their absolute levels of benefits and taxes they pay, and to compare these levels to their expectations. They were also asked about the fairness of the benefits and taxes. Finally, they were asked about the fairness of the procedures used to allocate benefits and determine tax rates.

The second issue examined was that of respondents' evaluations of public policy in the economic and social arenas. Respondents were asked whether the policies of the Reagan administration in each arena had helped them or hurt them, and about the distributive fairness of the policies. They were also asked about the procedural justice of the administration's policymaking procedures.[8]

As in the studies of experience already outlined, the first empirical issue to be addressed was the relationship between judgments of favorability of outcome and judgments of fairness. In the case of benefits and taxes the magnitude of the relationship was low (mean r = .17). With policy issues the mean correlation was .36 (similar in magnitude to that found in Tyler 1984). In other words, judgments based on fairness were distinct from those that were not, but not independent of them. Those placed at an advantage with respect to outcome were more likely to view the administration's policies as fair.[9]

Judgments based on fairness were found to have a greater influence on evaluations of the president and government than did judgments not based on fairness.[10] This was true both when the judgments considered were about government policies and when they were about benefits received and taxes paid. Judgments about personal gain and loss from the administration's economic and social policies, or of personal gain or loss from the administration's allocation of benefits and taxes, explained virtually no independent variance in support for Reagan or for the government itself (the average R-squared was less than 1 percent). In contrast to judgments not based on fairness, judgments of the relative fairness of policies and of benefits and taxes explained a substantial amount of independent variance (the average R-squared was 24 percent). In the case of satisfaction with benefits and taxes and agreement with policies, outcomes were slightly more important, but still less important than fairness judgments (the average R-squared for outcomes was 3 percent, for fairness judgments 13 percent).

If the influence of distributive fairness is distinguished from that of procedural fairness, the latter is found to be the key to evaluations both of President Reagan and of the government. In evaluations of President Reagan, judgments of distributive justice are also found to have a small influence. Citizens seem to care a great deal about issues of fairness when making general evaluations about government. Within the realm of fairness, procedural fairness seems the key issue, especially in judgments of legitimacy.

As before, path analysis was used to examine the direct and indirect influences of judgments based on outcome on satisfaction with benefits and taxes, agreement with policies, evaluations of the incumbent administration, and evaluations of the government system itself. Again the purpose of this analysis was to test the possibility that outcomes exert an indirect influence through their direct influence on judgments of fairness. The results show evidence of indirect influence by outcomes on judgments of justice, and of major, direct influence of judgments of justice on evaluations of the incumbent and government. Evidently, outcomes do exercise some indirect influence on evaluations, but only through their influence on judgments of fairness.

Unfortunately the literature reviewed has focused primarily on the effects on peoples' attitudes rather than on their behavior. Several studies suggest, however, that the effects of procedural justice may also extend to behavior. [11]

Friedland, Thibaut, and Walker (1973) examined in two studies the influence that judgments of procedural justice have on obedience to the law: one study was conducted in the laboratory, the other in the field. Both examined the effects of procedural justice and the severity of penalties on compliance with rules. The studies compared rules that were enacted fairly with others that were enacted unfairly. They found that procedural justice enhanced compliance, and that this enhancement was greater when the authority involved was enacting the rules fairly. Two other field studies indirectly confirm that procedural justice can enhance the acceptance of decisions made by an authority. McEwen and Maiman (1984) studied compliance with mediated and adjudicated settlements of disputes in small claims court. They found that litigants are more likely to comply with judgments that they perceive to be fair. Although McEwen and Maiman do not directly assess procedural fairness, their data show indirectly that procedural fairness is important in the effect of fairness that they found. [12]

A second field study by Adler, Hensler, and Nelson (1983) has findings similar to those of McEwen and Maiman in the context of nonbinding arbitration administered by the courts. They found that the satisfaction of litigants was an important determinant of whether an award was accepted. This satisfaction was found in turn to be linked to judgments of the perceived fairness of the procedure used to resolve the dispute. Again procedural justice was found to influence behavior indirectly, although the direct relationship between procedural fairness and acceptance was not measured.

In discussing reactions to experience, I have assumed that people always react to their experience in the same terms. This assumption is consistent with the research finding that the effects of procedural fairness are widespread in legal, political, industrial, educational, and interpersonal settings (for reviews see Lind and Tyler 1988; Tyler, Rasinski, and Griffin 1986). It is also true, however, that the degree of procedural influence has been found to vary, both in absolute terms and relative to the influence of distributive justice and concerns not based in fairness (see Tyler 1986a). In other words, those affected by decision-making procedures are not always equally concerned with their fairness. The further question of when procedural justice influences people's reactions to decisions might also be explored.

Ideally a test of the hypothesis that the importance of procedural justice varies with circumstances should be based on a typology of situations or people (or both) that leads to theoretically derived predictions about variations induced by circumstances. No such typology has yet been developed either for the study of moral issues (Kurtines 1986) or for the area of conflicts resolved by third parties. As a result, the dimensions used in the Chicago study and predictions about their effects were derived more generally from the literature on procedural justice and the resolution of conflict. Two hypotheses about when procedural justice matters were tested. One links the question to situational variations; the other links the question to the stakes involved.

Situational Variations

Past studies have found that procedural justice matters more when the authorities have imposed themselves on a person than when contact with the authorities has been freely chosen (Tyler and Folger 1980; Tyler, Rasinski, and McGraw 1985). Several studies suggest that this dimension of experiences may affect the importance of procedural justice. When citizens were asked to evaluate contacts with the police (Tyler and Folger 1980), it was found that procedural justice is a more important issue when citizens have been stopped by the police than when they have called the police for help. In the political arena, procedural justice was found to be more important with respect to the constrained aspects of a citizen's relationship to government, such as taxes, than with respect to the voluntary aspects, such as benefits (see Tyler, Rasinski, and McGraw 1985).

Finally, similar findings emerged from a study by Lissak and Sheppard (1983), in which decision makers were interviewed about the criteria they viewed as important in resolving disputes. In the first phase of the study, involving managers' evaluations of disputes in the workplace, procedural fairness did not emerge as the most important criterion. Similar results were obtained in a second phase of the study, involving evaluations of disputes in the workplace by people who were not managers. In the third phase of the study fairness was found to be the key factor in evaluations by the police of procedures used to intervene in disputes. If these procedures are more coercive than those of managers in work disputes, then constraint is again found to heighten attention to procedural justice. Of course these situations also differ in other ways: for example, managers have continuing social relationships with those they manage, whereas police officers seldom know or expect to see again the people they deal with. Because the nature of the social relationship influences judgments about justice, such differences could be quite important (Lind and Tyler 1988).

Thibaut and Walker (1975) studied procedural justice within a particular setting: trials conducted to resolve disputes between parties. Although these are very important symbolically, most of the dealings that people have with legal authorities involve the police, not the courts, and do not have to do with disputes. How important is procedural justice to the larger universe of people's experiences with legal authorities? To test the generalization of Thibaut and Walker two features of the experience must be considered: whether the authorities involved were police officers or judges, and whether there was a dispute between parties. If respondents have received a favorable outcome, they may be expected to evaluate their experience in procedural terms. If on the other hand they received a poor or unfair outcome, they might focus on that issue rather than on procedural fairness.

A second situational variation that might influence the degree to which respondents are concerned with procedural justice is the importance of the outcome involved. Several social scientists believe that people are less concerned about fairness when outcomes are more important (Heinz 1985; Lerner 1971). An extreme example is the case of those on trial for serious crimes, who may care more about the outcome of the trial than about its procedures. This possibility is supported by some evidence (Heinz 1985) and contradicted by other evidence (Casper, Tyler, and Fisher 1988; Landis and Goodstein 1986).

In summary, the ability of legal authorities to function effectively depends on their sensitivity to the concerns of those with whom they deal. Although it has been widely assumed that such concerns are instrumental, there are alternative perspectives to an instrumental view. The Chicago study focuses on one such alternative, a perspective based on normative justice. It explores how people's concerns with distributive and procedural justice influence their reactions to their experiences with police officers and judges. Recent studies cast doubt on whether an instrumental perspective is adequate for explaining people's reactions to their experiences. Issues of justice are uniformly found to have an important role in shaping such reactions. In particular, issues of procedural justice dominate generalizations from experiences to views about law and authority.

CHAPTER 7

Measuring the Psychological Variables

The Chicago study addresses two issues. The first is the relationship between the favorability of outcomes and judgments of distributive and procedural fairness. If normative judgments are not distinct from instrumental judgments, they cannot make an independent contribution to how people react to their experiences. Nothing new would be added to the ability to understand reactions to experiences by knowing whether those involved in the experience thought that the procedures were fair or unfair, beyond what would be learned by knowing whether the people had won their case or had their problem solved.

The second question is the extent to which judgments of fairness influence reactions to experience. If fairness judgments are distinct from issues of the favorability of outcomes, they can potentially exercise a separate influence on people's reactions to their experiences; this of course does not mean that they do exercise such an influence.

Given the similarity of the questions addressed here to those examined in the research discussed in the preceding chapter (Casper, Tyler, and Fisher 1988; Tyler 1984; Tyler, Casper, and Fisher 1989; Tyler, Rasinski, and McGraw 1985), why is this study needed? One important extension beyond earlier work is the larger scope of this project: its inclusion of the impact of experience on compliance with the law, and its more complex examination of the meaning of procedural justice. Another contribution of the Chicago study is its inclusion of a broader range of experiences than has been considered in earlier studies. Some have focused exclusively on defendants in court (see Tyler 1984; Casper, Tyler, and Fisher 1988; see also Casper, Tyler, and Fisher 1989), others only on citizens' encounters with the police (Tyler and Folger 1980). The Chicago study explores the full range of citizens' experiences with both judicial authority and police authority.

It is particularly important to consider a broader range of citizens' dealings with legal authority when addressing the role of their judgments about procedural justice in how they react to experiences with legal authorities. The focus of Thibaut and Walker on formal courtroom trials has continued to dominate more recent studies of procedural justice. Because recent research has found that the scope of procedural justice effects may be much broader than courtroom trials (Lind and Tyler 1988; Tyler 1987c; Tyler and Bies, in press), it is important to explore a broader range of experiences.

The Chicago study also expands the range of independent variables considered to include violations in procedural expectancies. Although the idea of procedural expectancies not based on questions of fairness is clear, the impact of violating such expectancies has not been studied. Again, research has followed the framework established by Thibaut and Walker (1975) and focused on aspects of procedures that are related to judgments of their fairness. But there are many elements of procedure that are not necessarily linked to fairness (see Lissak and Sheppard 1983; Tyler 1987c); for this reason the Chicago study attempts to capture this procedural focus, by measuring violations in procedural expectancies. [1] The range of the dependent variables considered is also expanded in the Chicago study. In particular, the impact of experiences on the legitimacy of legal authorities is assessed. Because legitimacy has a direct influence on behavioral compliance with the law (see part I), it is possible by measuring the impact of experience on legitimacy to test the hypothesis that experience has implications for citizens' overall behavioral orientation toward the law.

The Chicago study's approach to understanding citizens' concerns in dealing with police officers and judges focuses on specific experiences with legal authorities, and their effect on citizens' views about the legitimacy of authority and citizens' behavior toward the law. The advantage of an approach that focuses on experience is that it asks respondents to describe and direct their evaluations toward a concrete event rather than to make global assessments about authorities. Past studies have suggested that citizens have difficulty distinguishing various aspects of the actions of authorities on a global level. [2]

An important presumption of an approach based on experience is that what is experienced as an adult influences the citizen's views on the legitimacy of legal authority. Theories of legitimacy oriented toward socialization have emphasized that such views are acquired in childhood and may or may not be modifiable in later life (see Easton and Dennis 1969), so it cannot be presumed that such an influence based on experience will be found. For the approach based on experience to be reasonable, it is first necessary to show that experiences do in fact influence citizens' evaluations of legal authorities. [3]

Earlier research on citizens' satisfaction with political and legal authorities has been concerned with two distinct populations: "ordinary" citizens (such as those studied in Katz et al. 1975), and special populations, such as the defendants in felony cases (Casper 1978). The Chicago study focuses on the former; the encounters studied are of the type that most citizens have with legal authorities. It is important to recognize that the findings of the Chicago study may not generalize to major criminal trials and defendants facing long terms in prison or large fines (for efforts to deal with this question see Casper, Tyler, and Fisher 1988; Tyler, Casper, and Fisher 1989), or to contacts between citizens and police that are extremely serious in nature. Similarly, studies of major trials may not generalize to the more mundane encounters that form the bulk of the contact that ordinary citizens have with legal authorities.

Because the Chicago study focuses on the mundane, everyday experiences of citizens, it is especially important to demonstrate that these experiences do influence views about the legitimacy of legal authority. If the results of the study show the mundane, everyday experiences to have little or no influence on citizens' views about the legitimacy of the police and courts, then the focus on adult experiences is inappropriate. In that case studies of legitimacy should be directed at the socialization process or toward the major encounters with the police and the courts that are infrequent but potentially more influential.

Given that the effects of experience on general compliance are likely to be weak and indirect, why study those effects rather than compliance with a specific judicial decision? The reasons flow from the focus on political psychology underlying the approach taken in this book. A focus on political psychology leads to a concern with civic attitudes, such as views about the legitimacy of legal authority, which are essential to the effective functioning of society. This general civic culture supports the activities of the police and courts, and is expected to lead people to be more law-abiding in their everyday lives. This research, in other words, is not concerned with criminology. It does not focus on criminals with extensive experience with the legal system. It focuses on the ordinary citizens whose everyday compliance with the law is crucial to the effectiveness of the legal system.

What Types of Experiences Did People Have?

One type of experience that people had was initiated when they called the police. People called the police for a wide range of reasons: to report accidents, because of disturbances, problems, and suspicious activities in their neighborhood, and to report crimes against property and violent crimes. An examination of the calls to which the police responded (for the first wave n = 303) suggests enormous variation in the importance of the issues of concern to the callers. People themselves varied in their estimation of the seriousness of the problems. In all, 40 percent felt that their problem was very serious, 19 percent that it was quite serious, 32 percent that it was somewhat serious, and 10 percent that it was not serious at all. When asked how important it was to them that the police solved the problem, 54 percent said it was very important or quite important.

Most people whose calls were responded to in person felt positively about how quickly the police came: 67 percent said the police had responded very quickly or quite quickly, and only 15 percent said they had responded "not quickly at all." Beyond believing that the police had responded to their calls, 69 percent of the respondents knew specifically what actions the police had taken: 65 percent of those who knew what the police had done said the police had solved the problem. Of those who knew what the police had done and said the police had not solved the problem, 43 percent said the police had done everything they could to try to solve it. Therefore, 79 percent of those who knew what the police had done felt that they had either solved the problem or done everything possible to do so. Further, of the 46 percent who thought that in addition to solving the problem at hand the police could have done something to prevent similar problems in the future, 55 percent said that the police had taken some preventive action. Given these feelings, it is not surprising that 71 percent of all respondents should have expressed satisfaction with the outcome of their call; of those who said their problem was very serious or quite serious, 67 percent expressed satisfaction.

Respondents also felt that the way the police treated them mattered (70 percent said this was very important to them). In general, people said they had been well treated: 95 percent said the police had been polite; 88 percent said the police had shown concern for their rights; 93 percent said they were honest; 86 percent said they did nothing that was improper; 89 percent said they listened to the caller's description of the problem before acting; and 85 percent said they considered the caller's opinions in making decisions about how to handle the problem. Interestingly, the responses were less favorable when people were asked to infer "how hard" the police had tried to be fair to them: only 66 percent said the police had tried very hard or quite hard. Overall, however, 86 percent of all respondents expressed satisfaction with the way they had been treated by the police.

A second type of experience with the police occurred when the police stopped citizens, primarily for traffic offenses (this contrasts with telephone calls to the police, which varied widely in content and severity). Most respondents (86 percent) rated those offenses as "not serious at all" (62 percent) or somewhat serious (24 percent), and 86 percent knew the outcome of their experience. Of this group 59 percent were cited for a violation of the law, although most of the violations were trivial. Of those cited 56 percent called the violation of the law not serious at all and 35 percent called it only somewhat serious. Only 17 percent were arrested or taken to a police station. The incidents of being stopped by the police were also different from the telephone calls in that 45 percent of the respondents were dissatisfied with the outcome of their experience, which reflects that most received at least a traffic ticket. Although dissatisfied, 73 percent of respondents called their outcome fair, suggesting that many respondents felt they deserved the ticket they received. A majority of respondents (60 percent) said they felt it was very important that they be well treated by the police; an additional 16 percent said this was quite important. This is essentially the same proportion as was found when respondents were asked about the importance of the outcome (65 percent said it was very important or quite important).

Respondents generally felt less fairly treated when stopped by the police than they did when they had called the police for help. Only 65 percent said the police had been polite; 60 percent said they had showed concern for their rights; 75 percent said they had been honest; 69 percent said they had done nothing improper; 42 percent said they had listened before acting; and 40 percent said the police had considered what they had said. Finally, only 32 percent felt that the police had tried very hard or quite hard to be fair to them. Despite these grievances, 77 percent of respondents indicated that they were very satisfied or somewhat satisfied with the police, 65 percent said the procedures used by the police were fair, and 69 percent said they had been treated fairly by the police.

The final type of experience with legal authorities occurred when respondents went to court. This happened for many reasons, including debt collections, disputes between tenant and landlord, disputes with neighbors and business associates, and family problems. The problem that brought about an appearance in court was described as very serious or somewhat serious by 38 percent of the respondents, and 67 percent said whether they won their case was very important.

Of all respondents, 67 percent felt they had appeared in court voluntarily, although 72 percent were in fact defending themselves against the claims of other persons;[4] 30 percent were represented by an attorney. In most instances the case was dismissed (57 percent), whereas 13 percent settled informally, 11 percent pleaded guilty, and 11 percent had a trial.

Of the 84 percent of respondents who knew what the judgment was in their case, 50 percent were very pleased with the outcome and 25 percent were somewhat pleased. Similarly, 70 percent expressed overall satisfaction with the outcome of their case, and 78 percent called it fair. Despite this general satisfaction, 36 percent also said they thought there were additional things the judge could have done to reach a "better" outcome.

Eighty-five percent of respondents said how they were treated by the judge was important to them (67 percent called it very important). Eighty-eight percent said the judge was polite; 76 percent said he or she showed concern for their rights; 82 percent said he or she did nothing improper. On the other hand, only 49 percent felt they had an opportunity to state their case; only 57 percent said their views were considered; and only 45 percent said the judge had tried to be fair to them. Overall, 77 percent felt that the procedures used by the judge were fair, and 80 percent felt that they were treated fairly.

Unfavorability of outcome was measured absolutely and relatively. The absolute quality of the outcome was determined by coding respondents' statements about the outcomes that resulted from their experience. In the case of calls to the police, respondents were asked whether the police had solved the problem at hand. Where respondents had been stopped by the police, they were asked whether the police had cited them for a violation of the law, and, if the police had done so, whether they had arrested the respondents or taken them to a police station. With court cases respondents were asked to evaluate the favorability of the outcome of their cases.

Respondents' judgments of the positive or negative quality of their outcomes were weighted by the self-reported seriousness of the problem (very serious 27 percent, quite serious 13 percent, somewhat serious 27 percent, not serious at all 33 percent), to produce a scale of the absolute unfavorability of the outcome. In each case the scale of unfavorability ranged from 1 to 8, with high scores indicating unfavorable outcomes. The way ratings of favorability or unfavorability were distributed for each type of contact shows that respondents were most likely to report negative outcomes in cases where they called the police (34 percent), or when they were in court involuntarily (35 percent). Being stopped by the police produced higher levels of outcomes (81 percent positive), as did going to court voluntarily (81 percent positive; see appendix C for data on frequency).[5]

Respondents also rated the unfavorability of the outcome of their contact with legal authorities in relation to four standards: what they expected before the contact, what they had received in the past, what they thought others generally received in similar cases, and what their friends, family, or neighbors had received in the past.[6] Unfavorability in relation to prior experiences was assessed by asking respondents to compare their outcomes to other outcomes they had received in the past. Fifty-five percent of respondents said that their past outcomes had been similar, 18 percent said they had been better, and 10 percent said they had been worse; 15 percent had had no past experience. Unfavorability in relation to the outcomes of other people "in similar situations" was also assessed. Sixty-four percent of respondents said their outcomes were similar to those received by others, 28 percent said theirs were better than those of others, and 9 percent said theirs were worse than those of others. Assessments of unfavorability in relation to expectations showed that 43 percent of respondents received the outcomes they expected, 32 percent received better outcomes than they expected, and 25 percent worse outcomes than they expected.

Finally, unfavorability was assessed in relation to the recent experiences of family, neighbors, and friends. Of those respondents interviewed, 33 percent said they knew of other such experiences during the past year. Fifty-four percent said that they had received an outcome similar to that of their family, neighbors, or friends, 32 percent said their outcome was better, and 14 percent said their outcome was worse.[7]

Respondents rated not only the favorability of their outcomes according to these standards, but also the favorability of their treatment by the authorities (see Tyler 1986a).[8] Respondents first compared their treatment to their past experiences. Fifty-four percent said that their treatment was the same as it had been in the past, 21 percent that it was better, and 11 percent that it was worse (15 percent had had no past experience). Respondents then compared their treatment with what other people received in similar situations. Sixty-eight percent felt that their treatment had been similar to that received by others, 22 percent that it had been better, and 10 percent that it had been worse. On comparing their treatment to what they had expected before the experience, 46 percent of respondents said they had been treated as they expected they would be, 32 percent that they had been treated better, and 22 percent that they had been treated worse.

Finally, respondents compared their treatment to that recently received by neighbors, friends, or family. Of those aware of other such cases, 58 percent said their treatment was similar to that of others, 38 percent said it was better, and 4 percent said it was worse.[9]

The many relative judgments of outcome and treatment made by the respondents in the Chicago study are strikingly similar (see appendix C). In all cases the most common result is that people find the experience in question to be similar to others, whether those other experiences are personal experiences of the past, the experiences of other people, or experiences foreseen in the future. The evaluations that differ from the general pattern also show a striking similarity: in all cases respondents are more likely to say that their experience was better than the comparison standard than that it was worse. Thus if people evaluate their experiences primarily in relative terms, evaluations of the police and courts should grow more positive with experience. This is the case because most people think they are treated as well as the comparison standard or better (irrespective of what that standard is).

In addition to judgments about the absolute and relative favorability of outcomes and the relative favorability of treatment, respondents were asked to judge the fairness of the outcomes they received. Fairness of outcomes was assessed through two questions: one asked for a judgment of the fairness of the outcome the respondent received (57 percent called it very fair, 23 percent somewhat fair, 8 percent somewhat unfair, and 13 percent very unfair); the other asked whether the authorities gave the case or problem the attention it deserved (58 percent said yes, 14 percent said they gave it more attention than it deserved, and 28 percent said they gave it less attention than it deserved).[10] Procedural fairness was assessed by asking respondents how fair the procedures used by the police or courts were and how fairly the respondents were treated. Most respondents called the procedures fair (54 percent called them very fair, 24 percent somewhat fair, 11 percent somewhat unfair, and 10 percent very unfair) and said they had been fairly treated (49 percent said very fairly, 32 percent somewhat fairly, 9 percent somewhat unfairly, and 10 percent very unfairly).[11]

Conceptualizing Relative Judgments

Of the judgments outlined, relative judgments were the most difficult to conceptualize. The problem is that one does not know which referent is being used when people make relative judgments. In other words, with what do people compare their experience when they are judging its relative favorability? The Chicago study used four possible standards against which experience might be compared. What is not clear, however, is which of these standards ought to be used in the analysis. To decide which relative judgments to use in the study, each was compared to the others and to the dependent variables in question (see appendix C). In addition, each was compared to an overall index representing the average of the judgments. By examining the relationship of judgments to the dependent variables it was found that violations of expectations best predicted the dependent variables. Because this single index was better than an average index, it was used in the later analysis.[12]

The first question to address is whether respondents distinguished between outcome or procedural favorability and outcome or procedural fairness. By examining the correlation among items measuring those concepts one sees that the two concepts are distinct but not independent (see appendix C). To some extent those receiving more favorable outcomes or treatment do rate those outcomes or procedures as fairer (mean $r = .46$). The correlations among the justice indicators also suggest that distributive and procedural justice are distinct but related.[13] They are distinct because the internal consistency of each is higher than the relationship between the two, and they are related because of their nonzero correlation (mean $r = .62$). It is obvious that respondents see distributive and procedural justice as closely intertwined.

As with the data from the first wave of interviews, the most immediate question concerning the data from the second is whether the indices of outcome and favorability of procedure, and of outcome and fairness of procedure, are different in the minds of the respondents. Again the two concepts are distinct but not independent (see appendix C). Those receiving more favorable outcomes or treatment rate the outcomes or treatment as fairer (mean $r = .46$). But unlike the data from the first wave of interviews, the correlations from the second wave do not suggest that distributive and procedural justice represent two distinct judg-ments.[14] What prevents the two constructs from being clearly distinct is a lower correlation between the two distributive justice items than is found in the sample from the first wave. Despite this lack of empirical separation, for theoretical reasons the two concepts were kept separate in this analysis.

Two types of dependent variable were considered: personal satisfaction and evaluation of authorities. Questions about satisfaction assessed citizens' personal satisfaction with their outcomes (46 percent were very satisfied, 23 percent somewhat satisfied, 11 percent somewhat dissatisfied, and 20 percent very dis-satisfied) and with their treatment (53 percent were very satisfied, 23 percent somewhat satisfied, 12 percent somewhat dissatisfied, and 12 percent very dissatisfied).

Respondents were also asked about the influence of their experience on their feelings toward the authorities with whom they dealt. They were asked to indicate whether they felt anger (22 percent said yes) or frustration (32 percent said yes), or were pleased with the authorities (55 percent said yes). Finally questions were asked to elicit the degree to which respondents generalized from their experi-ences to views about the overall type of authority they had dealt with, rating the quality of performance of the police and courts (as outlined in the previously outlined evaluation scale) and the legitimacy of legal authority (again, in the manner previously described).[15]

To assess evaluations, respondents were given a score for the authority with which they had dealt (police or courts). This approach was found to explain more of the variance than would have been found simply by giving everyone an average evaluation score (38 percent of the variance was explained by experience, as opposed to 27 percent with the average score).

The data were found to be generally suitable for a test of the theories outlined above. Consequently, the results of the analysis allow both key issues of the Chicago study to be addressed. First, the relationship between judgments of favorability and judgments of fairness can be explored. Second, the role of each of these judgments in shaping reactions to experience can be established. With respect to measurement, the most troubling aspect of the data is the strong correlation between items measuring distributive fairness and items measuring procedural fairness. Although these two concepts can be clearly distinguished theoretically, the data suggest that they are closely intertwined in the minds of the respondents of the Chicago study.

CHAPTER 8

Does Experience Influence Legitimacy?

In this chapter I explore the impact of experience on views about legal authority. Regression analysis was used to examine the influence of judgments about experience both on evaluative reactions to the experience itself and on generalizations from personal experiences to broader views about legal authority. Two samples were used: the 652 respondents in the first wave of interviews with recent personal experience, and the 291 respondents in the second wave with recent personal experience. In the regression equations used to explore the impact of judgments about experience (assessments of the quality of the outcome received, and judgments of distributive and procedural fairness) were included as independent variables, and reactions to experience were dependent variables. Two types of reaction were considered: personal reactions (satisfaction with outcome, satisfaction with treatment, affect toward the authorities dealt with), and generalizations to views about the legitimacy and quality of performance of legal authorities.

As would be expected, judgments about experiences were found to influence satisfaction with the experiences. Sixty-one percent of the variance in satisfaction with outcome was explained by judgments about experience in the first wave, as were 65 percent of satisfaction with treatment and 55 percent of affect toward the authorities dealt with. Judgments about the legitimacy of the police and courts are also affected by experience (R-squared = 4 percent in the first wave), as are performance evaluations (R-squared = 34 percent in the first wave). These findings confirm that personal experience with police officers or court officials affects general views about the legitimacy of these authorities and the quality of their job performance. The data also suggest that the effect of experience on performance evaluations is much stronger than its effect on legitimacy. People's views about the legitimacy of legal authorities are more strongly insulated than performance evaluations are from the influence of a good or bad experience with police officers or a judge.

Of course, the regression analysis already outlined does not take advantage of the panel design of the study, which allows the influence of experiences between the two waves to be examined. It allows the impact of experience on people's views about the legitimacy of legal authority to be examined if one controls for prior views about the legitimacy of legal authority. Panel analysis is more sensitive than cross-sectional analysis. In a cross-sectional study it must be assumed that differences in the views expressed after an experience are due to the nature of the experience rather than to views held before the experience. A panel design allows this assumption to be directly tested, because both factors can be included in the analysis.

The first question is whether a more sensitive analysis of the type allowed by the panel data reveals any influence of experience on views about legal authority. The 291 respondents who were interviewed at two points in time and who had had a personal experience with the police or courts in the year between the two interviews were used to test this possibility. Looking first at people's views about the legitimacy of legal authorities, legitimacy scores computed before their experiences were found to explain 15 percent of the variance in their assessments of legitimacy made after their experiences. Adding the experiential judgments in a second stage increased this explanatory power to 18 percent (that is, there was an increment of 3 percent in the amount of variance explained; $F(1, 179) = 6.52$, p $< .05$). Adding both the experiential judgments (favorability of outcome, distributive justice, procedural justice) and evaluations specific to the experiences (satisfaction with outcome, satisfaction with treatment, affect) brought the level of explained variance 4 percent above that achieved by using the views held before the experiences (to 19 percent; $F(1, 176) = 8.70$, $P < .001$).

As for evaluations of the quality of the police and courts, measures of evaluation taken before the experience explained 40 percent of the variance in evaluations after the experience. When measures resulting from experience are added to the equation, 8 percent more variance is explained ($F(1, 154) = 23.53$, p $< .001$). Adding both the experiential variables and the evaluations specific to the experiences (satisfaction with outcome, satisfaction with treatment, affect) brought explained variance to a level 10 percent above that achieved using views held before the experiences ($F(1, 151) = 30.30$, p $< .001$).

In both instances judgments at the first wave significantly influenced those at the second. In other words, what people thought after their experience about the legitimacy and quality of performance of the police and courts was influenced by what they thought about them before their experience: experience did not overwhelm prior views. In addition, in both instances judgments based in experience also affected opinions held after the experiences: prior views did not overwhelm experience. Both the cross-sectional analysis and the panel analysis suggest that people's experiences influence their general views about the legitimacy of legal authorities and their evaluations of the general quality of the authorities' performance. The panel data suggest that this effect occurs even when the influence of prior views is removed.

Given that experience has been found to influence assessments of legitimacy, one can also ask which of the models outlined best explains what about experience accounts for its influence on satisfaction and evaluations. The two basic models that might explain reactions to experience include an instrumental one, according to which the key influence on reactions to experience is the favorability of outcome of that experience, and a normative one, according to which judgments of distributive and procedural fairness also are important influences on these reactions.

Regression analysis was used to isolate the influence of different aspects of experience.[1] The independent variables in this regression analysis were judgments about experience related and unrelated to fairness. The dependent variables were reactions to experience and generalizations from experience to views about legal authority. In the case of judgments specific to experience (satisfaction with outcome, satisfaction with treatment, affect toward the authorities dealt with), as well as with generalizations to evaluations of performance and legitimacy ratings, regression analysis shows that fairness judgments are the key to evaluations of both the experience and the authorities. One example of the influence of fairness is the case of satisfaction with outcome. The usefulness analysis shows that fairness judgments explain 21 percent of the variance beyond that explained by judgments unrelated to fairness.[2] By contrast, judgments unrelated to fairness explain only 1 percent of the variance beyond what can be explained by those related to fairness. Once the influence of fairness issues has been taken into account, little is added by considering favorability of outcome. Affect toward the authorities dealt with is similarly dominated by fairness issues (22 percent of the variance is uniquely explained by fairness, 1 percent by favorability of outcome). Satisfaction with treatment is also dominated by fairness issues, but not as strongly (judgments related to fairness explain 27 percent of the unique variance in judgments; those unrelated to fairness explain 1 percent). This is also true of generalizations about the quality of performance of the authorities and views about their legitimacy.[3] In these two cases judgments unrelated to fairness explain no unique variance, whereas judgments related to fairness explain 18 percent of the unique variance in the case of performance evaluations and 4 percent in the case of legitimacy.

Although fairness judgments dominate reactions to experiences, it is also important that direct outcome effects do emerge. These effects are consistently related to one factor: relative judgments of outcome. A significant positive influence on the part of relative judgments of outcome is found for satisfaction with outcome, satisfaction with treatment, and affect. Although consistently found, this effect of relative outcomes is small.[4] Neither the absolute favorability of outcomes nor the relative favorability of procedures influences any type of reaction to experiences. In the earlier discussion of relative judgments it was noted that research has focused on violations of expectancy in the area of outcome, but has ignored the possibility of violated procedural expectations. The Chicago study tested this possibility by examining the effects of procedural expectancy terms on reactions to experience. The results reveal no such effects. People do not seem to react to violations in expectations about how they will be treated, although they do react to the more traditionally studied issue of violations in expectations about what outcomes they will receive.

Within the general framework of fairness, procedural concerns consistently take precedence over distributive concerns. The only exception is the case of satisfaction with outcome, which not unexpectedly is more responsive to issues of outcome than to those of procedure. Affect, evaluation of performance, and legitimacy are all more strongly influenced by procedural fairness than by favorability of outcome or fairness of outcome. This finding accords with other recent evidence suggesting that citizens' evaluations of the authorities are heavily influenced by their judgments about the fairness of the decision-making procedures used by the authorities (Tyler, Rasinski, and Griffin 1986).[5]

It is possible that judgments unrelated to fairness have an effect, but one that is indirect: that is, their direct effects are on judgments related to fairness. Such indirect effects have been found in other recent studies of procedural justice (Tyler 1984; Casper, Tyler, and Fisher 1988; Tyler, Casper, and Fisher 1989; Tyler, Rasinski, and McGraw 1985). A causal model was used to examine this possibility, and as in earlier studies indirect effects emerged.[6] The nature of the indirect effect of judgments unrelated to fairness was as would be expected. Favorability of outcome and violated expectations of outcome influence judgments of distributive fairness more strongly than they influence judgments of procedural fairness. Violations of procedural expectations, on the other hand, influence judgments of procedural justice more strongly than they influence judgments of distributive justice.

That outcome indirectly affects judgments about justice raises an important question about the model being elaborated. Because outcomes influence judgments about justice, which in turn influence reactions to experience, favorability of outcome and procedure appears to be driving the reactions to experience. In fact, the results of the causal modeling initially suggest that favorability of outcome and procedure is the key determinant of judgments of distributive and procedural justice. Are judgments about justice more than justifications for favorable or unfavorable outcomes? This issue is directly addressed in the final section of this book, which focuses on the meaning of fair procedure and contrasts outcomes with other potential determinants of the fairness of a procedure.

The regression analysis does not take advantage of the panel aspects of the Chicago study; causal modeling does. The modeling uses the 291 respondents

**Fig. 8.1 Panel analysis of the impact of experience on views
about legal authority**

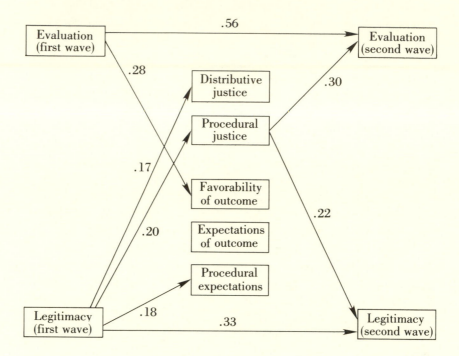

who had a personal experience with legal authorities during the year between the
two interviews. It focuses on the two dependent variables that involve generalization from personal experience to overall views: performance evaluation and
legitimacy. The causal model shows that controls for prior evaluations and legitimacy ratings do not eliminate the effects of procedural fairness on evaluation and
legitimacy (fig. 8.1). In addition, it suggests that prior views (in particular, prior
assessments of legitimacy) shape assessments of the fairness of experience.
Those who view the authorities they deal with as more legitimate before their
experience feel that they have received fairer outcomes and treatment in later
experiences.[7]

Does Procedure Provide a Cushion of Support?

The large sample involved in this study (n = 652) allows a realistic
test of the ability of fair procedures to mitigate the effects of negative outcomes. In
particular, one can examine the extent to which receiving procedural justice

provides a cushion of support when the outcomes are quite unfavorable. The full range of the unfavorable ratings on the scale measuring unfavorability of outcome was used to examine the effect of delivering negative outcomes through a fair or unfair process. Rather than the complete scale, ranging from very positive (1) to very negative (8), a six-point scale was used. This included all four points in the positive range, but because of the smaller number of negative outcomes, the four points in the negative range were collapsed into two: somewhat negative (5, 6, and 7) and very negative (8). (Because 15 percent of all respondents received a score of 8, this score could be preserved as a single category.)

In the analysis, the average affect scores for respondents receiving each level of outcome were examined by means of a procedure that they judged to be either fair or unfair (see figs. 8.2–8.4).

Fig. 8.2 Influence on affect

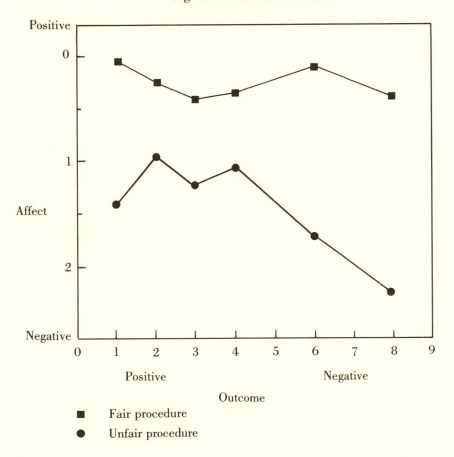

■ Fair procedure

● Unfair procedure

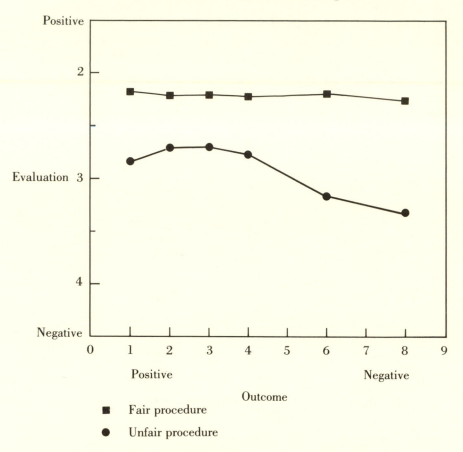

Fig. 8.3 Influence on evaluation of performance

The cushioning effects of procedural justice are quite robust. In no case involving a fair procedure did affect become less positive as outcomes became more negative. On the other hand, when the procedures involved were unfair, there were noticeable drops as outcomes became more negative. Declines following negative outcomes delivered through unfair procedures occurred with affect (fig. 8.2) and evaluation (fig. 8.3), but not with legitimacy (fig. 8.4). This means that legitimacy ratings are largely independent of issues of outcome. The effect of experience on legitimacy is driven by procedural judgments and is unrelated to outcome.

The cushioning effects of fair procedure can also be seen by looking at the correlation between unfavorability of outcome and the level of dependent variables within the categories of fair and unfair procedure. Among those re-

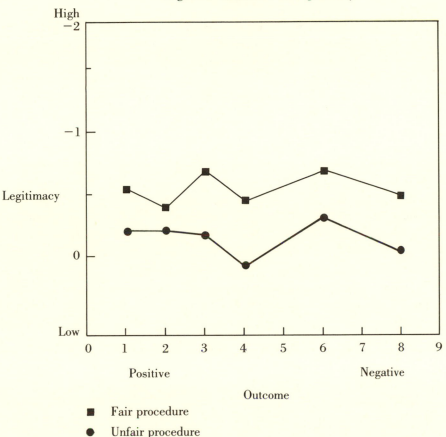

Fig. 8.4 Influence on legitimacy

■ Fair procedure
● Unfair procedure

spondents experiencing unfair procedures there is a strong relationship between level of outcome and affect ($r = .29$, $p < .001$) and between level of outcome and evaluation ($r = .26$, $p < .001$), although no relationship is found for legitimacy ($r = .03$, n.s.). Among those experiencing fair procedures, however, no relationship is ever found between outcome level and the dependent variables (for affect, $r = .14$, n.s.; for evaluation, $r = .02$, n.s.; for legitimacy, $r = .01$, n.s.). In the cases of affect ($z = 1.76$) and evaluation ($z = 2.73$) the correlations between the group subject to unfair procedure and that subject to fair procedure were significantly different. In the case of legitimacy ($z = .22$) they were not. In other words, if people receive fair procedures, outcome is not relevant to their reactions. If they do not, it is. As was hypothesized, fair procedures are a cushion of support against the potentially damaging effects of unfavorable outcomes.

Experience, Legitimacy, and Compliance

The analysis has dealt so far with two separate issues: the relationship between legitimacy and compliance, and the effects of experience on legitimacy. Although it is reasonable to separate these two issues, they are related. This analysis treats the two issues together. It examines a causal model that accounts for the effects of experience on legitimacy and compliance. Such an analysis makes it possible to measure the impact of experience on compliance directly, and indirectly through its effect on legitimacy. A combined causal model can first be tested by using the cross-sectional data from the 652 respondents in the first wave of the survey who had had recent personal experience with the police or courts. By so doing one finds that there are no direct paths from judgments about experience to behavioral compliance (fig. 8.5). Instead, judgments about the fairness of the procedures used during respondents' personal experiences influenced views about the legitimacy of legal authorities. These views of legitimacy in turn influenced compliance. Thus the two-stage approach of the study accords with the natural process of generalization.

A more complex causal model that tests for direct effects on compliance of judgments based on experience can be constructed by using the panel sample of

Fig. 8.5 Experience, views about legal authority, and compliance

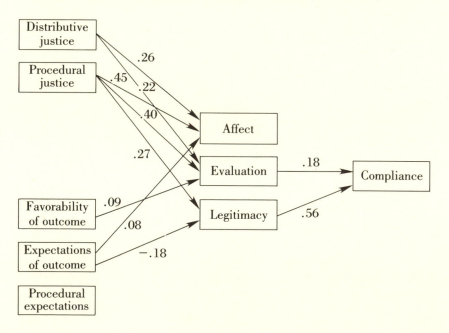

291 respondents who had experience between the two interviews. Such a model would make it possible to examine respondents' evaluations of performance and views about the legitimacy of legal authority both before and after their experience, as well as their compliance with the law at both points in time. In addition, it would account for respondents' judgments about their experiences (see fig. 8.6). Again there is little direct effect on compliance of judgments based on experience. Instead, experience influences compliance through its effect on judgments about legitimacy.

The modeling of the panel data demonstrates that the controls introduced through the use of a panel study do not eliminate either the link between legitimacy and compliance or the influence of procedural justice on legitimacy. The results still show that judgments of procedural justice influence judgments about the legitimacy of legal authorities, which in turn influence behavioral compliance with the law. It is also interesting to note the direct effect on behavior of judgments about distributive justice. This accords with the finding of other studies in the literature on procedural justice that assessments of distributive justice influence behavior more strongly than they influence attitudes. Alexander and Ruderman (1987), for example, found that procedural justice was more important than

Fig. 8.6 Panel analysis of experience, views about legal authority, and compliance

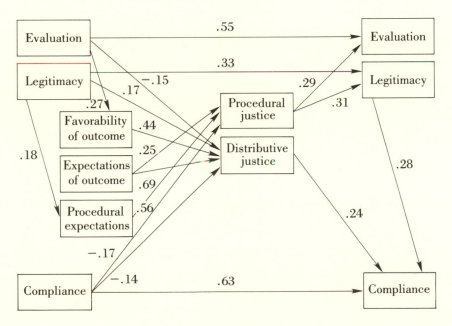

distributive justice in employees' evaluations of their organization. Those same employees, however, were more strongly influenced by distributive justice than by procedural justice when deciding to leave their job and find another.[8]

When Does Procedural Justice Matter?

The results of the Chicago study support the finding of earlier research that procedural justice is generally important. When people react to their dealings with police officers and judges they focus their attention sharply on questions of procedural justice. It may be that people do not always focus on procedural justice to the same degree: in some circumstances their attention may turn to other issues. Two elements of experience might influence the importance of procedural justice. The first is the nature of the event to which the experience relates: whether it involves the police or the courts, whether there is a dispute, whether there is voluntary contact, and whether the outcome is favorable. In addition, respondents may differ in their subjective assessments of the importance of the outcome.

To analyze the influence of all these potential dimensions, a set of regression equations was built for each of the six dimensions of the experience. Each equation had terms for the three independent variables found to influence legitimacy: procedural justice, distributive justice, and relative favorability of the outcome. In addition, each equation had a main effect to represent the dimension of the experience being examined and interaction terms for the interaction of that dimension with procedural justice, distributive justice, and relative outcomes. These interaction terms were used to assess whether procedural justice, distributive justice, or relative outcomes have a significantly different influence at varying points along the dimension of experience under consideration. The dependent variable in each analysis was legitimacy.

One type of variation that might influence the importance of procedural justice is variation in the situation. All four of the situational dimensions considered were found to affect the degree to which the procedural justice of an experience influenced the impact of that experience on views about the legitimacy of legal authority. Respondents focused more heavily on procedural justice when their experience involved the courts, was a dispute, was voluntary, and had an unfavorable outcome.

Thibaut and Walker studied procedural justice within one setting: that of formal courts. They also studied disputes between two parties. As has already been noted, most experiences that people have with legal authorities do not occur in courts and do not involve disputes. How would the conclusions of Thibaut and

Walker about the importance of procedural justice be different if they had studied all contacts rather than focus solely on disputes settled in courts?

If the concern is with the impact of experience on the legitimacy of legal authorities, a dependent variable not considered by Thibaut and Walker, then the results of the Chicago study are very consistent. Thibaut and Walker studied procedural justice in a setting where the effects of procedural justice on legitimacy are very strong. When the courts are compared with the police, these effects are found to be significantly stronger with the courts. When disputes are compared with experiences not involving disputes, the effects of procedural justice are found to be significantly stronger with disputes. Thibaut and Walker seem to have identified an excellent setting in which to demonstrate the importance of procedural justice to the impact of experience on legitimacy. The most surprising finding is that procedural justice matters more when experiences are voluntary. As has been noted, research has found that procedural justice matters more in situations of constraint, where the authorities impose themselves on others. These findings have led to the prediction that procedural justice will matter more when the interaction is not voluntary. But this prediction is not supported by these data: on the contrary, procedural justice mattered less in such a situation.

The final hypothesis, that procedural justice matters less when the respondents feel that the stakes are high, can be tested by looking at the importance of the outcome or the importance of treatment. When the role of procedural justice in reactions to experience is examined among respondents who have rated the outcome to be of greater or lesser importance, the results contradict the suggestion that procedural justice matters less when the outcomes are more important: in fact it matters at least as much. Procedural justice matters more when outcomes are more important, but the difference is not statistically significant. And as far as importance of treatment is concerned, procedural justice matters more when treatment is important, and in this case the difference is statistically significant.

With both of the variables that are "stakes," the importance of procedural justice remains similar or increases as the stakes grow. This suggests that people do not care less about procedural justice when the outcomes are more important: they care more. Of course the stakes involved in the experiences studied were not large, even in the serious incidents. But the results are consistent with those of another study (Casper, Tyler, and Fisher 1988), which concerned the procedures used to settle cases of felony defendants. These people faced substantial penalties (as much as twenty years in prison), and it was found that even among them, satisfaction with the disposition of cases was influenced by issues of fair procedure. Further, this concern with procedural justice was stronger among defendants who received more severe sentences.

How people view the legitimacy of legal authority is influenced by their experiences with police officers and judges. About 5 percent of the variance in people's views about the legitimacy of legal authority can be explained by the nature of their most important recent personal experience with the police and courts. Personal experience does have political impact. The judgments of adults about their obligation to follow legal authorities respond to their experiences with particular police officers and judges. Because experience influences legitimacy, legal authorities cannot take citizens' allegiance for granted. It can be eroded by unsatisfactory experiences with police officers or judges. And legitimacy will be eroded if the legal system consistently fails to meet citizens' standards. On the other hand, the existing reserve of legitimacy can be increased over time by positive personal experiences with police officers and judges.

Given that the experiences considered in the Chicago study represent only the most recent of the many potential contacts that an adult might have with the police and courts during his or her life, it is not trivial that the nature of such contact influences 5 percent of the variance in general views about the legitimacy of legal authority. It is also important that the figure of 5 percent is almost certainly an underestimate of the true influence of legitimacy. Corrections for reliability of measurement show consistently that legitimacy is more important than is shown in analyses that ignore the poor quality of its measurement. A causal model using panel data, for example, continues to display an influence of around 5 percent even though it controls for prior views, because it also adjusts for reliability of measurement.

The effect of experience on legitimacy makes it important to explore what it is about experience that determines its impact. The Chicago study shows that the impact of experience on views about the legitimacy of legal authorities is mediated not by the outcome of that experience, but by assessments of the fairness of the procedures used to deal with the problem. These results are consistent with those of other studies, which deal with citizens' encounters with police officers (Tyler and Folger 1980) and judges (Casper, Tyler, and Fisher 1988; Tyler 1984). These studies found that assessments of the fairness of the procedures used to solve problems or handle disputes affect people's reactions to their experiences, especially in the area of generalizations to views about legal authority.

The distinction between these two models of the person, one based on fairness and the other not, has important implications for law and public policy (see Tyler, Rasinski, and Griffin 1986). The public choice model of the person, which has dominated discussions in law, political science, and public policy, seems to be incomplete and ignores an important influence on people's reactions to their experiences with legal authorities: that influence is fairness and in particular procedural justice. The importance of procedural justice has been revealed before, but for several reasons the results of the Chicago study are especially compelling. First, the study is based on a larger and more diverse sample of people and experiences than has been studied before. Second, it includes a panel subsample, the analysis of which allows one to control for the effects of attitudes held before the respondents' experiences. Such controls do not change the nature of the conclusions: procedural justice is still found to be the primary factor mediating the impact of experience on views about legitimacy.

The important role of procedural justice in mediating the political effects of experience means that fair procedures can act as a cushion of support when authorities are delivering unfavorable outcomes. If unfavorable outcomes are delivered through procedures viewed as fair, the unfavorable outcomes do not harm the legitimacy of legal authorities. There may well be limits to this cushion of support. For example, if a "fair" procedure continually delivers unfavorable outcomes, its fairness may ultimately come under scrutiny. This may in turn undermine the ability of the procedure to cushion the system against the negative effects of unfavorable outcomes. Interestingly, research in procedural justice has found little evidence of erosion as a result of such scrutiny. Social psychology research typically finds that receiving unfavorable outcomes does not influence judgments of the fairness of a procedure, even when several unfavorable outcomes are received (Lind and Tyler 1988).

But studies of the cushioning effects of fair procedure are limited in their scope. They do not examine situations where people receive unfavorable outcomes over a long period. For example, do the poor continue to believe in the allocation procedures of a society that continually deals them unfavorable outcomes? Research on the poor in the United States suggests that to a large extent they do (Tyler and McGraw 1986). Therefore the ability of a fair procedure to cushion the effects of unfavorable outcomes seems fairly robust. Of course the procedural cushion is never absolute. People who have received negative outcomes are more likely to view the procedure by which they received them as unfair. Outcome does have some indirect effects, although they are smaller than the direct effects of judgments about justice that are the focus of the Chicago study. Nonetheless, such indirect effects will gradually undermine procedures over time.

It is also interesting that prior views about the legitimacy of authorities influence interpretations of the procedural justice of experiences with police officers and judges. Positive prior views are therefore another resource on which authorities can draw for discretionary authority. When authorities are viewed as legitimate, their actions are more likely to be seen as fair.[9] The legal authorities studied in Chicago generally benefited from the effect of prior views on the interpretation of experience, but such benefits need not always occur. If the authorities are viewed as illegitimate, their actions are more likely to be seen as unfair. In these circumstances police officers and judges who behave fairly will be frustrated by the tendency of those they deal with to interpret their actions unfavorably. The two potential sources of discretionary authority, positive prior views and the use of fair procedure, can both work in favor of the authorities. Positive prior views are of course beyond the control of any particular authority: police officers and judges cannot by themselves influence whether citizens generally view legal authorities as legitimate. They can, however, use fair procedures in dealing with citizens.

This Chicago study also shows a direct link between experiencing fair procedures in dealing with police officers and judges, and subsequent behavior in relation to the law. If people feel unfairly treated when they deal with legal authorities, they then view the authorities as less legitimate and as a consequence obey the law less frequently in their everyday lives. Experiencing unfair procedures also leads people to base their compliance less strongly on assessments of legitimacy. Although procedural issues are the primary concern when people evaluate their experiences with legal authorities, it is also important to note that they are not the only concern. People are also affected by issues of distributive justice and favorability of outcome.

Perhaps the most striking relationship is that between distributive justice and compliance with the law. This relationship is strong and direct: it does not flow through legitimacy, as does the effect of procedural justice. Unfortunately, the nature of this effect is not clear. Are there other general attitudes besides legitimacy that are affected by distributive justice and in turn affect behavior? Is the effect of distributive justice an affective reaction? Because the Chicago study focused on procedural justice, these issues were not explored. The existence of strong effects on behavior on the part of distributive justice suggests the need for further research in this area.

Why a Procedural Focus?

There are several reasons why people may focus on procedures rather than outcomes when evaluating authorities. The most straightforward reason is simplicity. Although it may seem simple to make evaluations based on the quality of one's outcomes, in reality it is quite difficult. In complex organizations, such as our society, people receive a wide range of benefits. They are also restricted in some ways and incur many types of cost. How can a person combine judgments of all these outcomes into any single evaluation of authorities, rules, or institutions?

Such complex decisions can be avoided by making organizational evaluations based on the procedures of allocation and resolution of disputes. If the procedures are fair, people will believe that over time their interests are reasonably protected by membership in the group. This has been called the "process politics" view of evaluations (Ophuls 1977).[10]

Another reason to focus on procedure is that procedure reflects the diverse values of distributive justice found in such a pluralistic society as the United States. Because there is no single, commonly accepted set of moral values against which to judge the fairness of outcomes or policies, such evaluations are difficult to make. People can however agree on the fairness of procedures for decision making. Evaluations of authorities, institutions, and policies therefore focus on the procedures by which they function, rather than on evaluations of their decisions or policies (Bellah et al. 1985; Schwartz 1978). If the consensus that binds together society is in fact a procedural consensus, then authorities need to be especially concerned with maintaining fair procedures for making allocations and resolving disputes. Of course, the argument that people simplify decision making by focusing on procedures assumes that there is some common agreement about what is a fair procedure for making decisions. (The extent to which such a common agreement exists is explored in the final section of this book.) That a procedural consensus exists raises the question of the origin of such commonly held views about fair procedures. How do people come to know what constitutes a "fair" procedure, especially in the many cases where rules are informal and not clearly articulated by authorities?

Views about what constitutes a fair procedure are distinct from issues of short-term self-interest. It seems likely that these views develop during the process of cultural socialization, as people acquire their basic political and social values. At this time little is known about the origin of procedural preferences, however, other than that such preferences are related to basic political and social values (Rasinski 1987).

Implications for Policy

In addition to having differing implications for how citizens evaluate their experiences with legal authorities, these models differ in their implications concerning the nature of public dissatisfaction with the courts and the law, the likelihood that future increases in the caseload of the courts will further increase public dissatisfaction, and the manner in which legal rules and changes should be implemented. Past treatments of public dissatisfaction with the courts and the law have emphasized public dissatisfaction with the outcomes that the courts produce. Examples of this focus on outcomes include concerns about the failure of the courts to dispose of cases quickly, or to give sentences of adequate length. According to a perspective based on justice, citizens' concerns should be viewed as part of their general view about fairness of procedure and fairness of outcome. It may be that procedural irregularities, such as criminals being let free on "technicalities," are particularly important in feeding public dissatisfaction with the courts.

A model based on justice also has different implications for citizens' reactions to increasing caseloads in the courts and the problems that result from them. According to such a model, citizens will accept these delays without withholding their support for the courts if they believe that there is fairness in the trial process and in the allocation of the benefits and burdens of litigation (Austin 1979; Friedman 1975; Flacks 1969; Kelman 1969). Citizens are also more likely to accept procedures designed to deal with problems of overload, such as court-annexed arbitration, if the procedures' design is sensitive to citizens' judgments about fair procedures to resolve disputes (Adler, Hensler, and Nelson 1983).

The procedural basis of citizens' evaluations of legal authorities suggests that the procedural aspects of legal decision making should be carefully scrutinized by legal authorities. A procedure such as plea bargaining is often justified in terms of outcome (it is an efficient method for settling cases). If the procedure is experienced by defendants as unfair, however, it may weaken their support for the legal system.[11] Similarly, a procedure such as no-fault insurance may make sense in economic terms, but be destructive of the moral consensus underlying citizens' commitment to the law (Lempert and Sanders 1986).

That fair procedures enhance commitment to the legal system has been recognized by the Supreme Court. In *Morrissey* v. *Brewer* (1972) the Court ruled that hearings to revoke parole must be conducted using due process. Their reasoning was that to do otherwise would undermine prisoners' commitment to legal authority, and that "fair treatment in parole revocations will enhance the chance of rehabilitation." The results of the Chicago study confirm that the fairness of procedures enhances or diminishes the legitimacy of legal authorities and future compliance with the law. When legal authorities attempt to implement policies, public conceptions of fair procedure are particularly important. According to a perspective based on procedural justice, people will accept or reject policies according to how they assess their fairness rather than in terms of costs and benefits. In the case of obedience to the law, recent studies have found that creating a moral climate of support for a law will alter compliance more effectively than will changing estimates of the certainty or severity of punishment. Schwartz and Orleans (1967), for example, found moral appeals to be four times as effective as threats of sanction in inducing people to pay taxes.

A perspective on policy implementation based on procedural justice has positive implications for legal authorities. If they had to change incentives every time they wanted to change public behavior, their ability to implement new policies would be very limited. But seemingly the authorities can draw on the public's willingness to comply with their decisions; this willingness can be most effectively tapped if the authorities make decisions in ways that the public views as fair. The perspective based on procedural justice also bodes well for the ability of the authorities to function during periods of crisis, when they most need public acceptance of their decisions. It is also during such periods, however, that authorities are least able to generate the resources needed to alter people's incentives. During recent periods of energy crisis, for example, leaders needed to reduce energy use by the public, but there were no incentives in place to reward the conservation of energy, or disincentives to punish the overuse of energy (Sears et al. 1978).

For leaders to gain the benefits of voluntary compliance, they need to understand the public's views of what is fair. This means they must understand both the public's views about fair procedures for decision making and the public's views about distributive justice. By identifying principles of fairness, social scientists can provide authorities and policy makers with important information. But although public views about fairness are important, there are dangers in simply making decisions based on public preferences. One important function of experts is to be aware of information that may not be known to the public. Legal authorities, for example, may be aware of procedures that might be used to resolve problems but that are not known to the public. Similarly, they may have information about the consequences of using different procedures. Hence public views should be only one input into the design of decision-making procedures.

There are also dangers for the public in the perspective based on procedural justice. If public satisfaction is linked to procedural fairness rather than to direct or tangible outcomes, authorities may be tempted to appear fair rather than to solve problems or provide help (Greenberg, in press). If people are satisfied with objectively poor outcomes because they believe they were generated by a fair process, this may reflect a false consciousness that is not desirable. Such a false consciousness would be lessened if people focused directly on outcomes. But this would introduce other problems. As already noted, people find it difficult to calculate outcomes. Further, membership in a group is a long-term proposition, and when thinking about outcomes people need to be careful not to focus too strongly on short-term ones. A focus on short-term outcomes might lead an individual to reject the participation of the group in a situation where participation in the group could bring about long-term benefits. It is of course concerns of this type that lead people to focus on procedures in evaluating authorities and organizations.

For the social critic it is important to distinguish between evaluations of the enactment of decision-making procedures and evaluations of the procedures themselves. For example, a trial can be conducted in a "fair" manner: the judge can be neutral, the witnesses honest, the jury unbiased. A person would therefore judge the trial to be fair. But the same person might feel that it is unfair to resolve disputes by means of an adversarial trial procedure, and that mediation would be better. People are clearly capable of making this distinction; the extent to which they do so in practice is explored in the last section of this book.

Until now I have dealt with two distinct issues: the role of legitimacy in compliance and the influence on legitimacy of different aspects of experience. The findings of research directed at these issues have a common characteristic: in each case noninstrumental concerns are found to be important. In the case of legitimacy, compliance with the law is influenced by judgments about the legitimacy of legal authority. When people's reactions to their experiences are examined, judgments of distributive and procedural fairness are found to have an important effect beyond any influence of the favorability of outcome. Beyond the general suggestion that norms matter, the results strongly support an orientation toward process in the study of normative issues. Research on distributive justice has focused on normative theories of fair outcomes; people, on the other hand, focus on fair process.

PART FOUR

The Meaning of Procedural Justice

CHAPTER 9

The Psychology of Procedural Justice

In the final section of this book I explore how people decide whether a procedure they have experienced is fair. Although the literature on procedural justice is extensive (see Lind and Tyler 1988), it has been directed primarily at showing that whether a procedure is fair affects people. It is equally important to examine what about a legal procedure leads those involved in it to feel that it is fair—to explore what procedural justice means to those evaluating procedures they have experienced.

Most efforts to understand the meaning of fair procedure have used the control theory of procedural justice originally articulated by Thibaut and Walker (1975). The nature of the control exercised by disputants over the forums used to resolve their disputes is the central construct in Thibaut's and Walker's model of what litigants mean by procedural fairness. As a consequence, issues of control have dominated more recent discussions about the meaning of procedural fairness. Thibaut and Walker based their theory of control on the distinction between decision control (the control over actual decisions made) and process control (control over the opportunity to state one's case to a third-party decision maker before a decision is reached).

In addition to suggesting that the distribution of control is the key to people's judgments about whether they have experienced a fair procedure, Thibaut and Walker presented a psychological model of control that they used to guide their work on procedural justice. Their model of procedural preference flows from the earlier social exchange model of Thibaut and Kelley (1959), according to which people maximize personal gain in their interactions with others and behave in their social interactions in ways that they think will lead to that goal. To pursue this objective, people seek to maximize their control over the decisions made about outcomes that affect them (Thibaut and Kelley 1959). For this reason people resist the intervention of third parties in disputes and bargaining. In some cases, however, people recognize that without a third party they will be unable to reach an agreement or settle a dispute, and consequently be unable to receive the benefits that would result from a successful settlement. In such circumstances they may give to a third party some control over the decision.

If disputants give up control to a third party in an effort to resolve their dispute, they will still seek to maintain as much control as they can. They will do so indirectly, by controlling the presentation of evidence (that is, through voice or process control). The model of procedural justice advanced by Thibaut and Walker links evaluations of the procedural justice of an experience to issues of decision control. While people are not reacting directly to the favorability of their outcome or to their control over that outcome, they are reacting to their ability to control the outcome by controlling the presentation of evidence. Thibaut's and Walker's model stems from an instrumental perspective on control. It emphasizes having indirect control of decisions by having the chance to state one's case. People are viewed as wanting to achieve desired outcomes and as judging the value of their opportunities to speak by the degree to which those opportunities facilitate achieving those outcomes (Brett 1986; Lind and Tyler 1988; Tyler and Lind 1986). Process control has value to the extent that it leads to decision control.

The contrast between instrumental and normative views has already been noted in connection with the question of why people follow the law, and how they react to their experiences with legal authorities. Here the same distinction occurs in defining the meaning of procedural justice. One study (Tyler, Rasinski, and Spodick 1985) found that process control has an importance not linked directly or indirectly to decision control: people value having the chance to state their case, irrespective of whether their statement influences the decisions made by the authorities. This view emphasizes the noninstrumental aspects of procedural justice—the normative issues that define procedural justice. The key to differentiating between instrumental views of control and normative views is process control. Does process control have effects that are independent of the level of decision control? According to both instrumental and normative views of control, people will feel more fairly treated if they have an opportunity to state their opinions. But according to instrumental views, such an opportunity will be valuable only to the extent that those stating their opinions think they are influencing outcomes.

Research on control has distinguished between process control and decision control and examined the impact of each on judgments of procedural justice. The results suggest that process control has an independent impact on satisfaction and perceived fairness (Houlden et al. 1978; Kanfer et al. 1987). The most striking evidence is found in two recent studies. The first (Lind, Lissak, and Conlon 1983) found that satisfaction in simulated trials was linked only to process control, not to decision control. The second (Tyler, Rasinski, and Spodick 1985) found that increased process control heightens judgments of procedural justice at low levels of decision control. That people value the opportunity to state their views to a decision maker regardless of the influence of those views on the decision is consistent with a noninstrumental perspective on process control.

The research I have described deals only with the general question of whether noninstrumental effects occur. It has not explored the possibility that such effects might occur in some circumstances and not others. One hypothesis is that noninstrumental effects will occur only where the stakes are trivial or unimportant, and where those affected by the decision would not care a great deal about the outcomes (Heinz 1985). This is similar to the general view (already disputed) that justice will matter only when the outcomes involved are not important (de Carufel 1981; Tyler 1986a). Although it seems untrue that justice matters less when outcomes are more important, it is still possible that people think about the meaning of justice in more instrumental terms when outcomes are more important.

Noninstrumental effects surely seem to exist, but it is not clear why giving people heightened process control leads them to feel more fairly treated if what they say has little or nothing to do with what the authorities decide. These effects have been called "value-expressive" (Tyler, Rasinski, and Spodick 1985) because they are not related to receiving favorable outcomes. What the preconditions are for these value-expressive effects is not clear, although three possible preconditions have been proposed: impartiality, good faith, and the consideration of one's views. The first of these is a belief that the authority involved is not behaving in a biased or self-interested manner. Folger notes that objective evidence of bias in a decision maker might produce frustration: process control without decision control might actually lessen feelings of procedural fairness (Folger 1977; Folger et al. 1979). He argues that participants who see evidence of bias by the authorities may imagine that they would have done better under a "fairer" procedure and consequently feel angry and dissatisfied (Folger 1986a, 1986b). To the extent that bias provokes such negative comparisons, decision makers must maintain the appearance of impartiality if process control effects are to occur. That impartiality may matter has also been noted by other writers. Impartiality is one aspect of what has been referred to as the fair enactment of a procedure ("interactional" justice; see Bies and Moag 1986), and is mentioned in Leventhal's theory of procedural justice (Leventhal 1980). Its potential importance has been suggested in several areas of research (Adler, Hensler, and Nelson 1983; Pruitt 1981; Sarat 1977; Tyler 1984, 1986c).

A second hypothesis is that those affected by decisions focus on the intentions of the decision maker and whether that person seems to have acted in "good faith." Cohen argues that those who view themselves as having "common interests" with the authority, as is often the case in legal settings, will feel that the decision maker desires to be fair and helpful (Cohen 1983, 1986). In a situation of conflict people will not necessarily view the authority as motivated to help them, so process control will not occur. The third hypothesis is that value-expressive effects depend on citizens' assumptions that their views are taken into account or considered by the decision maker, even if they do not influence the decision. Their views may be given this attention because of an effort on the part of the decision maker to be fair, or it may reflect the decision maker's concern with solving problems, balancing interests, or finding feasible solutions to problems. According to the group value conception of procedure, people who deal with third parties seek evidence that the authorities are trustworthy, benevolent, and caring (Lind and Tyler 1988). These attributes are connected to the belief that people's views are being considered by the third party. Therefore, for value-expressive effects to occur, people must believe that their views are being considered.

The results of the Chicago study can be used to examine whether there is a value-expressive component to procedural justice effects and, if there is one, whether it exists even when outcomes are important. Finally, they can be used to test three explanations that have been put forward to account for value-expressive process control effects.

Leventhal's Theory of Procedural Justice

Leventhal proposes a larger framework within which to view the meaning of procedural justice than that of Thibaut and Walker (1975). His theory notes six criteria against which the fairness of a procedure may be evaluated: representativeness, consistency, suppression of bias, accuracy, correctability, and ethicality.[1]

Leventhal's theory differs to a striking degree from that of Thibaut and Walker, in that he moves beyond issues of control and offers criteria unrelated to control as potential bases for evaluating the justice of a procedure. But the two theories do overlap in the area of representation, which is the degree to which the parties affected by a decision are allowed control of the decision-making process. In Leventhal's treatment of representation all affected parties should have both process control and decision control at all stages of decision making. This is roughly equivalent to the conception of control of Thibaut and Walker. But even here it is unclear whether representation refers to process control, decision control, or both. Leventhal is ambiguous on this point, suggesting that representation means that "the concerns of those affected should be represented in all phases of the allocation process" (1980, 43). The other issues raised by Leventhal are not discussed by Thibaut and Walker.

Consistency refers to similarity of treatment and outcomes. Consistency toward people generally takes the form of equal treatment for all affected parties. In a baseball game, for example, the umpire should define the same strike zone for all players. Consistency over time requires that the procedure follow the same rules and be enacted in the same way each time it is used. For example, the amount of physical contact that a basketball referee considers a foul should remain the same throughout the game.

The ability to suppress bias entails the ability of a procedure to prevent favoritism or external biases. Leventhal focuses on two of the many types of bias that may occur. The first is for the decision maker to have a vested interest in the outcome: if the referee in a basketball game had bet on one side before the game, he or she would have a vested interest in the outcome. The second type of bias occurs if the decision maker relies on prior views rather than the evidence—for example, if a juror votes to convict a defendant because of his or her belief that most defendants are guilty, rather than on the basis of the testimony and evidence presented during the trial. The accuracy of a decision is the ability of a procedure to reach solutions that are objectively of a high quality, and this depends on using accurate information and informed opinion. For example, decisions about pay and promotion should be based on detailed, well-kept, and accurate records of the work accomplished by employees. Correctability is the existence of opportunities to correct unfair or inaccurate decisions. The availability of procedures to voice appeals or grievances means that a decision that is unfair or arrived at unfairly can be adjusted by other decision makers. Of course, the appeal procedures must themselves meet the other criteria of procedural fairness. Finally there is ethicality, the degree to which the decision-making process accords with general standards of fairness and morality. Leventhal mentions many ways in which a procedure can fail to meet such standards: it may involve deception, bribery, or spying. Another example is torture, which is commonly excluded from judicial procedures because it violates basic moral codes of conduct.

Leventhal's possible criteria of procedural fairness can be used to examine three issues surrounding the meaning of fair procedure: the importance of different criteria of fairness to the assessment of the justice of a procedure; the relationship of these criteria of procedural fairness to one another; and the universality of the importance ratings given to criteria of procedural fairness from one type of experience to another, and from one type of person to another.

Because there are six criteria that might be used in evaluating the fairness of a procedure, it is important to know the weight that those affected by decisions place on each of these different criteria in defining the meaning of procedural justice. Research developing from both of the theoretical frameworks outlined above has addressed this issue. The most extensive exploration of the meaning of procedural justice is found in the work of Thibaut and Walker and their students, which focuses on trials. Their work suggests that both process control and decision control are important in procedural evaluations (Thibaut and Walker 1975), and recent research supports this suggestion.

A second area of research explores the importance of the six criteria of procedural justice proposed by Leventhal. Four studies have examined their importance to those affected by decisions, and all have found that consistency is the major criterion used to assess procedural justice (Barrett-Howard and Tyler 1986; Fry and Leventhal 1979; Fry and Chaney 1981; Greenberg 1986a). Further, consistency across people was found to be more important than consistency across time (Barrett-Howard and Tyler 1986).

Although the criteria used by Leventhal and by Thibaut and Walker have generally been examined separately, a recent study by Sheppard and Lewicki (1987) offers an exception. Managers and management students in their study considered incidents of fair and unfair treatment by a supervisor that they had experienced recently, and formulated the principle that led them to feel their treatment was fair or unfair. Three of the principles outlined above emerged as especially important: consistency, representation, and accuracy.

Overall, there is considerable convergence of results in prior studies of criteria of procedural justice, which find an emphasis on consistency (Barrett-Howard and Tyler 1986; Fry and Leventhal 1979; Fry and Chaney 1981; Greenberg 1986a; Sheppard and Lewicki 1987). In addition, accuracy is important (Barrett-Howard and Tyler 1986; Cornelius, Kanfer, and Lind 1986; Sheppard and Lewicki 1987), as is the related issue of suppressing bias (Barrett-Howard and Tyler 1986). Finally, work in the tradition of Thibaut and Walker finds that representation is important (Houlden, LaTour, Walker, and Thibaut 1978; Lind, Lissak, and Conlon 1983; Sheppard and Lewicki 1987; Tyler 1987a; Tyler, Rasinski, and Spodick 1985), a result consistent with the findings of Sheppard and Lewicki (1987).

The Chicago study combines the criteria for assessing the fairness of a procedure proposed by Thibaut and Walker (1975) with those of Leventhal (1980), and examines the importance of each criterion to citizens who have had personal experiences with the police or courts. Only one study has included such an examination before, and it was limited by a methodology that did not allow the rated importance of the criterion outlined to be directly examined (Sheppard and Lewicki 1987). The existence of varying criteria of procedural fairness also raises the question of how those criteria are related to one another. The importance of understanding the relationship among criteria emerges when people are choosing procedures for making decisions. In the literature on distributive justice the decisions of leaders have been regarded as trade-offs between objectives that cannot be simultaneously realized. For example, many have argued that society cannot simultaneously have a maximum of productivity and a maximum of social harmony. As a result, policymakers must trade off differing rules of distributive justice, each of which emphasizes one objective at the expense of another (see for example Okun 1975).[2] Here I am concerned with the extent to which such trade-offs also occur with procedures.

An example of value trade-offs in the criteria of procedural fairness can be found in the literature on the psychology of judicial sentencing, where it is argued that judges can reach good decisions that give appropriate punishment to each defendant only if they have wide latitude to sentence inconsistently, giving very different sentences for the same crime (Galegher and Carroll 1983). According to this argument, consistent sentences are in conflict with good sentences, if the latter are defined as sentences that will effectively rehabilitate individual criminals.

The major existing effort to explore the interrelationship among criteria of procedural justice is the work of Thibaut and Walker (1975), who focused on one subissue of this general question: the relationship between process and decision control. Their studies and those of later authors have consistently found a positive relationship between these two criteria of procedural fairness. Unfortunately, studies developing out of Leventhal's framework have not explored the interrelation of his criteria of procedural justice. The question of the relationship among criteria of procedural fairness leads into another issue: the possibility of underlying dimensions for evaluating procedures. Although a set of potentially important criteria have been elaborated for assessing the fairness of procedures (in the work of Thibaut, Walker, and Leventhal), these varying criteria may actually reflect several basic dimensions of procedural evaluation.

Another important issue is the degree to which the meaning of procedural justice is universal—the extent to which the fairness of procedures is always judged against the same criteria. Two extreme positions might be imagined. One would have stable criteria, with people always judging the fairness of procedures the same way, irrespective of the nature of the people or problem; the other would emphasize the relationship between the characteristics of the respondent, or of his or her recent personal experience, and the criteria used to evaluate the fairness of the procedures.

Research has found that the meaning of procedural justice will vary depending on the nature of the dispute or allocation (Barrett-Howard and Tyler 1986; Sheppard and Lewicki 1987). In situations varied along four basic dimensions of interpersonal relations (Deutsch 1982; Wish, Deutsch, and Kaplan 1976), respondents in formal situations were found to place more emphasis on suppression of bias, quality of decision, consistency, and representation (Barrett-Howard and Tyler 1986). In cooperative situations they focused more on consistency, quality of decision, and ethicality. Sheppard and Lewicki (1987) similarly found that the fairness criteria most important to people differed depending on the nature of the organizational roles they occupied (see also Sheppard, Saunders, and Minton 1988).

The Chicago study tested the degree of variation in the meaning of procedural fairness by examining the effect on the criteria that people use to evaluate whether they received a fair procedure of variations in the nature of the experience with the police and courts, and of variations in the type of people involved.

Several types of variation in the experience can be explored. The first variation is the type of authority encountered (police or courts). Thibaut and Walker examined formal courtroom settings; here the study of procedural justice was extended to less formal contacts with the police. My hypothesis is that judgments of informal encounters with the police will focus more on police efforts to be fair and less on adherence to formal issues of rights (that is, on ethicality). This is based on the supposition that in the more formalized environment of the courtroom, more attention will be drawn to issues of rights and ethical standards will be clearer.

A second extension of the original work of Thibaut and Walker moves beyond the arena of disputes. Their focus on courtrooms led them to focus on disputes. In many cases, however, citizens have contact with legal authorities for other reasons; for example, citizens may call the police for help. Because disputes involve contending factions, they lead citizens to place greater weight on whether they have an opportunity to state their case, on bias (favoring one party over others), and on consistency. In situations not involving disputes one would expect respondents to pay more attention to judgments about the quality of decisions.

The third variation is whether the experience is voluntary (as when a person initiates contact with the police or courts) or constrained (as when a person is stopped by the police). Citizens will presumably be more concerned with the quality of decisions when the contact is voluntary and more concerned with attention to their rights when it is not. A fourth aspect of the experience that may influence citizens' views of the meaning of procedural fairness is the favorability of its outcome. Those who have received poor outcomes may focus more on issues of bias, consistency, or dishonesty. Such judgments would allow them to determine whether they would have received better outcomes under alternative procedures for resolving disputes (Folger 1986a, 1986b). Those who receive favorable outcomes are expected to focus more on abstract issues such as ethicality: they can afford the luxury of being more abstract and of thinking about issues like politeness and concern for their rights.

Citizens may also differ in the importance they place on receiving favorable outcomes and treatment from the police and courts, and these variations in perceived importance may influence how they define the meaning of procedural justice. Those to whom outcomes matter more might focus more on aspects of procedure related to outcome, such as consistency, rather than on issues of ethicality.

Two types of personal characteristics are presumed to influence people's views about the meaning of procedural fairness: background characteristics and prior views. Six background characteristics particularly likely to be important are race, education, income, sex, age, and liberalism or conservatism. Those who are more highly educated and more liberal are expected to pay more attention to issues of ethicality in deciding if procedures have been just (McClosky and Brill 1983; Sullivan, Piereson, and Marcus 1982). Minorities are expected to define procedural justice more strongly in terms of issues of bias and inconsistency of treatment, because they are more likely to suffer from them. Predictions for sex, age, and income are not clear.

The prior views or expectations of respondents about the police and courts might also affect their views about important criteria of a fair procedure. Differences in their views were examined by using citizens' assessments of the equality of treatment they received from the police and courts. Each citizen was asked whether the police and courts generally treated citizens equally, and whether they treated people of the citizen's age, sex, race, or nationality worse than others. These two general assessments may be expected to lead to variations in the importance of bias to the assessment of the meaning of procedural justice. If citizens expect unequal treatment, or know that it occurs, they will assess the fairness of their own experience in terms of their bias or lack of bias.

The six criteria of fair procedure suggested in Leventhal's theoretical discussion of procedural justice form a basis for exploring the meaning of fair process. Three issues are addressed: the importance of the six different criteria, the relationship of the six criteria to one another, and the degree to which variations in the characteristics of the situation or people involved affect the relationship of the six criteria to judgments about the fairness of the procedure.

Normative Perspectives versus Instrumental Perspectives

In this chapter I have extended the contrast between normative and instrumental perspectives to the issue of the meaning of procedural justice. Specifically, I have contrasted the original conception of Thibaut and Walker of the meaning of procedural justice, which is instrumental, to a view that emphasizes the normative functions of having control. These value-expressive functions are not instrumental in character and do not depend on the influence of the decisions made by the third party.

I have used the same contrast between instrumental and normative views of the meaning of procedural justice to explore the larger framework proposed by Leventhal, which defines six possible aspects of experience that might be related to procedural justice. Some of those aspects of experience, such as the consistency of one's outcome or treatment with that of others, focus directly on outcomes. Other aspects, such as being treated politely, are related only marginally to obtaining favorable outcomes. According to an instrumental perspective, consistency should be very important, and politeness should be secondary at best. Those skeptical toward theories of procedural justice have often held that procedural justice judgments are simply ways of rationalizing post hoc about the favorability or unfavorability of the outcome of an experience. This instrumental view of procedure can be directly tested by examining the ability of noninstrumental criteria of fair procedure to explain variance beyond what can be explained by favorability of outcome.

CHAPTER 10

The Influence of Control on the Meaning of Procedural Justice

The control theory of the meaning of procedural justice put forth by Thibaut and Walker suggests that control matters. Research supports the suggestion, but has raised questions about how to understand the control effects that have been found. To address this question, I compare in this chapter the instrumental model of control of Thibaut and Walker to a noninstrumental, value-expressive model of control. One may infer from earlier studies that judgments of process control will be of primary importance when people form judgments about whether they received procedural justice. Two further issues about control are whether value-expressive effects occur when outcomes are important, and why value-expressive effects occur.

To examine control effects one must evaluate the responses of the 652 people in the Chicago study who had had recent personal experience with the police or courts. Process control was assessed by asking the respondents how much opportunity they had before decisions were made to present their problem or state their case. Decision control was assessed by asking respondents how much influence they had over the decisions made by the third party. Both assessments used a four-point scale that included the following responses: a great deal, some, a little, and not much at all.[1]

Most people felt they had high or moderate levels of process control: 43 percent said they had a great deal of opportunity to present evidence before decisions were made, and 20 percent said they had some. In contrast, most felt that they had little decision control (49 percent said they had not had much). Respondents were particularly likely to feel high process control when they had called the police (61 percent felt a great deal in such cases, compared with 30 percent in other cases), and those who called were more likely to feel that they had at least some decision control (65 percent felt so, compared with 42 percent in other cases).

Clearly, the conditions found in the Chicago study were ideal for comparing the instrumental and the value-expressive influences of process control. Respondents generally felt that they had high levels of process control: a chance to state their case. At the same time, they generally felt that they had little influence on the decisions made by the police and courts, and as a result a large group of the people interviewed felt that they had had high process control but low decision control. This group is ideal for testing the existence of distinct value-expressive effects, because the opportunity to state one's case is important from an instrumental perspective only if it is linked to influence over the decisions made.

Three dependent variables were considered. The first was the way the respondents judged the justice of the procedures used by the police or judge in their situation; the second was evaluations of the way the police or courts performed; and the third was views about the legitimacy of legal authorities. These scales were operationalized as they were in the analyses already outlined. The two components of legitimacy, obligation and support, were examined separately.

Control and Procedural Justice

To what degree are people's reactions to their experiences shaped by their judgments about their process control and decision control? Regression analysis was used to examine the effects of the level of each on assessments of procedural justice, evaluations of legal authorities, and views about the legitimacy of legal authorities. The regression analysis found that process control judgments dominate the influence of control judgments on assessments of procedural justice. Similarly, process control judgments dominate the impact of experience on evaluation. With support both effects are equally strong.[2] This means that when respondents react to their experiences with legal authorities, they focus more on their opportunities to state their case than they do on their influence over decisions.

The regression analysis also reveals a clear difference in the way process control affects the two components of legitimacy. No process control effect is found in the case of respondents' perceived obligation to obey the law, nor does decision control have any effect. Process control and decision control have effects only when the dependent variable is support for legal authorities; as a consequence, this component of legitimacy was used in other analyses of control.

Are there process control effects that are clearly separate from instrumental issues? This question can be examined in several ways. First, among all respondents, there is an independent influence of process control judgments once the effects of decision control have been removed. In fact, this independent influence dominates the equation: people care about process control beyond its relationship to decision control. Decision control also has an independent impact, but one that is typically smaller. By examining the means for the dependent variables at high and low levels of process control and decision control, one finds that process control increases the dependent variables as much at low levels of decision control as at high levels of decision control. People have more favorable attitudes toward legal authorities if they are allowed to state their case. The increase in favorability is as great when people do not think that what they say influences the decision as it is when they think that it does.

It is also possible to examine the influence of variations in process control at low levels of decision control, by dividing respondents into two groups: those with little decision control ("not much") and those who felt more control. Regression analyses conducted within each group show that process control continues to have an effect even when respondents feel that their opportunities to state their case have little or no effect on the decisions made by the third party. When decision control is low, variations in process control explain 18 percent of the variance in procedural justice (p < .001), 9 percent of the variance in evaluations (p < .001), and 4 percent of the variance in support (p < .01). This reinforces the suggestion that people value the opportunity to state their case and feel more fairly treated if they receive it, even if it does not affect the decisions made.

The difficulty with the regression analyses is that they do not take into account the effect of potential third variables—characteristics of the situation that might influence both process control and decision control. This might also be true of characteristics of the person. For example, situations where citizens create process control by approaching the legal authorities may differ from those where the authorities compel citizens to deal with them. Although the possibility of influence by third variables can never be completely eliminated, an explanation based on this influence will be made more implausible if logical third variables are shown not to cause confounding effects. In the Chicago study fourteen potentially confounding variables were tested, of which six were situational and eight personal. The situational variables were the authority dealt with; whether the contact was voluntary; whether the contact involved a dispute; the favorability of the outcome; the importance of outcome; and the importance of treatment. The personal variables were age, sex, race, education, income, liberalism or conservatism, whether the authorities gave citizens equal treatment, and whether the authorities were biased against one's demographic group.[3]

A third variable cannot be shaping the results of analyses involving process control unless it is related to judgments of process control. A regression analysis examining the influence of the six situational characteristics on judgments of process control showed a strong influence (R-squared = 16 percent, p < .001). The effect was also strong among those low in decision control (R-squared = 10 percent, p < .001). In both cases, the nature of the situation had an influence on whether citizens felt that they had process control. Situational controls should therefore be introduced.

An analysis of the influence of personal characteristics on judgments of process control suggests that personal characteristics have less influence on such judgments. Overall they explained 6 percent of the variance in process control judgments (p < .001), and 1 percent of the variance among those low in decision control (n.s.). In other words, different types of citizens felt only slightly differently about the extent to which they have process control, and controls on personal characteristics are less needed.

If the effects of process control and decision control already discussed are reexamined after introducing situational and personal controls, the effects of process control remain. Similarly, those at low levels of decision control continue to show the effects of process control when situational controls are introduced.[4] Even with situational controls, process control effects are found among those who believe they had little decision control.

A further refinement of the argument against the importance of the value-expressive component of process control effects is that the effects will occur only when the outcomes are trivial. To test this possibility respondents were divided into groups along two dimensions. The first division was made according to whether the respondents said that the outcome or good treatment was important, the second according to whether they received a favorable outcome. The importance of the outcome to the respondents was assessed by self-report, as was the importance of their treatment by the police or courts. Sixty-two percent of the respondents said the outcome was very important to them; 66 percent said how they were treated was very important to them.

Within each group, correlations between process control and the three dependent variables show that as the issues become more important to people and as the outcome becomes more unfavorable, people place greater weight on the degree to which they have process control.[5] As before, this effect remains when controls are placed on decision control. It seems clear that process control has value-expressive effects. Three factors have been suggested as preconditions for these effects to occur: the impartiality of the decision maker, the degree to which the decision maker is motivated to be fair, and the degree to which people think their views are considered by the decision maker. Are these elements of procedure in fact required to produce the value-expressive effects?

The impartiality of the decision maker was measured by asking respondents whether the officials they dealt with did anything improper or dishonest, whether they lied about anything, or whether they treated the respondents badly or gave them a poorer outcome than they would otherwise have received because of the respondents' age, sex, race, or nationality. Of those interviewed 28 percent felt that the officials they dealt with had not been impartial in one or more of these ways. The "good faith" of the officials involved was assessed by asking respondents how hard the officials tried to be fair. Forty-nine percent of the respondents felt that the officials tried very hard or quite hard to be fair; 51 percent felt that they tried only somewhat hard or not very hard. The extent to which respondents felt that their views were being considered was assessed by asking respondents how much consideration officials gave to their views before making their decisions. Sixty-three percent of the respondents felt that officials gave their views either a great deal of consideration or some; 37 percent felt that their views received only a little or not much consideration.

When the relationship of the three attitudes outlined to process control and decision control is examined, two factors emerge as key to judgments of process control: consideration of people's views and being seen as making efforts to be fair.[6] If people believe that their views are being considered, they think that they have greater process control. Similarly, if they believe that officials are trying to be fair, they believe that they have greater process control. Examining the correlates of judgments of process control does not directly test the preconditions needed for value-expressive process control effects, because judgments of decision control are not controlled for. To control for decision control a causal model was devised that included both process control and decision control (see fig. 10.1).

Fig. 10.1 Effects of control

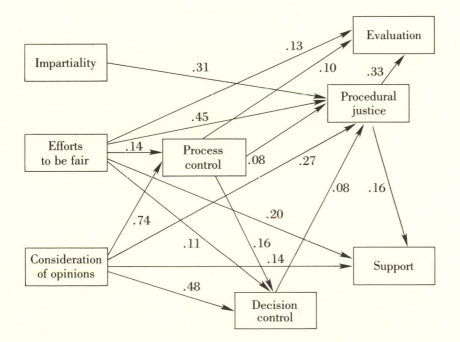

As in the case of the correlational analysis, the results of the causal model suggest that judgments of control are influenced both by consideration and by inferences that the third party is trying to be fair. The value-expressive component of process control is most responsive to the element of consideration. Whether people feel that what they say has been considered has a very strong effect on whether they feel they have had process control, even when the influence of decision control is removed. The results shown in fig. 10.1 also suggest that judgments of control do not capture the totality of the psychology of procedural fairness. All three of the attitudinal factors—impartiality, effort, and consideration—have direct paths to procedural fairness that are not mediated by judgments of control. Therefore, these results also suggest that there is more to procedural justice than is captured in control models.

The belief of citizens that their views are being considered by the authorities and that the authorities are trying to be fair clearly enhances their feeling that they have process control and decision control. Of these two beliefs, consideration is linked more directly and strongly to issues of control. Consideration also influences more directly whether control has a value-expressive effect.[7]

Preconditions for Voice Effects

Although the results already reported strongly support the idea of value-expressive voice effects, methodological concerns raised by the correlational nature of the Chicago study limit confidence in the results already outlined. In particular, it is possible that some of the dependent variables, such as the evaluation of legal authorities, do not flow from experiences. Instead, they might exist before the experiences and influence the way citizens interpret their experience with legal authorities. If people expect fair treatment from the legal authorities they may believe that their views are being considered, irrespective of the way the police and courts actually behave. It has already been noted that prior views about legitimacy influence judgments about experiences, such as judgments of how fairly one has been treated.

To test the possibility that prior views shape the interpretation of experience, one can use data from the full panel study. This makes it possible to control for the influence of prior views and expectations when examining the impact of experiences. If the findings outlined earlier are confirmed, this will increase confidence in their validity. The questions used to assess control in the second wave of interviews were identical to those used in the first wave, and the various scales used in the first were reconstructed in the same way for the second. The focus was on the support component of legitimacy, as in the first wave. Most of those interviewed in the second wave who had recent personal experiences (n = 291) felt they had had high levels of process control (48 percent said they had had a great deal of opportunity to state their case before decisions were made). Similarly, most respondents felt they had had little decision control (46 percent said they had had not much influence at all on the decisions and 8 percent said they had had only some influence). Owing to the smaller size of the panel, these two categories were combined to form one group that had low decision control.

The first question to be addressed is whether process control has value-expressive effects even after controls have been introduced for attitudes and expectations that existed before the experience. In analyzing this question, different controls were used to measure the effect of experience on judgments specific to the experience, and on general views of authority. For judgments specific to the experience, three questions were posed that were directly related to the respondent's experience: the procedural justice of the experience, satisfaction with treatment, and affect toward the authorities encountered. For these questions the control variable was an index of expectations; this was devised by using questions from the first wave of interviews that dealt with whether citizens felt they would receive fair treatment if they sought out legal authorities in the future, and whether they felt the authorities typically treated citizens fairly. In each case the scale used items from the first wave that were appropriate to the authority later encountered by the citizen (the police or judges). The result was a scale of expectations that measured whether respondents felt in the first wave of interviews that future contacts with the legal authorities would involve fair treatment.

To generalize from experience to views about authority, the level of support or evaluation measured at the first wave is used as a control; support is used as a control in analyzing support after the experience, and evaluation is used as a control in analyzing evaluation after the experience. As before, each analysis used the ratings for the authority eventually encountered by each respondent. A regression analysis that controls for expectations and that measures the influence of process control and decision control on the dependent variables specific to the experience at hand indicates that variations in process control strongly affect judgments of procedural justice, satisfaction, and affect toward the authorities.[8] Decision control is also found to have a smaller effect. Because this is a regression analysis, the influences of process control are independent of any influence of decision control on the dependent variables. A similar effect was found for the evaluation and support indices from the second wave when evaluation and support from the first wave were included as controls, although the pattern is somewhat more complex. In the case of evaluations, process control and decision control both have an effect. With support, a decision control effect is found, but there is no process control effect.

When only respondents who scored low on decision control were included in the analysis, the results were similar to those already outlined, but process control had a stronger effect. Among those who scored low on decision control, variations in process control influenced both evaluations specific to the experience (procedural justice, satisfaction, and affect) and generalizations to views about legal authority (evaluation and support). As with the overall sample, process control had a very strong effect for evaluations specific to the experience and a weaker one for generalizations. Process control continues to have an effect even when controls are introduced for attitudes held before the experience. The results also suggest that expectations and evaluations made at the first wave of interviews exerted an influence on the way citizens interpreted their experience. It is therefore possible that expectations influence the manner in which citizens react to experiences over which they have process control but not decision control.

The influence of expectations on the effect of process control in such situations can also be explored by dividing respondents into two groups: those who said in the first wave of interviews that they expected to receive fair treatment if they had future contact with legal authorities, and those who said they did not expect fair treatment. One would examine only those respondents who later had an experience with legal authorities in which they had little decision control.

Both those who expected fair treatment and those who did not showed statistically significant process control effects in reacting to experiences with legal authorities over which they had little decision control. These value-expressive effects were however not of similar magnitude: those who expected to receive fair treatment showed stronger process control effects. For example, variations in process control account for 41 percent of the variance in judgments of procedural justice among respondents who expected fair treatment ($p < .001$), but for only 10 percent of the variance among those who did not expect fair treatment ($p < .001$).

It is also possible to examine the influence of people's expectations and attitudes on their interpretation of experience, by looking directly at whether people with positive expectations interpret their experiences in a more positive way. This can be done by examining the influence of judgments made at the first wave of interviews on citizens' assessments of the characteristics of their later experiences. Doing so can measure the extent to which judgments of process control, consideration of views, decision control, and procedural justice are correlated with prior expectations. Two types of evaluation from the first wave were used in the analysis: general attitudes toward the police and courts (evaluation and support); and judgments about experiences that the respondents had before the first interview (evaluations of the procedural justice of encounters with the police or courts, and affect toward the authorities dealt with). The latter variables were assessed for the 199 respondents who reported an experience at both their first interview and their second.

The results show that the interpretation of experience is influenced by prior views.[9] In particular, when respondents are in a situation where they have little decision control, they are more likely to interpret that experience in a positive way if they have positive prior views. This is true in the case of their beliefs that their views were considered (R-squared = 7 percent, $p < .01$), that they were fairly treated (R-squared = 7 percent, $p < .001$), and that they were given an opportunity to express their point of view (R-squared = 5 percent, $p < .05$). It is interesting to note that assessments of decision control were not responsive to prior views (R-squared = 0 percent, n.s.).

In their original control theory of procedural justice, Thibaut and Walker emphasized an instrumental perspective on control. They viewed disputants as focused on outcomes and as seeking to exert either direct control or indirect control over outcomes by controlling the presentation of evidence. People were viewed as focusing as much as possible on gaining direct decision control, and, if they had to give up decision control, as seeking indirect decision control through process control. The literature since Thibaut and Walker has painted a picture of what litigants want from third parties considerably different from that contained in the original control model of Thibaut and Walker. People are found to focus heavily on issues of process control, whether or not control over the procedure translates into control over outcomes. In other words, people value the opportunity to state their case to a third party, irrespective of whether what they say influences the decision made by the third party.

The results of the Chicago study replicate earlier findings (Tyler, Rasinski, and Spodick 1985) that increased opportunities to state one's case before a decision is made heighten feelings that one has been involved in a fair procedure, and lead to positive feelings and support for police officers and judges, whether or not the actions of the authorities are influenced by the views expressed. The Chicago study therefore supports a value-expressive perspective on voice. Its findings are more compelling than those of the earlier study in that the larger sample allowed the variable of decision control to be examined when its value was essentially nil. In past research, small samples made it necessary to count those who felt they had some decision control among those who felt they had none. This blurred the conceptual distinction between having control over the outcome and lacking it. In addition, the Chicago study included a larger and more diverse sample of encounters with legal authority than did the earlier study.

The results of the panel analysis confirm the occurrence of value-expressive process control effects. They are found even when expectations and attitudes are controlled for. Thus value-expressive effects are not an artifact of method. The panel analysis also shows that the interpretation of experiences is influenced by expectations and attitudes. Citizens are much more likely to feel positively about situations where they had process control but no influence on outcomes if they are positively disposed toward the authorities. It seems that the reason prior views had an influence was that prior views affected citizens' judgments of the extent to which they had process control and the extent to which their views were considered. Views about consideration seemed in particular to be strongly influenced by prior attitudes. Because consideration of views was found to be a key construct through which value-expressive process control effects occurred, the influence of prior attitudes on consideration means that they play an important role in the occurrence of process control effects where decision control is low. Of course the role of prior attitudes should not be exaggerated: they do not, for example, influence citizens' judgments about the degree to which they had decision control.[10] People do not think they had more control over the decision of the police officer or judge just because they initially viewed the police officer or judge more positively.

The Chicago study agrees with earlier ones in finding evidence that the distribution of control when a person is dealing with a legal authority influences the person's assessment of whether procedural justice has occurred. At the same time, the study does not support an instrumental interpretation of control effects. Instead, it suggests that people seek to present their views to authorities for interpersonal reasons, as well as to influence the authorities' decisions.

A larger concern not dealt with in this examination of control is the extent to which respondents define the meaning of procedural justice in control terms. To address this issue, one must compare the importance of control with the importance of criteria of procedural justice that are not related to control. I do so in the next chapter.

CHAPTER 11

Beyond Control

What is it about legal procedures, formal and informal, that leads those involved in them to feel that they are fair? The question is related to three issues: the importance of different potential criteria of procedural justice; the relationship among those criteria; and the universality of the criteria used to assess the fairness of procedures.

Potential Criteria

The first two potential criteria of procedural justice are those proposed by Thibaut and Walker (1975): process control and decision control. They also constitute the dimension of representation of Leventhal, who also proposes five additional criteria of procedural justice. His first criterion of procedural justice is consistency. In the Chicago study, four types of consistency were examined: first, respondents compared their experience with experiences they had had in the past (consistency over time); second, they compared their experience with their expectations (consistency over time), however derived; third, they compared their experience with what they thought generally happened to other members of the public (consistency toward people); finally, they compared their experience with recent experiences of their friends, family, or neighbors (consistency toward people). The way these variables were operationalized in the study has already been discussed.[1] In the analysis being discussed here an average score was computed for all four scales.

Impartiality was first measured as a lack of bias in the authorities' behavior, by asking respondents whether their treatment or the outcome of their interaction was influenced by their "race, sex, age, nationality, or some other characteristic of them as a person." In addition, in cases of a dispute (17 percent of cases), respondents were asked whether the legal authorities involved had favored one party over the other. Eleven percent of respondents indicated at least one of these types of bias. To measure impartiality in terms of the intentions of the authority, respondents were asked how hard the authority tried to be fair to them. Respondents differed widely on this dimension: 37 percent said the authorities tried "very hard" to be fair, 12 percent said they tried "quite hard," 26 percent said they tried "somewhat hard," and 26 percent said they did not "try hard at all." Finally, impartiality was assessed as honesty, by combining responses to two questions: whether the authorities "did anything" improper or dishonest (21 percent said they had), and whether officials had lied to them (16 percent said they had).

The accuracy or quality of decision making was assessed in two ways. First, respondents were asked whether the authorities involved had "gotten the information they needed to make good decisions about how to handle" the problem (80 percent said they had). Second, respondents indicated whether the authorities had tried to "bring the problem into the open so that it could be solved" (63 percent said they had). Correctability was assessed by asking respondents whether they knew of any "agency or organization" to which they could have "complained" about unfair treatment (33 percent said they knew of such an agency). And ethicality was measured in two ways: by asking respondents whether the authorities had been polite (83 percent said they had), and whether the authorities had shown concern for their rights (76 percent said they had).[2]

The key dependent variable in the analysis of the meaning of procedural justice is the respondents' judgment about the fairness of the procedures they experienced with the police or courts. (The way this variable was measured has already been outlined). Respondents also assessed the fairness of the authorities themselves. They first assessed the fairness of "the way the Chicago police (courts) treat people and handle problems" (66 percent of those who had dealt with the police said the police were very fair or somewhat fair; 53 percent of those who had dealt with the courts said the same of the courts). They were also asked "how often the police (courts) treat citizens fairly and handle their problems in a fair way" (53 percent said usually or often for the police; 46 percent said so for the courts) and "how fairly" they would be treated if they dealt with the police or courts in the future (90 percent said very fairly or somewhat fairly for the police; 86 percent said so for the courts).

The importance of each of the six potential criteria of procedural fairness was tested by looking at the relationship between citizens' judgments that their experiences had the characteristics associated with that criterion and their judgments that fair procedures had been used. Two types of analysis were conducted. In the first the zero-order correlation between each potential criterion and judgments of procedural justice was computed. In the second the beta weight was computed for an equation in which all criteria were entered simultaneously. The latter number indicates the independent contribution of each factor, controlling for the influence of all the other factors. Two equations were examined: the first included potential indices of procedural justice; the second added favorability of outcome as an independent variable, to remove any influence that this factor might have on others in the equation (see tables 11.1 and 11.2).

The judgment of procedural justice was found to be complex and multifaceted. Citizens are not using any simple, unidimensional approach to assessing procedural justice. Instead, they pay attention to seven distinct aspects of procedure: the authorities' motivation, honesty, bias, and ethicality; their opportunities for representation; the quality of the decisions; and the opportunity for correcting errors. Each of these seven aspects of procedure has a significant independent influence on judgments about procedural justice. Both aspects of procedure related to decision making and those unrelated to it are important to judgments of procedural justice. The elements of procedural justice most directly linked to decision making are judgments about the neutrality of the decision-making procedure. People believe that decisions should be made by neutral, unbiased decision makers, and they expect the decision makers to be honest and to make their decisions based on objective information about the issues.

People also feel that procedures are fairer when they believe they have had some control in the decision-making procedure. Such control includes having the opportunity to present one's arguments, being listened to, and having one's views considered. As previously noted, this influence includes elements of control over

Table 11.1
Attributes of a procedure that lead citizens to see it as fair

	Judgments that the procedures were fair				With control on outcome	
	R	Rank	Beta	Rank	Beta	Rank
Representation	.62***	3	.17***	4	.17***	4
Consistency	.32***	7	.04	—	.02	—
Impartiality						
Bias	.43***	5	.07**	7	.04	—
Dishonesty	.59***	4	.23***	2	.22***	2
Effort to be fair	.71***	1	.30***	1	.28***	1
Quality of decisions	.37***	6	.17***	5	.15***	5
Correctability	.04	—	.14***	6	.12**	7
Ethicality	.69***	2	.21***	3	.21***	3
Outcome	—	—	—	—	.13***	6
R-squared			.69***		.70***	

Table 11.2

Attributes of a procedure that lead citizens to see the authorities as fair

					With control on outcome	
	R	Rank	Beta	Rank	Beta	Rank
Representation	.35***	3	.12***	3	.11*	5
Consistency	.16***	—	.03	—	.20***	3
Impartiality						
Bias	.26***	5	.05	—	.00	—
Dishonesty	.34***	4	.11*	4	.09	—
Effort to be fair	.45***	1	.27***	1	.24***	1
Quality of decisions	.15***	6	.02	—	.02	—
Correctability	−.03	—	.00	—	.07	—
Ethicality	.41***	2	.15***	2	.16***	4
Outcome	—	—	—	—	.23***	2
R-squared			.26***		.30***	

the decisions made, but also includes interpersonal issues not directly linked to decision making. Procedural fairness is further linked to interpersonal aspects of the decision-making procedure. People place great weight on being treated politely and having respect shown both for their rights and for themselves as people. In addition, assessments of procedural fairness are strongly linked to judgments about whether the authorities being dealt with are trying to be fair. These interpersonal factors were not of minor importance. Inferences about the effort to be fair were the most important criterion of procedural fairness; concerns about politeness and rights (jointly labeled ethicality) were the second-most important. Clearly, there are important noninstrumental elements to the meaning of procedural justice.

The criteria used to assess the fairness of an experience are found to be similar to those used to assess the fairness of the authorities. In both cases the effort to be fair and ethicality were key factors. The major difference was that dishonesty was less important in assessments of the general fairness of the police and courts. Because the correlation between judgments of the procedural fairness of the experience and judgments of the procedural fairness of authorities is .51 (p < .001), finding similar effects is not surprising. It is possible to examine further the instrumental and noninstrumental aspects of procedural justice by looking at procedural justice effects independently of the favorability of outcome. According to an instrumental perspective, people seek control to gain favorable outcomes, and the favorability of the outcomes people receive should therefore directly shape their reactions to experiences. If such favorability is controlled for, according to an instrumental perspective other influences on procedural justice should be weak or nonexistent. Introducing outcome controls directly addresses the question of whether procedural justice judgments are simply post hoc justifications for favorable or unfavorable outcomes. A regression analysis makes it possible to test the importance of favorability of outcome if the analysis controls for the favorability of the outcome that people receive in their interaction. With judgments of procedural justice, outcome controls are found to have no effect on the conclusions already outlined. Favorability of outcome is not a major predictor of procedural fairness (it ranks sixth in importance), and its introduction into the equation does not change the relative importance of the other factors.

In the case of judgments about the justice of the authorities involved, introducing favorability of outcome has a stronger influence on the meaning of procedural justice. In the case of judgments of the fairness of the authorities, favorability of outcome is the second-most important criterion in terms of its impact on the dependent variable. Its introduction into the equation also changes the relative importance of other criteria of fair procedure, causing consistency to be more important and representation and ethicality less important.

These findings are inconsistent with an instrumental perspective on procedural justice, such as that found in the theory of control of Thibaut and Walker. First, interpersonal elements are more important to people than aspects of the procedure more directly linked to its outcome. Second, controls for favorability of outcome have little influence on the importance of these interpersonal elements of procedure. The extent of this noninstrumental influence can be further explored by using a usefulness analysis, to compare the magnitude of noninstrumental and instrumental influences on procedural justice. A regression analysis examining the ability of different clusters of variables to explain variance not explained by other variables suggests that in judgments of procedural justice the absolute and relative favorability of one's outcome explained 1 percent of the variance beyond what can be explained by the other criterion of procedural justice.[3] In contrast, the noninstrumental criteria of fair procedure explained 47 percent of the variance in judgments of procedural justice beyond what could be explained by favorability of outcome. Noninstrumental issues dominate judgments of procedural justice.[4]

If one examines the role of favorability of outcome in shaping judgments that the authorities follow fair procedures, the procedural justice criteria again dominate. They explained 18 percent of the variance beyond what could be explained by outcomes, whereas outcomes explained only 6 percent of the variance that could not be explained by the procedural justice criteria. In this case, however, favorability of outcome clearly plays a more important role relative to issues unrelated to outcome than is true with judgments of procedural justice.

In an earlier analysis it was found that procedural justice is particularly important relative to other issues when the dependent variable is a person's generalizations from particular experiences to overall views about legal authorities; procedural justice is therefore the key to the political impact of experience. The results examined here seem to mitigate that conclusion. Although judgments of procedural justice may be especially dominant in generalizations from experience to views about legal authority, the judgments themselves may be more heavily influenced by outcome issues when they are focused on legal authorities. Here judgments of the procedural fairness of authorities are more heavily influenced by favorability of outcome than are judgments about the procedural justice of experiences. Outcomes thus have less direct effect, but a greater indirect effect when the dependent variable is judgments about legal authorities.

The Relationship among Criteria of Procedural Justice

A second important question is that of the relationship among the varying criteria of procedural justice. An examination of the correlations among the criteria of procedural justice under consideration reveals that they generally have a positive overlapping quality (mean r = .36). In other words, citizens judge the fairness of procedures by using a variety of positively interrelated criteria. These findings confirm the idea of positively interrelated clusters of procedural criteria. Their existence suggests that the choice of procedures for resolving disputes or solving problems does not require making the trade-offs discussed in the literature on distributive justice. Procedures that are viewed as leading to decisions of a higher quality, for example, are also more ethical and allow more influence by citizens. Thus from the citizen's perspective, procedures exist that will simultaneously promote all aspects of procedural justice. This does not mean that all criteria can be fully attained at one time; they cannot. But the harsh trade-offs described in the literature on distributive justice do not appear here.

The various criteria of procedural justice that have been examined may be definable in terms of a smaller number of underlying dimensions. To identify such dimensions the criteria were analyzed by factor, and two underlying factors were found. The first is made up of judgments based on experience. The second consists of judgments that involve comparing the experience at hand to other experiences (consistency) or to external ethical standards (ethicality; see table 11.3).

The third issue to be considered is the extent to which citizens use different criteria to assess the justice of a procedure in different circumstances. To test for variations in the meaning of procedural justice a regression analysis was conducted, in which the eight criteria measuring potentially important elements of procedural justice were used to predict judgments of procedural justice (as in earlier analyses). In addition, terms were entered for the interaction of each criterion with the situational and personal variables under consideration. Finally, a term was entered for the main effect of the situational or personal variable under consideration. The interaction terms are important because they can reveal a significant difference in the weight given to a criterion in different situational and personal conditions. For example, if the personal variable involved were sex and an interaction effect were found for consistency, this would show that men and women place a significantly different weight on consistency in judging procedural justice.

Table 11.3
Factor analysis of the attributes of a procedure

	Factor one	Factor two
Representation		
Process control	.78	—
Decision control	.58	—
Consistency		
Outcomes	—	.42
Procedures	—	.75
Impartiality		
Bias	.42	—
Dishonesty	.49	—
Effort to be fair	.75	—
Quality		
Of decisions	.66	—
Effort to solve problem	.76	—
Correctability	—	—
Ethicality		
Politeness	—	.78
Concern for rights	.43	.73

NOTE. Entries are from a factor analysis using Varimax rotation. Only loadings over 0.4 are shown.

In addition to the analysis outlined above, respondents were divided into two groups for each of the situational and personal variables under consideration, and a separate regression analysis was then performed for each group. Within each group, the eight criteria of procedural justice were used to predict judgments of procedural justice. The six situational characteristics examined were as follows: the authority involved, whether the situation was a dispute, the importance of the outcome, the importance of the procedure, whether the situation involved choice, and whether the outcome was positive. Eight personal characteristics were also examined: two were indices of prior views about the fairness of the authorities, and the others were education, race, sex, age, liberalism or conservatism, and income. Six situational characteristics and eight criteria of procedural justice produced forty-eight interaction terms. Of these, sixteen were statistically significant at the $p < .10$ level or greater (33 percent, a proportion higher than would be expected by chance, with $p < .001$). This suggests that the nature of the situation influences the meaning of procedural justice. In different situations citizens judge the fairness of procedures using different criteria of fairness (see table 11.4).

In the case of personal characteristics eight characteristics were considered, leading to sixty-four interaction terms. Of these only five (8 percent) were significant, a level not different from that which would be expected by chance. There is therefore no evidence that different types of people think differently about the meaning of procedural fairness.

The first situational characteristic examined was the extension to experiences outside the courtroom and to situations that are not disputes. In the first case, it was found that citizens who deal with the courts are significantly more concerned with quality of decision, bias, and correctability than are citizens who deal with the police. There was no evidence for the greater attention to ethicality in courtrooms that was hypothesized. Instead, ethicality mattered both inside and outside the courtroom. Why might ethicality not have mattered more in dealings with the courts? One possible explanation is the generally low esteem in which the courts in Chicago are held by the public. Citizens approaching the courts may not think of them as places where individual rights are a major issue. In contrast, the police are viewed more positively.

In the second case, procedures for resolving disputes were found significantly more likely to be judged in terms of control (as hypothesized), but no bias effect was found. Situations that were not disputes were significantly more likely to be judged in terms of the efforts made by the police officer or judge to be fair. Choice also showed an effect on the meaning of procedural justice. Citizens who voluntarily sought out the police or courts focused more heavily on the quality of the decisions reached by police and courts (as hypothesized), and on issues of bias and correctability. Those without choice were more concerned with the consistency of decision making. When citizens received a favorable outcome they were significantly more concerned with ethicality, as predicted. Those who received negative outcomes evaluated procedural justice more heavily in terms of bias, consistency, and the effort of the authorities to be fair. Those who received poorer outcomes looked beneath the surface and attempted to judge whether the authorities they had dealt with were motivated to be fair. They also looked for surface evidence of bias or inconsistency on the part of the decision maker.

The importance of outcome was found to have only one influence on the meaning of procedural justice. When the outcome was judged to be more important, issues of honesty became more important. Importance of treatment produced two effects: those who regarded being well treated as more important paid more attention to ethicality (to whether the behavior of the police and courts conformed to general rules of proper conduct) and to the quality of the decisions made.

These results show that the meaning of procedural justice changes in response to the nature of the experience that citizens have with legal authorities. Apparently, individuals do not have a single schema of a fair procedure that they apply on all occasions, but instead are concerned with different issues in different circumstances. As a result, it is likely that there are no universally fair procedures for allocation and the resolution of disputes.

In the earlier discussion of control theories of fair procedure it was found that prior attitudes about the authorities influenced judgments about control: those who believed before the experience that the authorities were competent were more likely to believe that their own views were considered. It is possible that other criteria of procedural justice are also affected by prior views, and the results bear this out. Prior views about the legitimacy of legal authorities have a strong effect on people's judgments about whether the authorities were biased ($r = .29$, $p < .05$), as well as influencing many other judgments about the experience. Prior evaluations of quality of performance influence assessments of honesty ($r = .33$, $p < .001$) and of the effort to be fair ($r = .23$, $p < .01$).

Prior views about the authorities have only a small influence on judgments about experience that are most directly linked to issues of outcome. Both absolute and relative judgments of favorability of outcome are only weakly linked to prior views about the legitimacy of legal authorities and prior evaluations of the quality of their performance. The one exception is the relationship between prior evaluations and favorability of outcome ($r = .21$). Those who believe in advance that the authorities perform poorly are more likely to receive an unfavorable outcome. In general, however, prior views seem to have little influence on judgments about the quality of the outcome of experience. This finding is similar to the finding that

Table 11.4
Attributes of a fair procedure in varying circumstances

	Authority			Dispute			Choice		
	Courts	Police	Difference	Yes	No	Difference	Yes	No	Difference
Representation	.15**	.18****	—	.38*****	.17*****	#	.13**	.20***	—
Consistency	.04	.05	—	.12*	.03	—	.02	.08*	#
Impartiality									
Bias	.13*	.02	#	.06	.00	—	.14***	.04	#
Dishonesty	.21***	.26****	—	.15**	.23****	—	.22*****	.23****	—
Effort	.26****	.31*****	—	.07	.36*****	#	.35*****	.24*****	—
Quality	.26***	.14**	#	.16	.08*	—	.29*****	.03	#
Correctability	.25***	.10**	#	.08	.09**	—	.23****	.05	#
Ethicality	.29****	.20****	—	.21**	.23*****	—	.13***	.27****	—
R-squared	67%	71%		75%	67%		67%	66%	

| | Outcome | | | Importance | | | | | |
| | | | | Outcome | | | Process | | |
	Good	Bad	Difference	High	Low	Difference	High	Low	Difference
Representation	.15***	.18****	—	.18****	.17***	—	.15****	.19****	—
Consistency	-.04	.09***	#	-.04	-.04	—	-.04	-.07	—
Impartiality									
Bias	.00	.09***	#	.04	.13**	—	.05	.08	—
Dishonesty	.31****	.21****	—	.26****	.15***	#	.23****	.25****	—
Effort	.20***	.32****	#	.29****	.32****	—	.29****	.28****	—
Quality	.12*	.18***	—	.19****	.10	—	.18****	.12**	#
Correctability	.09	.16***	—	.13***	.14**	—	.17****	.03	—
Ethicality	.39****	.15***	#	.19****	.27****	—	.25****	.18***	#
R-squared	74%	66%		71%	66%		72%	63%	

*p<.10; **p<.05; ***p<.01; ****p<.001

NOTE. Entries are beta weights when all criteria are entered at the same time. All R-squared entries are the adjusted squares of the multiple correlation coefficients. The significance of the difference in weights is assessed by using a regression equation which includes main effects and interaction terms for all eight criteria. The symbol # in the difference column means that the interaction terms were significant at a level of $p < .10$ or greater.

prior views have little impact on assessments of decision control ($r = .02$, n.s.; see the chapter on control).

The findings reported here provide further support for the important role of noninstrumental issues in people's reactions to their experiences. It has already been noted that people react to their experiences based on normative judgments, not instrumental ones. Several aspects of this analysis further support this conclusion. First, judgments about the justice of procedures are found to be affected by a variety of aspects of experience, not simply by outcomes. Some of these aspects, such as the consistency of the outcome with other outcomes, are directly linked to favorability of outcome. Others, like politeness, are linked only remotely to instrumental issues. It seems that the more instrumental criteria of procedural justice are not the most important. On the contrary, several of the key criteria—ethicality and the effort to be fair—are those furthest removed from issues of favorability of outcome.

In addition, statistical controls introduced for the favorability of outcomes have almost no influence on the importance of other (normative) criteria of procedural justice. If other criteria of procedural justice were simply indirect extensions of favorability of outcome, their influence should be diminished or eliminated when favorability of outcome is controlled for. This does not happen. Finally, a direct comparison of the influence of instrumental and noninstrumental criteria of procedural justice suggests that noninstrumental factors explain more of the variance in procedural justice judgments than can be explained by such criteria as favorability of outcome. This direct comparison is striking: neutrality, representation, ethicality, and the effort to be fair explain 47 percent of the variance in judgments of procedural justice beyond what can be explained by the instrumental issues of absolute and relative favorability of outcome. These outcome issues explain only 1 percent of the variance that cannot be explained by criteria unrelated to outcome.

Thibaut and Walker (1975, 1978) discuss the meaning of procedural justice in terms of control. According to their control model, people seek maximum attainment of favorable outcomes, either through direct decision control, or through indirect decision control by means of process control. The Chicago study agrees with earlier research in its finding that control influences judgments of procedural justice. But it also supports earlier research in raising questions about the instrumental interpretation by Thibaut and Walker of control effects. Process control is found to be the major issue of control that matters to disputants, and its influence is maintained even when the influences of decision control are removed. When the opportunity to present evidence is not linked to control over outcomes, process control effects are still found. People have a tremendous desire to present their side of the story and value the opportunity in and of itself.[5]

If citizens are allowed to convey to authorities their suggestions for solving problems, they feel that their experience is procedurally fairer, and this judgment in turn leads their experience to have positive effects on their views about legal authorities. Such process control effects are larger than the effects of control over the decisions made by the third party. In addition, process control effects increase in magnitude as the outcomes involved become more important. When people feel that they had an opportunity to present their evidence but that they had no influence over the decisions made by the authorities, they may have several possible reactions. First, they may feel a lack of influence and decision control, and these feelings may lead to a loss of support for the authorities that made decisions without heeding their views. This reaction reflects an instrumental perspective. It is a reaction based on the lack of correspondence between the person's advocated outcomes and the outcomes actually obtained. Alternatively, people may react favorably to the opportunity to present their views, even if their views had no effect on the decision made. This has been called the value-expressive effect (Tyler, Rasinski, and Spodick 1985) because the value of process control is not linked to its impact on outcomes.

That process control without decision control generally enhances judgments of fairness and support for the authorities is a result consistent with the value-expressive perspective on process control. People do not seem sensitive only to whether their opportunity to speak influences decisions made by a third party. The implication for legal authorities is that they can gain public support by setting up decision-making structures that allow opportunities for process control. Irrespective of whether their long-term accountability is based on the quality of the outcomes they produce, authorities can clearly obtain short-term support from their constituents by providing opportunities for process control. For authorities motivated to follow policies that are sound in the long term, this discretionary authority gives them the flexibility to do so (see Tyler, Rasinski, and Griffin 1986).

Unfortunately, value-expressive effects also provide opportunities to authorities less interested in helping people: opportunities to mislead and beguile the public by providing chances to speak not linked to any short- or long-term influence over decisions (Tyler and McGraw 1986). If the focus on having opportunities to speak draws people's attention away from the tangible benefits they might receive from the authorities, it makes "false consciousness" possible. People may be satisfied in situations that should be viewed as unfair if judged on objective grounds.

The study of procedural justice is neutral about the quality of the existing legal system. It is beyond the scope of this book to evaluate whether those studied "ought" to be more or less satisfied than they are with legal authorities. The results of the Chicago study simply suggest that value-expressive effects can occur, which means that people are potentially open to the development of false consciousness.

Authorities can recognize the value that people place on participation and process control, and establish decision-making procedures that increase people's control of decision making and effect on decision making. Their doing so would make the legal system both seem and be fairer—it would lead to "true" consciousness. Authorities can also recognize the value-expressive elements of process control effects and use these effects to beguile the public. Because research into procedural justice does not examine the motives of authorities, it does not reveal how frequently each of these two types of reaction will occur.

The potential openness of people to value-expressive effects has long been recognized by authorities. For example, a manual written in 2300–2150 B.C. advises Egyptian judges as follows:

> If you are a man who leads
> Listen calmly to the speech of one who pleads;
> Don't stop him from purging his body
> Of that which he planned to tell.
> A man in distress wants to pour out his heart
> More than that his case be won.
> About him who stops a plea
> One asks "Why does he reject it?"
> Not all one pleads for can be granted,
> But a good hearing soothes the heart.
>
> (cited in Mashaw 1981)

Ultimately, heightened self-awareness is the answer to a false consciousness of value-expressive effects. If people recognize their propensity for accepting symbolic gestures and focus not on such gestures but on the tangible benefits that flow from decisions made by third parties, they are less susceptible to false consciousness. The first step in this process is to identify the psychological mechanisms that operate in this situation; that is the goal of this book.

A recent analysis of the content of the speeches of revolutionary leaders found that the speeches focused heavily on distributive justice as opposed to procedural justice (Martin, Scully, and Levitt 1986). Perhaps revolutionary leaders recognize that successfully undermining the legitimacy of existing authorities involves directing people's attention toward distributive injustices.

The Psychology of Value-Expression

The Chicago study also provides insight into the psychological mechanisms underlying value-expressive process control effects. The most important factor shaping people's reactions to having process control is their assessment of the degree to which their views are considered by the decision maker (see also Tyler 1987a). Simply providing structural opportunities to speak is not enough to produce value-expressive effects: citizens must also infer that what they say is being considered by the decision maker. Because of this requirement, the prior views that citizens use as a basis for interpreting the actions of the authorities they deal with are an important determinant of whether process control without decision control enhances feelings of fair treatment. If citizens believe that the authorities are fair, they are more likely to interpret favorably a situation of high process control and low decision control. In such a situation those with positive prior views about the authorities are more likely to infer that their views were considered by the decision maker.

Authorities can enhance the acceptance of their decisions by the way they present them to affected parties. The justifications that leaders offer for their actions seem to affect the responses of subordinates to the actions (see Tyler and Bies, in press). According to the Chicago study, one type of justification is likely to be effective in explaining a lack of decision control: the argument that the citizen's views were considered but (unfortunately) could not influence the decision made. Of course, prior views about the authorities involved will influence the extent to which citizens accept such explanations.

The noninstrumental component of process control effects is of key importance. Citizens do not evaluate their experiences with the police and courts by examining their short-term control over outcomes (Tyler, Rasinski, and Spodick 1985). If they believe that their views are being considered by the authorities, citizens accept a lack of decision control if they have been given the opportunity to state their case.

Although process control effects clearly do not advance self-interest in the short term, it is not clear whether the value-expressive effects of process control found in the Chicago study are noninstrumental in character, or whether they are linked to assessments of long-term self-interest. According to a perspective grounded in long-term self-interest, citizens recognize that they cannot always influence the actions of the authorities. Their allegiance to the group is based on their belief that over time their membership in the group will give them a reasonable level of positive outcomes. This belief can be maintained only if citizens believe that their concerns are being considered by decision-making authorities (Easton 1965; Tyler 1986a). If their views are not considered, citizens will not believe that the authorities are attempting to deal with them in a reasonable way, and long-term allegiance will be called into question.

An alternative perspective on process control focuses on the noninstrumental character of value-expressive effects. According to a noninstrumental perspective, people value the opportunity to address authority figures, irrespective of the effect on decisions of what they say. This perspective emphasizes the interpersonal dimensions of process control, its effect on self-esteem. Studies in the legal, managerial, and political arenas have found that citizens place great value on being treated politely and having respect shown for their rights; these aspects of the interaction reinforce citizens' positive self-image and sense of personal worth (Bies and Moag 1986; Lane 1986; Tyler 1986a; Tyler and Folger 1980). These concerns also emerge in the Chicago study.

The elements of interaction with the authorities that enhance self-esteem depend on the belief that the authorities are paying attention to what the citizen is saying. Self-esteem is not enhanced by being ignored. The key point is that having one's views considered is important because it is a message about one's standing in a social group, not because it means that one's views will necessarily prevail. The Chicago study does not allow the effects of judgments of long-term self-interest to be disentangled from noninstrumental effects. The finding that citizens focus on whether their views are considered by the decision-making authority can be explained by the model of process control effects that is based on self-interest, as well as by that which is not. A study that distinguishes between these two potential models of process control is needed, but the clear implication of the studies that have been conducted is that people do not simply respond to their short-term control over decisions and outcomes.

That value-expressive effects occur implies that there is more to procedural justice than can be captured in an instrumental model. Contrary to the predictions of such a model, people seem generally insensitive to instrumental issues; the interpersonal issues raised by their interaction with third parties seem to be of major importance. This discussion of process control must be placed in the larger context of issues of procedural justice. Although process control and decision control have been studied thoroughly as a result of the emphasis placed on them by Thibaut and Walker (1975), they are only two of many potential criteria of fair procedure. Leventhal (1980) refers to process control and decision control as representation, which he calls one of six criteria of fair procedure. Therefore, in addition to efforts to understand process control, efforts are needed to place it in the larger context of fair procedure. This can be done by directly comparing the importance of Leventhal's six criteria. It is important not to assume that discussions of process control or decision control encompass all or even most of the concerns that citizens have when assessing the fairness of procedures.

Leventhal's Six Criteria of Fair Procedure

The thesis of Thibaut and Walker that issues of control influence judgments of procedural justice is borne out by the Chicago study. The study suggests further that a variety of other issues also influence judgments of procedural justice. Control is important, but it is not the only issue influencing people's reactions to their experiences, or even the most important one. Other important factors include inferences that the authorities are trying to be fair, judgments of honesty, opportunities for representation, assessments about the quality of the decisions made, opportunities for correcting errors, and the absence of bias. Thibaut and Walker emphasized the decision-making functions of procedures, and this also was strongly supported by the Chicago study. Such issues as the neutrality of the decision maker and the quality of the decision influence people's sense that procedures are fair or unfair. Concerns about the decision-making functions of procedures are central to both legal discussions of procedure and popular images of legal justice.

Judgments about "how hard" the authorities try to be fair emerge as the key overall factor in assessing procedural justice. This type of judgment represents an attribution of motive and requires the respondent to think about whether the official is trying to be fair. One might expect such a judgment to be avoided, because it requires more effort than simpler, behavioral judgments. Instead, citizens focus on this assessment, in this case even though inferences of traits are especially difficult to draw and are less reliable when observers can rely only on information from a single interaction (Heider 1958). Others have noted the desire of citizens to infer the intentions of authorities. Lane (1988) notes that citizens focus strongly on inferences about the "benevolence" of political leaders; Bies suggests that workers are very concerned with the "sincerity" of managers (Bies and Shapiro 1987). These concerns reflect a desire on the part of followers to understand the dispositional tendencies of those making decisions. If they infer a positive disposition, they can trust that authority in the long run will serve their interest. It is for this reason that trust is such an important component of legitimacy (Barber 1983; Tyler 1986b).

The emphasis that people place on attributing motives to the authority they are dealing with suggests that the personal qualities of the authority are crucial. This helps to explain why people are often as satisfied with informal forums, such as mediation, as with formal trials. If they make positive inferences about the intentions of the third party in either case, people will feel fairly treated. This also raises the more general question of what makes a third party an authority to people with a problem or dispute to be resolved. Is it the position that person occupies (such as that of judge or police officer), or is it the inference that the person has certain characteristics, such as sincerity or competence? In other words, does legitimacy reside in a social role, or in characteristics of the person? (See Merry and Silbey 1984.) According to the Chicago study, legitimacy is based on both social roles and personal characteristics. Legal authorities have legitimacy because people feel that they ought to obey them, and this is due to the social role that the authorities occupy. In addition, particular police officers and judges can gain support by communicating to those they deal with that they are trying to treat them fairly.

Concern with issues of ethicality has not figured prominently in past psychological discussions of procedural justice, but it is one of the criteria mentioned by Leventhal (1980). Other social scientists have also suggested that ethical appropriateness is a key aspect of fair treatment. Lane (1988) has noted the importance of ethicality in politics. He argues that one of the most important aspects of procedural justice to citizens is that the procedures used support their sense of self-respect. Being treated politely and having one's rights as a citizen respected should strongly reinforce self-respect, the importance of which to overall psychological well-being has been discussed by others (Campbell 1980; Rosenberg 1979). The importance of self-respect in the specific context of citizens' encounters with legal authority was noted in a study that examined contacts between citizens and police; the study found that a key issue to citizens in such contacts is "recognition of citizen rights" (Tyler and Folger 1980, 292).

Similar evidence of a concern with interpersonal aspects of encounters with authorities has been found in research conducted in work environments. Bies and Shapiro (1987) discuss research into job applicants' reactions to their experiences in corporate recruiting. They report that job candidates react to aspects of the interviewing experience that are interactional (that is, that relate to being treated politely and decently), as well as to such issues as honesty, consistency, and bias. An extreme example of the importance of interpersonal issues is provided by the problem of burglary. If a home is burglarized, the police typically have little likelihood of recovering any stolen property. Fortunately for the police, the way they are evaluated will not be linked to their ability to solve the problem. If the police come to a person's home, treat the person politely, and fill out a burglary report, the person is likely to have positive feelings about the police (Parks 1976). People feel entitled to having their problem taken seriously by the authorities.

In the Chicago study the concept of ethicality was viewed in two potentially distinct ways: as politeness and as concern for one's rights. These two items were combined into one index because they were found to be highly correlated ($r = .59$). If they are separated, concern for one's rights is more strongly related to judgments of procedural justice ($r = .67$) than politeness is ($r = .58$).

The most striking deviation from predictions is the failure to find strong consistency effects in citizens' judgments of fairness. Citizens are not basing their procedural justice judgments on a comparison of their experience with other experiences, either of their own or of other people. Because consistency has been commonly found to be a major issue in past studies, its failure to be important here is puzzling. There are several possible explanations for this. One is that citizens lack the information necessary to judge consistency. There are many varied reasons why citizens may have contact with the police and courts, and to each corresponds an appropriate type of treatment by the authorities. As a result, citizens may be aware of several instances of police behavior or the behavior of judges, but may not know how the situation involved is related to their own. Because judgments of similarity are the key to processes of comparison (Festinger 1954), this makes it difficult for citizens to make judgments of relative outcomes and treatment. For example, how can the outcome of a call to the police to stop a neighborhood disturbance be compared with not receiving a ticket from the police when stopped for speeding?

Bies and Shapiro (1987) have proposed that citizens accept differences in treatment or outcomes that correspond to differences in the problems being dealt with. This is supported by the finding of Cornelius, Kanfer, and Lind (1986) that inconsistency of treatment does not lead to perceived unfairness if it is justified by differences in the task. A lack of awareness of the experiences of others may be a characteristic of only some populations. Special populations may have greater knowledge of others and may rely more on others' experiences when evaluating their own. One example of such a special group is criminals. Casper found from interviews with defendants in prison that career criminals have a great deal of knowledge about the typical behavior of the police and courts, and use consistency with their expectations as an important basis for evaluating their treatment and sentences (Casper 1972, 1978).

The difficulties that citizens face in acquiring the appropriate information for social comparison are similar to the more general difficulty that they have in drawing useful information from indirect sources such as the mass media. In the case of information about crime, for example, these difficulties can be traced in part to the failure of the mass media to present citizens with situational information they need. This leaves citizens unable to compare the circumstances of victims whom they read about or see on television with their own (Tyler 1984; Tyler and Cook 1984; Tyler and Lavrakas 1986), and unable as a result to assess their own risks. A second factor that may account for the lack of influence of consistency in the Chicago study is that many of the contacts examined were not disputes among several parties. In the courtroom settings studied by Thibaut and Walker, for example, one party is presented with a very clear focus of social comparison: the other party to the dispute. In such a context inconsistency of treatment is very clear. Research that has found strong consistency effects has typically involved either disputes between parties or allocations among several parties (Barrett-Howard and Tyler 1986; Fry and Chaney 1981; Fry and Leventhal 1979; Greenberg 1986a).

If citizens lack the information needed to rely on consistency (that is, on cross-situational comparisons), their alternative is to rely on judgments that can be made with the information available. One type of information is that about the behavior of the officials, which leads to inferences about their efforts to be fair. Another is information about their apparent honesty. A third is ethicality, a judgment about whether the officials involved followed general ethical standards of conduct. The need to rely on judgments based on a single experience is one reason why ethicality had a strong influence on judgments of procedural justice. Consistency with ethical principles is a type of judgment that allows citizens to assess the quality of police and court conduct within the context of one experience. Irrespective of the problem or issue at dispute in such a contact, citizens can feel that the officials involved should follow general ethical guidelines. As a result, such judgments override the difficulties involved in social or temporal comparisons.

Formal and Informal Legal Procedures

Although decision-making issues are important in assessing procedural justice, the Chicago study shows that many other issues are also important. That they are important helps to explain the puzzling results of some studies of formal and informal means to resolve disputes; one of these is that informal means of resolving disputes, such as mediation, are typically regarded as fair procedures by those who use them to settle problems (Tyler 1989). Similarly, plea bargaining is considered by defendants to be as fair as a trial for settling cases (Landis and Goodstein 1986; Casper, Tyler, and Fisher 1988).

Legal scholars have raised various concerns about the procedural adequacy of both plea bargaining and unconventional means of resolving disputes. In contrast, those who use such informal procedures do not view them as more unfair than trials, and are no less satisfied with settling cases informally. Why might this be the case? The Chicago study suggests that aspects of procedure that are unrelated to decision making have important implications for judgments of their fairness. These aspects of procedure are linked only loosely to the formal character of the procedure; they therefore vary widely within procedures, and the type of procedure being used is not by itself a good predictor of whether people will feel fairly treated.

In some ways informal legal procedures may correspond more closely than trials to people's intuitions about what is a fair procedure. Such procedures offer greater opportunities for direct participation than formal trials do and may allow the decision maker more flexibility to be sensitive to people's interpersonal concerns. What is clear from the results of this study is that people assess the fairness of a procedure by using criteria quite different from those central to defining such formal legal procedures as trials. As a result, there is a sizable gap between forums that best satisfy people's naive psychology of fairness and those that follow legal rules (O'Barr and Conley 1985). The presence of this gap raises the possibility that people can go through "fair" formal legal procedures and end up feeling unfairly treated. Although the formal legal system may not conform to people's feelings about procedural fairness, this does not mean that procedures should necessarily be changed to reflect people's preferences. Those who experience an informal procedure may not be well informed about the alternatives to it. If they actually experienced these alternatives, they might prefer them.

Members of the public may also not be sensitive to the legal safeguards built into the law, because they may not be exploited by the legal authorities with whom they deal. Many elements of legal procedure are designed to protect people from situations where other people, either private citizens or authorities, have improper motives. Although such situations occur infrequently, they are very destructive to the social fabric when they do. But because such problems are infrequent, people may not think about them in their daily lives, and they may not figure prominently in how people react to dealings with the law and legal authorities. Because law develops through the codification of problems, when difficult situations occur they become important in the development of legal doctrine. The law is built around abuses of authority that have occurred and may again. And if the law is successful in discouraging such abuses, the abuses will not be salient to members of the public. For the public's concerns to diverge from those of the formal law is therefore not an indictment of either.

The divergence of views about procedure that has been outlined raises the question of who "owns" a problem or dispute. If members of the public are the primary focus, then procedures should be shaped by public concerns. If society is the primary focus, then procedures should advance societal objectives. In fact both issues are important and some balance must be struck. Society must make some effort to satisfy disputants, but procedures must also advance society's self-interest.

To what extent are people's concerns now represented in legal procedures?

Compared with legal forums in many societies studied by anthropologists, American legal procedures are not particularly responsive to popular desires. For example, in most cultures people are allowed fairly unrestricted opportunities to tell authorities about their problems in a form of their own choosing (O'Barr 1988). By comparison, American legal procedures are very constrained. In contrast to some of the more restrictive European procedures, on the other hand, American legal procedures seem very responsive to people's desires. Although Thibaut and Walker (1975) found that European citizens prefer adversary procedures, in their courts people may speak only to the extent and in the form dictated by the judge. People lack even the indirect control over trials that Americans have through their lawyers.

There are also practical difficulties stemming from any effort to be responsive to people's desires. The desire to present one's case, for example, clashes with the legal system's need to dispose of problems efficiently. Judges are under pressure to resolve cases quickly and may not feel that they have the freedom to allow litigants to speak their mind. Lawyers are similarly eager to dispose of cases and may not want to take the time to allow their clients to take part in negotiations. These issues are of real importance to legal authorities. The authorities need to recognize, however, that simply producing a good settlement for a person will not lead the person to feel fairly treated, nor necessarily enhance the image of the legal system in the eyes of the public.

Is the Meaning of Procedural Justice Universal?

Clearly, the meaning of procedural justice changes in response to the nature of people's experiences with legal authorities. Although the pattern of the research findings is complex, it points to the conclusion that individuals do not have a single schema of fair procedure to apply in all situations. Rather, they are concerned with different issues in different circumstances, and it is likely as a result that there is no universally fair procedure for allocation and for resolution of disputes. As has already been noted, Thibaut and Walker focused on issues of representation when examining the meaning of procedural justice (that is, on process control and decision control). The Chicago study suggests that they may have overgeneralized from the context of their own work, which centered on disputes, to a general theory of fair procedures. In the context of disputes representation is most important. If the context is broadened, however, other issues emerge.

It is also interesting that the characteristics of the person do not influence the criteria used to assess whether a procedure is fair. In other words, different types of people define the meaning of procedural justice in the same way. This suggests that definitions of the meaning of justice within particular settings may be part of the cultural beliefs shared by members of our society. This is supported by recent ethnographic studies of the courts (Merry 1985, 1986) and by studies of consensus in judging wrongdoing (Sanders and Hamilton 1987).

The lack of personal differences has very important consequences for interactions among citizens and between citizens and authorities. Because all parties to a problem have a common conception of the meaning of procedural justice, all will focus on similar issues in attempting to find a process for dealing with the question at hand. If this were not the case, police officers and judges would have to understand immediately the meaning of procedural justice to each party that appeared before them. To come to agreement on these issues before even attempting to choose procedures for resolving every problem that legal authorities face would be complex and time-consuming. The authorities are therefore aided in their efforts to resolve public problems by shared cultural values and shared views of the meaning of procedural justice. These common values reveal to them the public concerns they ought to address, and facilitate the acceptance of decisions once they are made. It seems likely that efforts to develop a typology that will clarify when procedural justice will have different meanings should focus on developing a situational typology. People think about procedural justice in a similar way even if characteristics of their backgrounds differ.

PART FIVE

Conclusions

CHAPTER 12

The Antecedents of Compliant Behavior

Authorities in social groups recognize that their effectiveness depends on their ability to influence the behavior of the groups' members. In the case of legal authorities effectiveness depends on the extent to which they are able to influence the public's behaviors toward the law. Laws and the decisions of legal authorities are of little practical importance if people ignore them. Because of the centrality of compliance to effectiveness as a legal authority, understanding why people follow the law is a central issue in law and the social sciences.

Two theories of compliance with the law have been advanced: the instrumental and the normative. In this book I have emphasized the importance of the normative perspective, which focuses on the values that lead people to comply voluntarily with legal rules and the decisions of legal authorities. Such values, if they exist, form a basis for the effective functioning of legal authorities. This is especially true of legitimacy—the belief that one ought to obey the law. If normative values are absent, authorities must use the mechanisms of deterrence that stem from instrumental control over reward and punishments. Such mechanisms are costly and in many cases may be inadequate. The Chicago study supports the normative perspective on compliance. Both personal morality and legitimacy are found to have an effect on people's everyday behavior toward the law, whatever type of analysis is conducted.

Legitimacy is the normative factor of greatest concern to authorities. According to a variety of theories advanced by social scientists, legitimacy is crucial if the authorities are to have the discretionary power they need to fulfill their roles. In the case of legal authorities, legitimacy underlies their expectation that the public will generally obey the law. The Chicago study confirms that legitimacy plays an important role in promoting compliance.

The Procedural Basis of Legitimacy

Given the centrality of legitimacy to compliance, it is important to understand how legitimacy is maintained or undermined among members of the public. The Chicago study explored this issue in the context of people's experiences with legal authorities, and examined the effects of experience with particular police officers and judges on views about the legitimacy of legal authorities. To be concerned with the impact of experiences on views about the legitimacy of legal authorities is to be concerned with the political impact of experience. If legitimacy diminishes, so does the ability of legal and political authorities to influence public behavior and function effectively.

Many aspects of experience could be important in determining the political impact of experience. The Chicago study contrasts the instrumental and normative perspectives on experience. The normative perspective that it emphasizes is represented by psychological theories of justice, according to which people react to social experiences in terms of the fairness of the outcomes they receive (distributive justice), and the fairness of the procedures by which those outcomes are arrived at (procedural justice). In contrast, according to an instrumental perspective people react to their experiences depending on the favorability of the outcomes of the experiences. The normative perspective is better able to account for people's reactions, especially when people use their experiences with particular police officers and judges to generalize about the overall legitimacy of legal authority. Procedural justice is the key normative judgment influencing the impact of experience on legitimacy. Similar evidence has been found in politics and the workplace (Lind and Tyler 1988; Tyler 1987c). Views about authority are strongly connected to judgments of the fairness of the procedures through which authorities make decisions.

That people are concerned with procedure is not a new idea. Past conceptions of the citizen have relied heavily on the principle that citizens evaluate government institutions and authorities in procedural terms (Anton 1967; Easton 1965; Edelman 1964; Engstrom and Giles 1972; Murphy and Tanenhaus 1969; Saphire 1978; Scheingold 1974; Wahlke 1971). The procedural effects found by the Chicago study may contradict the instrumental views now prevailing in legal studies, but they are consistent with a procedural school in the social sciences that is of long standing.

If one accepts the image of the person that is put forth by the Chicago study, one will look in a new way at how people react to decisions in political, legal, and work organizations. In the legal arena citizens will be seen as reacting to the procedures through which court decisions are made, as well as to the decisions themselves. In politics people will react to policies and politicians on procedural grounds. And in the workplace they will be concerned with how decisions are made about pay and promotions. Therefore, decision makers can gain public acceptance for their decisions and rules by making and implementing them in ways that the public thinks is fair.

One clear implication is that authorities are freer than they commonly believe to follow painful policies that are sound in the long term. Authorities often feel that their legitimacy is linked to their ability to deliver tangible positive outcomes to self-interested citizens. They reflect the assumptions of the economic model, and think that people affected by their decisions will react to the decisions based on the extent of their personal gain or loss. That people attend to matters of procedure gives authorities latitude to pursue long-term policies by stressing the fairness of the procedures through which they came about (Tyler, Rasinski, and Griffin 1986).

The Meaning of Procedural Justice

Given the importance of procedural justice to legitimacy, it is crucial to understand how people define fair procedures. Again, an instrumental perspective contrasts with a normative one. According to the instrumental perspective of Thibaut and Walker (1975), people define fairness primarily by the extent to which they are able to influence the decisions made by the third party. According to a normative perspective, there are many other aspects to the fairness of a procedure, which have little or nothing to do with outcomes or the control of outcomes. The Chicago study reinforces the normative perspective on the meaning of fair process. Judgments of procedural justice are found to be multidimensional. They involve many issues besides favorability of outcome and control of outcome. In fact, the criterion of fair procedure most closely related to outcomes (that is, consistency) is found to be of minor importance. In contrast, judgments about the social dimensions of the experience, such as ethicality, weigh very heavily in assessments of procedural justice. In the context of people's experiences with police officers and judges, the Chicago study found that seven different aspects of procedure independently influenced judgments about whether the procedure was fair.

One important element in feeling that procedures are fair is a belief on the part of those involved that they had an opportunity to take part in the decision-making process. This includes having an opportunity to present their arguments, being listened to, and having their views considered by the authorities. Those who feel that they have had a hand in the decision are typically much more accepting of its outcome, irrespective of what the outcome is. An additional advantage of procedures that allow both sides to state their arguments is that each side is exposed to the other. Because a party to a dispute is often unaware of the feelings and concerns of the other party, this exposure is very important (Conley 1988; Tyler 1987b).

Judgments of procedural fairness are also linked to judgments about the neutrality of the decision-making process. People believe that decision makers should be neutral and unbiased. They also expect decision makers to be honest and to reach their decisions based on objective information about the case. As is true of questions of participation, these issues are linked to settling the dispute or policy issue involved. Procedural fairness is also related to interpersonal aspects of the decision-making procedure. People place great weight on being treated politely and having respect shown for their rights and for themselves as people. The way people are dealt with by legal and political authorities has implications for their connection with the social group and their position in the community. It therefore has important implications for self-esteem (Lane 1988) and group identification (Lind and Tyler 1988). People are unlikely to feel attached to groups led by authorities who treat them rudely or ignore their rights. The treatment accorded by public officials is also an indication of the likelihood that people will receive help if they have problems in the future, and so has important implications for feelings of security. People will not feel identified with officials whom they regard as unresponsive to their problems and unwilling to help and protect them.

The importance that people attach to their relationship to authorities is reflected in the importance of another criterion of procedural justice: inferences about the motives of the authorities. The way people assess procedural fairness is strongly linked to their judgments of whether the authority they are dealing with is motivated to be fair. Because motivational inferences require considerably more cognitive effort than assessments of such surface features as honesty and bias, one might expect them to be avoided. Why are they instead central to assessments of procedural fairness? One advantage of inferences of motive or intention is that they reflect dispositional characteristics, that is, features of the person that are likely to predict their future behavior (Heider 1958). The centrality of such inferences to issues of procedural justice reflects people's concern with knowing how authorities will act toward them in the future.

Finally, the fairness of procedures is linked to whether the procedures produce fair outcomes. Procedural issues are not independent of questions of outcome. Fair outcomes are one thing that people expect from a fair procedure, and a procedure that consistently produces unfair outcomes will eventually be viewed as unfair itself.

Although the factors outlined typically emerge as central to judgments about procedural justice, it is also important that the same issues are not used to judge the fairness of procedures with regard to all issues. In different situations people evaluate the fairness of procedures against different criteria of procedural justice: there is no universally fair procedure that can be used to resolve all types of problems and disputes. At the same time, different types of people do not evaluate the fairness of procedures against different criteria. Within the context of a particular type of problem or dispute, different types of people generally agree about the criteria that should be used to judge the fairness of the procedure. This finding is consistent with other recent evidence that there is a substantial consensus among Americans about what is fair (Merry 1985, 1986; Sanders and Hamilton 1987).

The Normative Perspective

The Chicago study makes clear that normative issues are central to any effort to understand authority and compliance. In three areas normative issues were found to be important: the legitimacy of leaders is directly related to compliance; justice affects reactions to personal experience; and people think about justice in noninstrumental terms.

The instrumental perspective is clearly insufficient to explain people's views about the legitimacy of authority and their behavioral compliance with the law. Citizens act as naive moral philosophers, evaluating authorities and their actions against abstract criteria of fairness. The instrumental conceptions of the person that have recently dominated discussions of legal issues are incomplete. Explanations based on the image of people as entirely rational beings who maximize utility are insufficient to account for their behavior in social groups. Further, procedural justice plays a crucial role in the political impact of experience. The legitimacy of authorities is closely intertwined with the procedures they use when dealing with the public. These findings of the Chicago study reinforce the importance of "civic duty" in political science (Easton 1965), of normative issues in sociology (Gamson 1968; Schwartz 1978), and of distributive and procedural justice in psychology (Crosby 1976; Lind and Tyler 1988). Although issues of justice and legitimacy have long been given attention in each of these fields, more recently models of public choice emphasizing instrumental concerns have dominated. The Chicago study shows that a fuller description of citizens' behavior can be obtained by paying greater attention to normative questions.

A normative perspective can also give a differing approach to policy issues, such as the issue of how to implement public policies. In past discussions of policy implementation, it has been assumed that citizens' behavior is motivated by self-interest, and as a result the focus has been on the manipulation of behavior through the control of punishments and incentives. In light of the Chicago study, however, policymakers might also pay attention to the normative climate that surrounds legal authority and to citizens' conceptions of fair decision-making procedures in legal settings. The study does more than make the general suggestion that norms matter: it strongly supports a procedural orientation toward normative issues. Research on distributive justice has focused on fair outcomes, but people focus on fair procedure.

Implications for Theories of Public Choice

The Chicago study raises questions about the completeness of the theories of public choice that have guided earlier research on how people react to the law and legal authorities. Although it is possible to develop explanations for the findings of the study that are consistent with models that focus on outcome, it is much more straightforward simply to recognize that people are concerned about normative issues. This is of course not to suggest that people never care about outcomes. The Chicago study examined the political implications of experience, and it may be that people differentiate between political aspects of their experience and market aspects. According to traditional economic theory, market decisions are heavily influenced by concerns about self-interest (but see Kahneman, Knetsch, and Thaler 1986).

When considering the implications of the study it is important to distinguish between the model of subjective expected utility and the image of the person contained in theories of public choice. The model is used for combining various utility factors into a single behavioral propensity. The image of the person contained in theories of public choice is one of a person motivated primarily by short-term self-interest.

It is possible to deal with issues of fairness by incorporating them into an expanded model of expected utility, following the conceptual approach of Fishbein and Ajzen (1975; Ajzen and Fishbein 1980) or Leventhal (1976, 1980). To do so follows the pattern of recent research on deterrence, which has incorporated both informal sanctions by the social group and personal moral concerns into models that traditionally had included only judgments about the certainty and severity of punishment. Once the concept of an expanded model of expected utility is accepted, the issue becomes one of specifying when each of the terms in the equation will be important. The Chicago study sheds light on one factor: whether the judgment is one of personal satisfaction or an evaluation of authorities affects the values of the terms. Situational factors may also matter: for example, procedural justice matters more in dispute situations. Ultimately a model should incorporate all these elements into an overall theory of fairness.

In contrast to its minimal implications for models of expected utility, the Chicago study's implications for the image of the person contained in theories of public choice are troubling. The people studied in Chicago do not react to their experiences or behave in ways that can be easily explained by reference to their short-term self-interest. Instead, people seem concerned with normative issues. After the Second World War came a series of important developments in economics. Theories were formulated based on rational models of choice and decision making that were oriented toward outcome. The principal conceptual innovation was the articulation of expected utility and of a theory of how to assess it (Von Neumann and Morgenstern 1947). Models of expected utility allow the idea of people as personal maximizers of utility to account for social and political behavior. As a result of these developments, models of the person based on self-interest have come to dominate law, policy studies, and political science. It has been increasingly assumed that people are concerned primarily with the personal favorability of the outcomes they receive from legal and political authorities, and that they shape their behavior based on expectations about the rewards and punishments those authorities provide. This assumption is the key characteristic of models of public choice.

Models of public choice have had two influences on the study of law and public policy. First, they have influenced the political and social issues that are regarded as important enough to study. Second, they have influenced the image of the person that is used in examining the issues. One implication of the Chicago study is that there is a need to shift the questions that are studied by political psychologists. Theories of public choice have directed attention to issues that when viewed from a perspective of public choice appear paradoxical or problematic. That people vote, for example, is difficult to explain given the low expected gains of voting and its clear costs (Laver 1981; Mueller 1979). Another problem central to theories of public choice is that of noncompliance with government burdens, for example taxes. If people are viewed as motivated by personal gain, they will be expected to try to avoid obligations, as long as avoidance does not appear to have immediate personal costs. Therefore, all citizens will try to avoid paying taxes. If all succeed, society cannot function.

A normative perspective directs attention to a different set of concerns. In particular, it focuses the attention of researchers and policymakers on normative issues, and on the need to understand how people acquire the normative values that have such an important influence on how people evaluate the law and behave toward it. The Chicago study is unclear about the origins and evolution of beliefs about the legitimacy of authority. Earlier theories have emphasized that legitimacy develops during socialization in childhood. This initial belief in the legitimacy of authority then functions as a residue of support that cushions people against negative experiences during their adult life. The respondents in the Chicago study clearly had such beliefs, because an overwhelming proportion of respondents said they felt the law should be obeyed. But when their belief developed is unclear.

It is also important to study the origin of people's schemata for judging the fairness of outcomes and procedures. Researchers have found that people are almost always able to judge whether a procedure is fair or unfair, just as they can almost always judge this of an outcome. Thus people have well-established frameworks for making judgments about justice. Where do these frameworks come from? As has been noted, research has found that there is a consensus among Americans about what constitutes a fair procedure, and explanations of this have focused on socialization. In this regard, the results are similar to those that prevail with legitimacy. There too a consensus exists that people ought to follow the law. Still unanswered in both cases is the nature of the process of socialization underlying the effects. In addition to research aimed at understanding the origin of normative views, more research is needed about what those views are. Although the Chicago study makes clear that normative concerns matter, it is vague about their content. The perceived obligation to obey authorities was found to have a stronger relationship to compliance than support for the authorities has. Unfortunately, it is not clear why people feel obligated to obey the law and legal authorities, to whom they feel this obligation, or the range of behavior to which the obligation applies.

In addition, people's views about fairness are quite complex and sophisticated, in two ways. First, judgments about justice consider in general a variety of issues, some of which are quite subtle. For example, people rely heavily on inferences about the motives of the authorities. Second, people do not always consider the same issues. They recognize that different issues are relevant to the fairness of a procedure in different circumstances.

One approach to understanding the nature of values pertaining to justice is to begin with their connection to basic political and social values. An incipient effort to do so is the demonstration by Rasinski (1987) that values of justice are linked to basic political and social values. Models of justice also point up the need for a different view of the person in efforts to understand and deal with legal and political problems (Tyler, Rasinski, and Griffin 1986). In trying to understand why people follow the law, for example, we should not assume that behavior responds primarily to reward and punishment (as do traditional theories of deterrence; see Andenaes 1974 and Tittle 1980). Instead, we should recognize that behavior is affected by the legitimacy of legal authorities and the morality of the law. Similarly, the literature on implementing policy should not focus simply on manipulating penalties and incentives: it should also be concerned with creating a normative climate that promotes the acceptance of law and public policies.

The implications of accepting public concerns about justice are broad. To recognize them will help us to understand the nature of public discontent with the legal and political system, to design ways of implementing policies that will make the policies more widely accepted, to understand why people react to their dealings with police officers, judges, and other legal and political officials, and to understand the basis of public behavior—whether the public is obeying the law, rioting, or voting.

CHAPTER 13

The Psychology of Legitimacy

People generally feel that existing legal authorities are legitimate, and this legitimacy promotes compliance with the law. To understand why legitimacy leads to compliance requires a psychological model of the individual's relationship to social organizations. A starting point for examining people's relationships to organizations is the social exchange model (Thibaut and Kelley 1959), according to which people are self-interested. They join groups and stay in them because they gain by doing so. The idea that people seek to maximize their personal gain when interacting with others is a key feature of several social science and behavioral models of the person, including economic models (Laver 1981), models associated with learning theories, and sociological and social psychology models of social exchange and interdependence (Homans 1961; Kelley and Thibaut 1978; Thibaut and Kelley 1959). These models, which dominate law, public policy, and the social sciences, have widespread intuitive appeal and have proved to contain important assumptions in many studies of the behavioral and social sciences.

The image of the person developed by the social exchange model provides the underlying assumptions that shape the procedural justice model of Thibaut and Walker (1975). One of the basic ideas embodied in this model is that people who find themselves in conflict and have little success in negotiating a settlement turn to a third party to resolve their dispute. They then seek maximum control over the outcome of the effort to resolve the dispute by means of maximum control over their own presentation of evidence. The assumption underlying the control model of Thibaut and Walker is that people are fundamentally concerned with their own outcomes. As a result, procedural preferences develop in social settings out of the operation of self-interest. Basing models of justice on an image of a self-interested person is not unique to Thibaut and Walker. Walster, Walster, and Berscheid (1978) similarly develop their theory of equity (distributive justice) out of a conception of a self-interested person.

In these models of justice, people recognize that they must curb their self-interest to cooperate with others. Even in such simple interactions as bargaining, people are faced with the problem of balancing the desire for maximum self-interest and the desire to maintain the relationship with others. A child will prefer always to sit in the swing and for other children always to push, but such a relationship cannot be maintained. Even in simple situations, interaction is a game of mixed motives. In bargaining this is called the bargainer's dilemma. If one pushes harder to reach an agreement favorable to one's own interests, one may gain more, but this also increases the risk of disrupting the relationship and securing no agreement.

Given the limits of social interaction, why do people choose to engage in it? According to the perspective grounded in self-interest, in the long run people gain more through cooperation than they can gain alone, even with the compromises inherent in interaction. This logic of long-term gain applies to membership in small and informal groups as well as in large and complex organizations. Whether in the legal or political system, a social group, or a work organization, people join and remain in the group because they believe they can gain in the long run. In long-term relationships in social organizations the mixed motives of social interaction become complex. People are members of a legal and political system for many years, perhaps for their entire lives. Similarly, they belong to educational, work-related, and social organizations for long periods. How can people decide how well their interests are being served by the organization and its authorities, how loyal they should be to an organization, its rules, and its authorities?

When assessing loyalty toward groups people must consider whether the authorities allocating resources or restricting their actions are doing so in a way that will benefit the members in the long run. In organizations to which people have a long-term commitment involving many areas of exchange, calculations based on short-term self-interest are difficult. People typically receive many types of benefit and incur many types of cost through membership in the group. The literature on distributive justice demonstrates that people typically focus not on the absolute number of resources they receive, but on how their level of resources compares with that of others. In doing so they use some rule of relative fairness that tells them the level of resources they deserve.

A calculation of distributive justice of the type outlined is quite complex, for membership in organizations involves gains and losses in a variety of areas. How, for example, can the benefits of flexible work time be compared to a higher salary or a larger office? Further, such calculations are not typically short-term: people must assess the probable future benefits and costs of membership in the group. And how are people to know whether they are receiving a level of resources that is appropriate relative to the resources received by others? What makes people believe that they will fairly benefit in the long run from belonging to the group?

The problem people face in dealing with legal authorities is similar to the problem they face when dealing with authorities in general. They must decide how committed they should be to the organization to which they belong. One way they can decide this is by comparing the benefits received from the organization with the costs of membership. This comparison can be made either in absolute terms or relative to the costs and benefits of others. They can also focus on the procedures by which distributions are made. If the procedures are fair, it is reasonable to expect long-term gains even in the absence of short-term gains.

The Chicago study confirms that people settle issues of loyalty and obedience to organizational rules and authorities by focusing on the procedure by which the authorities make decisions. There are two types of evidence for this procedural orientation. The first is the finding that the procedural justice of experience determines its impact on views about the legitimacy of authority. The Chicago study supports the widespread view that the evaluation of authorities and institutions is shaped by concerns about procedural justice (Lind and Tyler 1988). When people generalize about legal authority based on their personal experiences, they focus most strongly on questions of procedural justice. Similar findings are obtained when one explores the effects of experience on the relationship of legitimacy to compliance. If people have an experience not characterized by fair procedures, their later compliance with the law will be based less strongly on the legitimacy of legal authorities. Therefore, not experiencing fair procedures undermines legitimacy.

Why might experiencing unfair procedures undermine the role of legitimacy in maintaining compliance? The obligation to obey is based on trust of authorities. Only if people can trust authorities, rules, and institutions can they believe that their own long-term interests are served by loyalty toward the organization. In other words, the social contract is based on expectations about how authorities will act. If authorities violate these expectations, the social contract is disrupted. It is interesting that people appear to connect the obligations of authorities to issues of fair procedure, not to outcomes. It is being unfairly treated that disrupts the relationship of legitimacy to compliance, not receiving poor outcomes. [1]

The importance of procedures to a long-term organizational perspective is illustrated in Easton's theory of support for political organizations (1965). Easton asks why citizens do not leave a political system or seek its overthrow when their candidate does not win an election. He argues that they do not because they feel that in the long run their interests are served by the political system to which they belong. They believe this because they have "diffuse" support for the political system, based on a faith in the procedures and institutions of government. Given that the underlying procedures of government are fair, people feel that over time they will receive reasonably good outcomes from the political system. As a result, the belief that decision-making procedures are fair promotes loyalty and good feeling toward the system.

The model that has been developed rests on an assumption that people ultimately care about issues of self-interest. In the context of organizational membership, simple short-term self-interest extends across a number of issues and over time. People want to feel that they will generally benefit from membership in the group. They judge whether they will by examining the procedures according to which allocations are made and disputes resolved. If the procedures are fair, people think they will receive positive outcomes.

The Group Value Model

It is not necessary to accept an instrumental view of the person as a framework for considering people's relationships to society and social groups. The relationship may be viewed according to the group value model (Lind and Tyler 1988). According to this model, people value identification with social groups. Such groups provide a source of resources, self-knowledge, self-identification, and social rewards. As a result, people join and take part in many social and work-related groups, as well as in the legal, political, and social structures of society. Through these involvements people identify with groups and with their relationships to them, and group members become important determinants of individual attitudes and behaviors.

Social psychologists have long held that people identify with groups and value their membership in them. People have been found to be affiliative in nature, seeking to spend time in groups. They have also been found to develop identification with groups based on minimum common characteristics (Brewer and Kramer 1986; Kramer and Brewer 1984; Messick and Brewer 1983; Orbell, van de Kragt, and Dawes 1988).[2] Once such an identification has developed people put aside their self-interest and act for the benefit of the group. In fact, this is so much the case that some psychologists have argued that group behavior cannot be explained simply by reference to self-interest and requires the assumption that group identification is a value in and of itself. What is clear is that people come to value status accorded by the group and membership within it. Being accepted and esteemed by others is rewarding; being rejected by members of a group is painful.

The value that people place on membership in the group and the status conferred by it creates a tension that they must resolve. The tension arises from their attraction to the group, which must be balanced against the fears they have of being exploited by others. As has already been noted, to participate in organized groups individuals must be willing to temper their motivation to seek maximum personal gain with a motivation to cooperate, so that members of the group receive some of the rewards they desire. It is because of this that there is an inherent tension in social relationships between the individual and the group.

Individuals must be sensitive to the possibility that their sacrifices are not being returned by the group, and able to reevaluate their loyalty to the group when they feel they are receiving inadequate returns for their loyalty. When people do not benefit from an organizational decision and see rewards and opportunities going to others, why do they continue to remain loyal to that organization?

It has been proposed that people resolve their concerns about loyalty to the group by focusing on the procedures of allocation and decision making in the group (Lind and Tyler 1988). This is strongly borne out by the Chicago study. The procedural focus stems from people's desire to reap the benefits of belonging to the group without being open to exploitation. If there is a mechanism to assure that outcomes are distributed fairly, long-term membership in the group will be rewarding; evidence that procedures for allocation are fair provides a basis for a continued belief in the value of organizational loyalty in the face of negative decisions.

In complex organizations procedures are not used simply to make decisions or resolve conflicts. Procedures specify the lines of authority and social processes that regulate the group's activity, and define the internal framework of the group, just as the group's identity defines it in relation to other, external groups. Because they regulate social processes, procedures are extremely important to the members of social groups. Procedures define social status, access to desired activities and resources, opportunities for participation in the group, and personal vulnerability or invulnerability to exploitation and harm. Because members of the group value their status and security within it, they are very concerned with the procedures used by the group to make decisions. Given their central role in defining status and authority in organizations, it is not surprising that procedural assessments are the key to evaluating authorities and institutions. When people assess their commitment and loyalty to a group they focus on the procedures through which the group functions, not on particular authorities.

Because procedural issues are so central to organizational evaluations, it might also be expected that organizational evaluations would influence procedural judgments. A member of a group who holds the group and its authorities in high esteem might be expected to evaluate decision-making procedures more highly. The Chicago study confirms this. The panel data make clear that prior views about authority have a strong influence on people's judgments about whether they have experienced fair procedures in dealing with legal authorities.

The Meaning of Procedural Justice

The most useful contribution of a conception of the individual's relationship to the group based on the group value model, beyond that which can be explained using a model based on self-interest, is that it helps to explain the findings of the Chicago study concerning the meaning of procedural justice. In their original conception of procedural justice, Thibaut and Walker viewed concerns about procedural justice as being instrumental in two ways. First, their conception focused on the decision-making aspects of interactions with authorities. To Thibaut and Walker a judge is a third party used to resolve a dispute, and procedure represents the things the third party does to resolve the dispute. Second, Thibaut and Walker suggested that people react instrumentally to the entire experience of resolving disputes. They focus on their direct or indirect control over third-party decisions. The Chicago study makes the conception of fair procedure of Thibaut and Walker seem too narrow: those involved with third parties are concerned with issues beyond control.

To begin with, people care about the decision-making process. They consider evidence about representation, neutrality, bias, honesty, quality of decision, and consistency. People's concerns about decision making are not simply instrumental. In the case of representation, for example, people focus on value-expressive issues in addition to their instrumental concerns. People also place great weight on inferences about the motives of the decision maker. They seem interested in the nature of the third party they are dealing with, not just in the decision the authority makes. The interpersonal context of the experiences people have with legal authorities also matters a great deal. People value being treated politely and having respect shown for their rights. These aspects of the experience are unrelated to the decision made by the third party. Finally, the aspect of experience most strongly related to its outcome—consistency of outcomes and procedures with various standards of reference—has little effect. Just as control over decisions has little direct effect on judgments of procedural justice, aspects of procedure most closely related to outcomes have only a small effect on these judgments.

How can the importance of normative aspects of the experience be understood? First, it must be recognized that when people deal with authorities more is involved than just the outcome of a particular allocation or dispute. The procedures experienced are viewed as information about the group that the authority represents and to which the parties to the dispute or allocation belong. When people approach authorities, their social standing and feelings of security within the group are on the line. They may have an experience that reaffirms their belief that they are valued, protected members of society who will receive benevolence and consideration from the authorities when they need it; they may also have an experience that makes them feel less valued and protected than they would like to believe. Dealing with authorities clearly raises issues far beyond those connected with the issue to be decided.

Consider the value-expressive functions of process control: people value their participation in organizations and the opportunities that it provides to affirm their status within the group. Procedures that allow them to present evidence on their own behalf affirm status, because they allow people to feel that they are taking part in their social group. Similarly, the willingness of the authority to listen to them and consider their arguments is a recognition of their social standing. If people are not allowed to express their views, they are being denied signs of their standing within the group, as well as opportunities for interaction with authorities that lead to positive beliefs about membership in the group.[3] People feel that their membership and status in the group are confirmed when their views are heard and considered, irrespective of the decisions made by the third party. An approach based on group value concerns therefore makes clear why consideration is the key precondition for the effectiveness of process control (Tyler 1987a).

Issues of politeness can also be viewed from a group perspective. Although politeness and concern for one's rights may seem like minor aspects of an interaction with a legal authority, they convey considerable information about status within the group. When the police harass members of minority groups, the poor, or the young, they are communicating to those groups that they have marginal social status. Members of these groups may be most concerned about their social standing, but everyone is concerned about social standing to some extent, and dealing with authorities, legal, political, or managerial, brings these concerns to the fore.

Socialization of Beliefs

How do people know whether allocation procedures are fair? For example, if a dispute is resolved in mediation rather than through a trial, how do people decide whether mediation was the fairer procedure? One important influence on such judgments is socialization, through which a society or organization communicates common values within a group concerning the meaning of "fair" procedures and "fair" outcomes. New members of groups learn such procedural values from older members.

An example of the role of socialization in the development of beliefs is provided in the work of Easton (1965; Easton and Dennis 1969). As has already been noted, Easton's theory argues for the separation of diffuse support from specific support. The second aspect to his theory is the suggestion that children acquire diffuse support for the political system as part of the socialization process of childhood. Such support develops as an affective attachment to the political system—that is, without any rational evaluation of the personal gains or losses that it might bring about. Once established, such support is a long-term affective predisposition that is coupled only loosely to issues of self-interest. For example, a child does not feel loyal to the American legal system rather than to the English, German, or Japanese system because of any rational calculation of costs and benefits. Children are socialized to value the legal procedures of their own countries, and to view these procedures as naturally and self-evidently fair. According to Easton these early affective attachments persist across adulthood, lending legitimacy to legal authorities. Adults continue to have an affectively based loyalty to their social group, irrespective of issues of short-term gain and loss.

Easton acknowledges the importance of having a perspective on diffuse system support that is based on long-term gain. He suggests that repeated failures of the political or legal system to solve problems or deliver positive outcomes would eventually lead to a loss of diffuse support. Socialization provides a cushion of affective attachment that helps maintain support. Affective loyalty can be eroded by repeated experiences of unfairness. Like the theories of Easton, psychological theories of socialization emphasize the importance of the socialization process to the development of basic moral values (Hoffman 1977). Members of a culture learn basic common values as children that condition their adult behavior. One core value for legal authorities is the perceived obligation to obey the law. As already noted, most Americans feel that obligation quite strongly. Socialization processes therefore seem quite effective in creating a predisposition to behave in a way that supports existing authorities and institutions (Tyler and McGraw 1986).

Although people may decide to follow legal rules either from fear of punishment (as in Kohlberg's preconventional stage) or as a result of reasoning about the purpose of rules (as in Kohlberg's postconventional stage), most adults do not do so. Instead, they have learned the value of following rules for their own sake (as in Kohlberg's conventional stage). The majority of adults express the strong belief that obeying rules has value in itself. If procedural issues are the key to legitimacy, socialization should have a strongly procedural character. Easton finds that political socialization has such a character, focusing on the "rules of the game" that define the processes of American government. In the area of law the content of socialization is less clear.

One interesting question is the extent to which socialization creates values as opposed to beliefs. Values define the basic objectives to be obtained. In law, for example, the importance placed on not convicting the innocent is a value. A belief is an understanding of facts—for example, the belief that the death penalty deters crime. Another is the belief that truth can best be found through an adversary trial system. To at least some extent, both the high level of legitimacy accorded legal authorities (values) and the beliefs about authority examined by the Chicago study are socialized attitudes. Like other attitudes, they may have been initially formed during childhood, and may as a result have taken on a life of their own and be resistant to disconfirmation.

There is already some evidence in favor of a perspective based on socialization: the subgroups studied in Chicago did not differ in their understanding of the meaning of procedural justice. There appears to be a consensus among members of the group studied about what fair procedure means in the context of a particular dispute or problem.

If people's concerns about fairness depend on their connections to social groups, then these concerns may have a limited range. People may feel less concerned about issues of fairness when they are dealing with others outside their group, however that group is defined. Deutsch (1985) raises this possibility, arguing that the rules of justice are applicable only in social relations "in which there is perceived to be a minimum degree of actual, normatively expected or potential cooperation" (36–37), and his suggestion has received recent experimental confirmation (Opotow 1987). What is unclear is how people judge the boundaries of the social groups to which they belong.

In Conclusion

The key implication of the Chicago study is that normative issues matter. People obey the law because they believe that it is proper to do so, they react to their experiences by evaluating their justice or injustice, and in evaluating the justice of their experiences they consider factors unrelated to outcome, such as whether they have had a chance to state their case and been treated with dignity and respect. On all these levels people's normative attitudes matter, influencing what they think and do. The image of the person resulting from these findings is one of a person whose attitudes and behavior are influenced to an important degree by social values about what is right and proper. This image differs strikingly from that of the self-interest models which dominate current thinking in law, psychology, political science, sociology, and organizational theory, and which need to be expanded.

A change in our image of the person also has practical implications. People are more responsive to normative judgments and appeals than is typically recognized by legal authorities. Their responsiveness leads people to evaluate laws and the decisions of legal authorities in normative terms, obeying the law if it is legitimate and moral and accepting decisions if they are fairly arrived at. Police officers and judges who recognize and respond to people's normative concerns can exercise their authority more effectively; their rules and decisions will be accepted and obeyed voluntarily.

Appendix A: Questionnaire Used in
First Wave of Chicago Study

ID #: _____

TIME STARTING: _____

AM 1
PM 2

CIRCLE SEX OF RESPONDENT:

Male 1

Female 2

1. Overall, how good a job are the Chicago police doing? Are they doing . . .

a very good job, ... 1
a good job, ... 2
a fair job, ... 3
a poor job, or 4
a very poor job? 5
REFUSED 7
DON'T KNOW 9

2. In general, how satisfied are you with how well the Chicago police solve problems and help those who call them? Are you ....

very satisfied, ... 1
somewhat satisfied, ... 2
somewhat dissatisfied, or 4
very dissatisfied? 5
NEUTRAL 3
REFUSED 7
DON'T KNOW 9

3. How satisfied are you with the fairness of the outcomes that people receive when they deal with the Chicago police? Are you ....

very satisfied, ... 1
somewhat satisfied, ... 2
somewhat dissatisfied, or 4
very dissatisfied? 5
NEUTRAL 3
REFUSED 7
DON'T KNOW 9

179

4. Some people say that the Chicago police treat everyone equally, others that they
favor some people over others. How about you, do you think that the police . . .

treat everyone equally, ... 1

or that they favor some people

over others? 2

REFUSED 7

DON'T KNOW 9

5. Do you feel that people like yourself, that is people of your age, race, sex, income
and nationality, receive the same treatment from the Chicago police as the average
citizen, or are people like yourself treated better or worse than the average citizen?

TREATED THE SAME 2

TREATED BETTER 1

TREATED WORSE 3

REFUSED 7

DON'T KNOW 9

6. Overall, how satisfied are you with the fairness of the way the Chicago police treat
people and handle problems? Are you . . .

very satisfied, ... 1

somewhat satisfied, ... 2

somewhat dissatisfied, or 3

very dissatisfied? 4

REFUSED 7

DON'T KNOW 9

7. In general, when people call the Chicago police for assistance, how often do you
think that the police provide them with satisfactory service? Do you think that the
police . . .

always, ... 1

usually, ... 2

sometimes, or 3

seldom provide

satisfactory service? 4

REFUSED 7

DON'T KNOW 9

8. When people are stopped by the Chicago police, how often do the police handle the
situation in a satisfactory way? Do they . . .

always, ... 1

usually, ... 2

sometimes, or 3

seldom handle the

situation satisfactorily? 4

REFUSED 7
DON'T KNOW 9

9. How often do citizens receive fair outcomes when they deal with the Chicago police? Do they . . .

always, ... 1
usually, ... 2
sometimes, or 3
seldom receive fair
outcomes? 4
REFUSED 7
DON'T KNOW 9

10. And how often do the Chicago police treat citizens fairly and handle their problems in a fair way? Do the police . . .

always, ... 1
usually, ... 2
sometimes, or 3
seldom treat
people fairly? 4
REFUSED 7
DON'T KNOW 9

11. How frequently do the Chicago police patrol the residential areas of your own neighborhood? Do they patrol . . .

very frequently, ... 1
somewhat frequently, ... 2
not very frequently, or 3
not frequently at all? 4
REFUSED 7
DON'T KNOW 9

12. Now let me ask you about the Cook County Courts, that is the courts that serve Chicago and its suburbs.

Overall, how good a job are the Chicago courts doing? Are they doing . . .

a very good job, ... 1
a good job, ... 2
a fair job, ... 3
a poor job, or 4
a very poor job? 5
REFUSED 7
DON'T KNOW 9

13. In general, how satisfied are you with how well the Chicago courts solve the problems that come to court? Are you . . .

very satisfied, ... 1

somewhat satisfied, ... 2

somewhat dissatisfied, or 4

very dissatisfied? 5

NEUTRAL 3

REFUSED 7

DON'T KNOW 9

14. How satisfied are you with the fairness of the decisions made by the Chicago courts? Are you . . .

very satisfied, ... 1

somewhat satisfied, ... 2

somewhat dissatisfied, or 4

very dissatisfied? 5

NEUTRAL 3

REFUSED 7

DON'T KNOW 9

15. Some people say that the Chicago courts treat everyone equally, others that they favor some people over others. How about you, do you think that the Chicago courts . . .

treat everyone equally, or 1

that they favor some people

over others? 2

REFUSED 7

DON'T KNOW 9

16. Do you feel that people like yourself, that is people of your age, race, sex, income and nationality, receive the same treatment from the Chicago courts as the average citizen, or are people like yourself treated better or worse than the average citizen?

TREATED THE SAME 2

TREATED BETTER 1

TREATED WORSE 3

REFUSED 7

DON'T KNOW 9

17. Overall, how satisfied are you with the fairness of the way the Chicago courts treat people and handle their problems? Are you . . .

very satisfied, ... 1

somewhat satisfied, ... 2

somewhat dissatisfied, or 3

very dissatisfied? 4

REFUSED 7

DON'T KNOW 9

18. In general, when people appear in the Chicago courts, how often do you think that their cases are resolved in a satisfactory manner? Are they . . .

always, ... 1
usually, ... 2
sometimes, or 3
seldom resolved
satisfactorily? 4
REFUSED 7
DON'T KNOW 9

19. How often do citizens receive fair outcomes when they deal with the Chicago courts? Do they . . .

always, ... 1
usually, ... 2
sometimes, or 3
seldom receive
fair outcomes? 4
REFUSED 7
DON'T KNOW 9

20. And how often do the courts treat citizens fairly and handle their problems in a fair way? Are the courts . . .

always, ... 1
usually, ... 2
sometimes, or 3
seldom fair? 4
REFUSED 7
DON'T KNOW 9

21. Please tell me if you agree strongly, agree, disagree, or disagree strongly with each of the following statements about the Chicago police and courts.

	AS	A	D	DS	RF	DK
a. I have a great deal of respect for the Chicago police.	1	2	3	4	7	9
b. On the whole Chicago police officers are honest.	1	2	3	4	7	9
c. I feel proud of the Chicago police.	1	2	3	4	7	9
d. I feel that I should support the Chicago police.	1	2	3	4	7	9
e. The Chicago police should be allowed to hold a person suspected of a serious crime until they get enough evidence to officially charge them.	1	2	3	4	7	9

f. The police should be allowed to stop
    people on the streets and require
    them to identify themselves.   1 . 2 . 3 . 4 .. 7 . 9

g. The courts in Chicago generally
    guarantee everyone a fair trial.   1 . 2 . 3 . 4 .. 7 . 9

h. The Chicago courts are generally too
    easy on criminals.   1 . 2 . 3 . 4 .. 7 . 9

i. The basic rights of citizens are well
    protected in the Chicago courts.   1 . 2 . 3 . 4 .. 7 . 9

j. Many of the people convicted of
    crimes in Chicago courts are actually
    innocent.   1 . 2 . 3 . 4 .. 7 . 9

k. On the whole, Chicago judges are
    honest.   1 . 2 . 3 . 4 .. 7 . 9

l. Court decisions in Chicago are almost
    always fair.   1 . 2 . 3 . 4 .. 7 . 9

22. How likely is it that you would call the police if each of the following situations
    came up in the future?

	VL	SWL	SWU	VU	RF	DK

a. If your home was burglarized
    would you be very likely,
    somewhat likely, somewhat
    unlikely, or very unlikely to
    call the police?   1 . 2 .. 3 . 4 . 7 . 9

b. What if you had a complaint
    against someone in your
    neighborhood?   1 . 2 .. 3 . 4 . 7 . 9

c. In an emergency?   1 . 2 .. 3 . 4 . 7 . 9

d. To report suspicious activity
    in your neighborhood?   1 . 2 .. 3 . 4 . 7 . 9

23. During the past year, have you attended any community meetings during which the
    police made a presentation?

                        YES 1
                        NO 2
                        REFUSED 7
                        DON'T KNOW 9

24. I would also like to ask you about several situations in which you might go to court.

	VL	SWL	SWU	VU	RF	DK

a. If you received a speeding
    ticket when you felt that you

were not speeding, and you
could either pay a fine or go
to court to defend yourself,
would you be very likely,
somewhat likely, somewhat
unlikely, or very unlikely to
go to court?   1 . 2 .. 3 . 4 . 7 . 9

   b. What if a business owed you
$300 and refused to pay it
to you?   1 . 2 .. 3 . 4 . 7 . 9

   c. And if a neighbor's dog dug
up your garden on several
occasions and the neighbors
refused to tie the dog up?   1 . 2 .. 3 . 4 . 7 . 9

25. If you called the Chicago police in the future, how satisfied do you think that you
would be with their handling of your call? Do you think that you would be . . .

very satisfied, ... 1
somewhat satisfied, ... 2
somewhat dissatisfied, or 3
very dissatisfied? 4
REFUSED 7
DON'T KNOW 9

26. How fair do you think the outcome you received from the police would be? Would it
be . . .

very fair, ... 1
somewhat fair, ... 2
somewhat unfair, or 3
very unfair? 4
REFUSED 7
DON'T KNOW 9

27. How fairly do you think that you would be treated by the police? Would you be
treated . . .

very fairly, ... 1
somewhat fairly, ... 2
somewhat unfairly, or 3
very unfairly? 4
REFUSED 7
DON'T KNOW 9

28. What about if you were stopped by the Chicago police in the future? How satisfied
do you think that you would be with police handling of their contact with you. Do
you think that you would be . . .

very satisfied, ... 1
somewhat satisfied, ... 2
somewhat dissatisfied, or 3
very dissatisfied? 4
REFUSED 7
DON'T KNOW 9

29. How fair do you think that the outcome you received from the police would be?
    Would it be . . .

very fair, ... 1
somewhat fair, ... 2
somewhat unfair, or 3
very unfair? 4
REFUSED 7
DON'T KNOW 9

30. And how fairly do you think that you would be treated by the police? Would you be
    treated . . .

very fairly, ... 1
somewhat fairly, ... 2
somewhat unfairly, or 3
very unfairly? 4
REFUSED 7
DON'T KNOW 9

31. If you appeared in a Chicago court as a party to a case in the future, how satisfied
    do you think that you would be with the outcome of your case? Do you think that
    you would be . . .

very satisfied, ... 1
somewhat satisfied, ... 2
somewhat dissatisfied, or 3
very dissatisfied? 4
REFUSED 7
DON'T KNOW 9

32. How fair do you think that the outcome you received from the court would be?
    Would it be . . .

very fair, ... 1
somewhat fair, ... 2
somewhat unfair, or 3
very unfair? 4
REFUSED 7
DON'T KNOW 9

33. And how fair do you that the judge would be in the way he treated you and handled your case? Would he be . . .

very fair,	1
somewhat fair,	2
somewhat unfair, or	3
very unfair?	4
REFUSED	7
DON'T KNOW	9

34. People have different opinions about how important it is to obey police officers, judges and the law. The following questions are concerned with your own feelings about obeying the law. Please tell me if you agree or disagree with each of these statements.

	A	D	NEUT	RF	DK
a. People should obey the law even if it goes against what they think is right.	1	3	2	7	9
b. I always try to follow the law even if I think that it is wrong.	1	3	2	7	9
c. Disobeying the law is seldom justified.	1	3	2	7	9
d. It is difficult to break the law and keep one's self-respect.	1	3	2	7	9
e. There is little reason for a person like me to obey the law.	1	3	2	7	9
f. It is hard to blame a person for breaking the law if they can get away with it.	1	3	2	7	9
g. If a person goes to court because of a dispute with another person, and the judge orders them to pay the other person money, they should pay that person money, even if they think that the judge is wrong.	1	3	2	7	9
h. If a person is doing something and a police officer tells them to stop, they should stop even if they feel that what they are doing is legal.	1	3	2	7	9

35. I'd also like to ask you about some things that most people have done at one time or another. We are trying to find out which of these things have been done by the largest number of people. Please tell me if you have done each of these things often, sometimes, seldom or never during that past year.

		some-					
	often	times	seldom	never	RF	DK	NA

a. Made enough
   noise to
   disturb your
   neighbors.   1 .. 2 ... 3 ... 4 .. 7 . 9 . 8

b. Littered in
   violation of
   the law.   1 .. 2 ... 3 ... 4 .. 7 . 9 . 8

c. Driven an
   automobile
   while
   intoxicated.   1 .. 2 ... 3 ... 4 .. 7 . 9 . 8

d. Driven over
   55 miles per
   hour on the
   highways.   1 .. 2 ... 3 ... 4 .. 7 . 9 . 8

e. Taken
   inexpensive
   items from
   stores without
   paying for
   them.   1 .. 2 ... 3 ... 4 .. 7 . 9 . 8

f. Parked your
   car in
   violation of
   the law.   1 .. 2 ... 3 ... 4 .. 7 . 9 . 8

36. If you did each of the following things, how likely do you think it is that you would
    be arrested or issued a citation by the police?

	VL	SWL	SWU	VU	RF	DK	NA

a. If you made
   enough noise to
   disturb your
   neighbors, is it
   very likely,
   somewhat likely,
   somewhat
   unlikely, or very
   unlikely that you
   would be arrested
   or issued a
   citation?   1 . 2 ... 3 . 4 .. 7 . 9 .. 8

b. What if you littered in violation of the law?   1 . 2 . . . 3 . 4 . . 7 . 9 . . 8

c. If you drove a car while intoxicated.   1 . 2 . . . 3 . 4 . . 7 . 9 . . 8

d. If you drove over 55 miles per hour on a highway.   1 . 2 . . . 3 . 4 . . 7 . 9 . . 8

e. If you took an inexpensive item from a store without paying for it.   1 . 2 . . . 3 . 4 . . 7 . 9 . . 8

f. If you parked your car in violation of the law.   1 . 2 . . . 3 . 4 . . 7 . 9 . . 8

37. Think about the five adults that you know best. If you were arrested for doing each of the following things, how much would they disapprove or feel that you had done something wrong?

	AGD	SW	AL	NMAA	RF	DK	NA
a. If you were arrested for making enough noise to disturb your neighbors would your friends disapprove a great deal, somewhat, a little, or not much at all?	1 .	2 .	3 .	4	. . 7 .	9 .	8
b. What if you were arrested for littering in violation of the law?	1 .	2 .	3 .	4	. . 7 .	9 .	8
c. Driving a car while intoxicated?	1 .	2 .	3 .	4	. . 7 .	9 .	8
d. Driving over 55 miles per hour on a highway?	1 .	2 .	3 .	4	. . 7 .	9 .	8
e. Taking an inexpensive item from a store without paying for it?	1 .	2 .	3 .	4	. . 7 .	9 .	8
f. Parking your car in violation of the law?	1 .	2 .	3 .	4	. . 7 .	9 .	8

38. Finally, think about your own feelings about what is right and wrong. How wrong do you think it is to do each of the following things?

	VW	SWW	NVW	NWAA	RF	DK	NA
a. First, disturbing your neighbors. Do you feel that it is very wrong, somewhat wrong, not very wrong, or not wrong at all to disturb your neighbors?	1 .	2 .	3 ..	4	.. 7 .	9 .	8
b. What about littering in violation of the law?	1 .	2 .	3 ..	4	.. 7 .	9 .	8
c. Driving a car while intoxicated?	1 .	2 .	3 ..	4	.. 7 .	9 .	8
d. Driving over 55 miles per hour on a highway?	1 .	2 .	3 ..	4	.. 7 .	9 .	8
e. Taking an inexpensive item from a store without paying for it?	1 .	2 .	3 ..	4	.. 7 .	9 .	8
f. Parking your car in violation of the law?	1 .	2 .	3 ..	4	.. 7 .	9 .	8

Now I would like to ask you several questions about your personal experiences with the Chicago police during the past year.

39. During the past year have you called or otherwise contacted the Chicago police to report a crime, make a complaint, or ask for help of any kind?

    YES 1
    NO 2
    DON'T KNOW 9

40. During the past year, have you been stopped by the Chicago police while on the streets or while in a car for routine questioning or due to a traffic violation?

    YES 1

NO 2

DON'T KNOW 9

41. Have you had any other type of contact with the Chicago police during the past year that you have not already mentioned?

	What type of contact was it?
1 .....YES →	_____
2 .....NO	_____
9 .....DON'T KNOW	_____

42. What about the Chicago area courts? During the past year, have you appeared in a Chicago court as part of a case you were involved in as a defendant or a plaintiff?

YES 1

NO 2

DON'T KNOW 9

43. During the past year have you appeared in court as a witness in another person's case, to observe another person's case, or as a juror?

1 ..... YES

2 ..... NO

9 ..... DON'T KNOW

44. Have you had any other contact with the Chicago courts during the past year that you have not already mentioned?

	What type of contact was it?
1 ..... YES →	_____
2 ..... NO	_____
3 ..... DON'T KNOW	_____

MULTIPLE EXPERIENCES 3

ONE EXPERIENCE 2

NO EXPERIENCE .... 1 (ASK NO
                                    EXPERIENCE)

ONE EXPERIENCE

POLICE ⟶ Now I would like to ask you about the recent experience with the police that you just mentioned.

CALLED THE POLICE .... 1 (ASK CALLS)

STOPPED BY THE POLICE .... 2 (ASK STOPPED)

COURT ⟶ Now I would like to ask you about the recent experience in court that you just mentioned.

COURT CASE .... 3 (ASK COURT)

MULTIPLE EXPERIENCES

Now I would like to ask you about the experience you had with the police or courts during the past year that was *most important* to you in shaping your views about the legal system.

Was that an experience that you had with the police or in court?

POLICE ⟶ Did you call the police or did they stop you?

CALLED THE POLICE .... 1 (ASK CALLS)

STOPPED BY THE POLICE .... 2 (ASK STOPPED)

COURT ....3 (ASK COURT)

NO EXPERIENCE

45. Have you *ever* called or otherwise contacted the Chicago police to report a crime, make a complaint, or ask for help of any kind?

YES 1
NO 2
DON'T KNOW 9

46. Have you ever been stopped by the Chicago police while on the streets or while in a car for routine questioning or due to a traffic violation?

YES 1
NO 2
DON'T KNOW 9

47. Have you ever appeared in a Chicago court as part of a case you were involved in as a defendant or a plaintiff?

YES 1
NO 2
DON'T KNOW 9

48. Have you ever appeared in court as a witness in another person's case, to observe another person's case, or as a juror?

YES 1
NO 2
DON'T KNOW 9

SKIP TO Q99

CALLS

49. Briefly describe what happened.

_____

_____

_____

_____

_____

_____

_____

_____

_____

_____

50. How many months ago did this incident occur? _____

51. How serious was the problem about which you called the police? Was it . . .

very serious, ... 1

quite serious, ... 2

somewhat serious, or 3

not serious at all? 4

REFUSED 7

DON'T KNOW 9

52. I would like to ask you about the *outcome* of your call, that is what happened in response to your call to the police. Overall, how satisfied were you with that outcome? Were you . . .

very satisfied, ... 1

somewhat satisfied, ... 2

somewhat dissatisfied, or 3

very dissatisfied? 4

REFUSED 7

DON'T KNOW 9

53. Did the police respond to your call in person?

YES .... 1 (SKIP TO Q53d)

NO .... 2 (SKIP TO Q53a)

REFUSED .... 7 (SKIP TO Q99)

DON'T KNOW .... 9 (SKIP TO Q53a)

53a. When you called the police, did they tell you . . .

that they would call you

back later about your problem, ... 1 (SKIP TO Q53b)

that you should come into the

police station to deal with

your problem, ... 2 (SKIP TO Q53c)
that you should contact some
other agency to handle your
problem, ... 3 (SKIP TO Q99)
that there was nothing they
could do to help you, or .... 4 (SKIP TO Q99)
did they tell you that they
would respond to your call
in person? .... 5 (SKIP TO Q99)

53b. Did the police call you back later about your problem?

YES .... 1 (SKIP TO Q53d)
NO .... 2 (SKIP TO Q53d)

53c. Did you go into the police station to deal with your problem?

YES 1
NO .... 2 (SKIP TO Q99)

53d. Do you know what the police did to deal with the problem?

YES 1
NO .... 2 (SKIP TO Q63)

53e. Did the police solve the problem about which you called?

YES .... 1 (SKIP TO Q53g)
NO 2
DON'T KNOW 9

53f. Could the police have done anything to try to solve your problem that they did not do?

YES 1
NO 2
DON'T KNOW 9

53g. How hard did the police try to solve the problem about which you contacted them? Did they try . . .

very hard, ... 1
quite hard, ... 2
somewhat hard, or 3
not hard at all? 4
REFUSED 7
DON'T KNOW 9

53h. How quickly did the police respond to your call? Did they respond . . .

very quickly, ... 1
quite quickly, ... 2
somewhat quickly, or 3
not quickly at all? 4

REFUSED 7
DON'T KNOW 9

53i. What was the racial or ethnic group of the police officers you dealt with?

WHITE ONLY 1
WHITE AND MINORITY 2
MINORITY ONLY................................. 3
DON'T KNOW 9
REFUSED 7

54. Was the outcome of your call to the police what you thought it would be when you called them or was it better or worse than you expected?

EXPECTED 2
BETTER THAN EXPECTED 1
WORSE THAN EXPECTED........................ 3
DON'T KNOW 9

55. When you compare the outcome of your call to the outcome people generally receive when they call the police with similar problems, did you receive about the same outcome as others, or did you receive a better or worse outcome than others usually receive?

THE SAME AS OTHERS .... 2 (SKIP TO Q58)
BETTER THAN OTHERS .... 1 (SKIP TO Q58)
WORSE THAN OTHERS 3
DON'T KNOW .... 9 (SKIP TO Q58)

56. Do you think that you received a worse outcome than others because of your race, sex, age, nationality or some other characteristic of you as a person?

YES 1
NO .... 2 (SKIP TO Q58)
DON'T KNOW .... 9 (SKIP TO Q58)

57. What characteristic?

_____
_____
_____
_____

58. When you compare the outcome of your call to the Chicago police to the outcome you have received when you have had contact with the police in the past, was the outcome about the same, better or worse than you have received in the past?

ABOUT THE SAME 2
BETTER 1
WORSE... 3
NO PAST EXPERIENCE 4
DON'T KNOW 9

59. How fair was the outcome of your call, that is the things the police did to deal with the problem about which you contacted them? Was the outcome very fair, somewhat fair, somewhat unfair, or very unfair?

    VERY FAIR .... 1 (SKIP TO Q61)
    SOMEWHAT FAIR 2
    SOMEWHAT UNFAIR 3
    VERY UNFAIR 4
    DON'T KNOW .... 9 (SKIP TO Q61)

60. What about the outcome led you to feel it was unfair?

    _____
    _____
    _____
    _____

61. Did the police give the problem about which you called . . .

    the attention it deserved, ... 2
    more attention than it deserved, or 1
    less attention than it deserved? 3
    DON'T KNOW 9

62. How important was it to you whether the police solved the problem about which you called? Was it . . .

    very important, ... 1
    quite important, ... 2
    somewhat important, or 3
    not important at all? 4
    DON'T KNOW 9

63. Now I would like to ask you about *the way you were treated* by the police officers who handled your call, that is whether they were polite to you, listened to your reasons for calling, and handled your problem in a fair way. Did you have any contact with the police officers who handled your call?

    YES 1
    NO .... 2 (SKIP TO Q95)
    DON'T KNOW .... 9 (SKIP TO Q95)

64. Overall, how satisfied were you with the manner in which the police treated you and handled your problem? Were you . . .

    very satisfied, ... 1
    somewhat satisfied, ... 2
    somewhat dissatisfied, or 3
    very dissatisfied? 4
    DON'T KNOW 9

	Yes	No	RF	DK	NA
65. Were the police polite to you?	1	2	7	9	8
66. Did they show concern for your rights?	1	2	7	9	8
67. Did they get the information they needed to make good decisions about how to handle your call?	1	2	7	9	8
68a. Did they try to bring the problem into the open so that it could be solved?	1	2	7	9	8
69a. Were the police honest in what they said to you and in their reporting of your call?	1	2	7	9	8
70. Did the police do anything that you thought was improper or dishonest?	1	2	7	9	8

71. Could the police do anything to try to reduce the chance of a similar problem in the future?

    YES 1
    NO .... 2 (SKIP TO Q73)
    DON'T KNOW .... 9 (SKIP TO Q73)

72. Did they do what they could to try to prevent similar problems in the future?

    YES 1
    NO 2
    DON'T KNOW 9

73. Did your call involve a dispute between you and other people?

    YES 1
    NO .... 2 (SKIP TO Q76)
    DON'T KNOW .... 9 (SKIP TO Q76)

74. Did the police try to reduce anger among those involved?

    YES 1
    NO 2
    DON'T KNOW 9

75. Did the methods used by the police . . .

    favor one person over another, or 1
    were they equally fair to everyone
    involved in the dispute? 2
    DON'T KNOW 9

76. Do you know of any agency or organization that you could have complained to if you had felt that the police were unfair?

    YES 1
    NO 2
    DON'T KNOW 9

77. How much of a chance or opportunity did the police give you to describe your problem to them before making any decisions about how to handle it? Did you have . . .

a great deal of opportunity, ... 1
some opportunity, ... 2
a little opportunity, or 3
not much opportunity at all? 4
DON'T KNOW 9

78. How much consideration did the police give to what you said when making their decisions about how to handle your call? Did they give your views . . .

a great deal of consideration, ... 1
some consideration, ... 2
a little consideration, or 3
not much consideration at all? 4
DON'T KNOW 9

79. How much influence did you have over the decisions made by the police? Did you have . . .

a great deal of influence, ... 1
some influence, ... 2
a little influence, or 3
not much influence at all? 4
DON'T KNOW 9

80. Overall, how fair were the procedures used by the police to handle your call? Were they . . .

very fair, ... 1 (SKIP TO Q82)
somewhat fair, ... 2
somewhat unfair, ... 3
or very unfair? 4
DON'T KNOW .... 1 (SKIP TO Q82)

81. What about the way your call was handled did you feel was unfair?

_____
_____
_____
_____
_____

82. How hard did the police try to be fair to you? Did they try . . .

very hard, ... 1
quite hard, ... 2
somewhat hard, or 3
not hard at all? 4

REFUSED 7

DON'T KNOW 9

83. Did the police treat you and handle your call in the manner that you expected they would when you called or did you receive better or worse treatment than you expected?

EXPECTED 2

BETTER THAN EXPECTED 1

WORSE THAN EXPECTED 3

DON'T KNOW 9

84. When you compare the way you were treated to the way the police generally treat people who call them with similar problems, did you receive about the same treatment that others receive, or were you treated better or worse than others?

THE SAME AS OTHERS .... 2 (SKIP TO Q87)

BETTER THAN OTHERS .... 1 (SKIP TO Q87)

WORSE THAN OTHERS 3

DON'T KNOW .... 9 (SKIP TO Q87)

85. Do you think that the police treated you worse than others because of your race, sex, age, nationality or some other characteristic of you as a person?

YES 1

NO .... 2 (SKIP TO Q87)

DON'T KNOW .... 9 (SKIP TO Q87)

86. What characteristic?

_____

_____

_____

_____

87. When you compare your treatment by the Chicago police to the treatment you have received when you have had contact with the police in the past, would you say that you received about the same treatment as in the past, or that you were treated better or worse than in the past?

ABOUT THE SAME 2

BETTER 1

WORSE 3

NO PAST EXPERIENCE 4

DON'T KNOW 9

88. Overall, how fairly were you treated by the police? Were you treated . . .

very fairly, ... 1

somewhat fairly, ... 2

somewhat unfairly, or 3

very unfairly? 4

DON'T KNOW 9

89. How important was it to you how well you were treated by the police? Was it . . .

very important, ... 1

quite important, ... 2

somewhat important, or 3

not important at all? 4

DON'T KNOW 9

90. How typical were the police officers you dealt with of Chicago police officers in general? Were they . . .

very typical, ... 1

quite typical, ... 2

somewhat typical, or 3

not typical at all? 4

DON'T KNOW 9

91. How much did your experience with the police tell you about how they would act if you called them in the future? Did it tell you . . .

a great deal, ... 1

something, ... 2

a little, or 3

not much at all? 4

DON'T KNOW 9

	Yes	No	DK
92. When you think about the experience, do you feel angry at the police?	1	2	9
93. Do you feel pleased with the police?	1	2	9
94. Do you feel frustrated with the police?	1	2	9

95. Do you know of any instances during the past year in which other members of your family or your neighbors or friends had contact with the Chicago police?

YES 1

NO . . . . 2 (SKIP TO Q99)

DON'T KNOW . . . . 9 (SKIP TO Q99)

96. When you compare the outcomes those people received from the police to the outcome you received, would you say that your outcome was about the same, better, or worse?

ABOUT THE SAME 2

BETTER 1

WORSE 3

DON'T KNOW 9

97. Would you say that the police treated you better, worse, or about the same way they treated these other people?

BETTER 1
WORSE 3
ABOUT THE SAME 2
DON'T KNOW 9

98. How similar are these people to you? Are they . . .

very similar, ... 1
quite similar, ... 2
somewhat similar, or 3
not similar at all? 4
DON'T KNOW 9

STOPPED

49. Briefly describe what happened.

_____

_____

_____

_____

_____

_____

_____

_____

_____

_____

50. How many months ago did this incident occur? _____

51. How serious was the problem about which the police stopped you? Was it . . .

very serious, ... 1
quite serious, ... 2
somewhat serious, or 3
not serious at all? 4
REFUSED 7
DON'T KNOW 9

52. I would like to ask you about the *outcome* of your contact with the police, that is what happened to you. Overall, how satisfied were you with the outcome of your contact with the police? Were you . . .

very satisfied, ... 1
somewhat satisfied, ... 2
somewhat dissatisfied, or 3
very dissatisfied? 4

REFUSED 7

DON'T KNOW 9

53. Do you know the outcome of your contact with the police?

YES 1

NO .... 2 (SKIP TO Q64)

DON'T KNOW .... 9 (SKIP TO Q64)

53a. Did the police arrest you or take you to a police station?

YES 1

NO 2

DON'T KNOW 9

53b. Did the police cite you for a violation of the law?

YES 1

NO .... 2 (SKIP TO Q53d)

DON'T KNOW .... 1 (SKIP TO Q53d)

53c. How serious was the violation of the law for which you were cited? Was it . . .

very serious, ... 1

quite serious, ... 2

somewhat serious, or 3

not serious at all? 4

REFUSED 7

DON'T KNOW 9

53d. What was the racial or ethnic group of the police officers you dealt with?

WHITE ONLY 1

WHITE AND MINORITY 2

MINORITY ONLY 3

DON'T KNOW 9

REFUSED 7

54. Was the outcome of your contact with the police what you thought that you would receive if stopped by the police or was it better or worse than you expected?

EXPECTED 2

BETTER THAN EXPECTED 1

WORSE THAN EXPECTED 3

DON'T KNOW 9

55. When you compare the outcome you received to the outcome people generally receive when they are stopped by the police for similar reasons, did you receive about the same outcome as others, or did you receive a better or worse outcome than others usually receive?

THE SAME AS OTHERS .... 2 (SKIP TO Q58)

BETTER THAN OTHERS .... 1 (SKIP TO Q58)

WORSE THAN OTHERS 3
DON'T KNOW .... 9 (SKIP TO Q58)

56. Do you think that you received a worse outcome than others because of your race, sex, age, nationality or some other characteristic of you as a person?

YES 1
NO .... 2 (SKIP TO Q58)
DON'T KNOW .... 9 (SKIP TO Q58)

57. What characteristic?

_____

_____

_____

_____

58. When you compare the outcome of your contact with the Chicago police to the outcome you have received when you have had contact with the police in the past, was the outcome about the same, better or worse than you have received in the past?

ABOUT THE SAME 2
BETTER 1
WORSE............................ 3
NO PAST EXPERIENCE.............. 4
DON'T KNOW 9

59. How fair was the outcome you received from the police? Was it . . .

very fair, ... 1 (SKIP TO Q61)
somewhat fair, ... 2
somewhat unfair, or 3
very unfair? 4
DON'T KNOW .... 9 (SKIP TO Q61)

60. What about the outcome led you to feel it was unfair?

_____

_____

_____

_____

61. Did you feel that you received the outcome you deserved, a better outcome than you deserved, or a worse outcome than you deserved?

DESERVED OUTCOME 2
BETTER THAN DESERVED 1
WORSE THAN DESERVED 3
DON'T KNOW 9

62. How important was it to you what outcome you received from the police when they stopped you? Was it . . .

very important, ... 1
quite important, ... 2
somewhat important, or 3
not important at all? 4
DON'T KNOW 9

63. SKIP

64. I would also like to ask you about *the way you were treated* by the police officers who stopped you, that is whether they were polite to you, listened to your side of the story, and treated you in a fair way.

Overall, how satisfied were you with the manner in which the police treated you and handled their contact with you? Were you . . .

very satisfied, ... 1
somewhat satisfied, ... 2
somewhat dissatisfied, or 3
very dissatisfied? 4
DON'T KNOW 9

	Yes	No	RF	DK	NA
65. Were the police polite to you?	1	2	7	9	8
66. Did they show concern for your rights?	1	2	7	9	8
67. Did they get the information they needed to make good decisions about how to handle the situation?	1	2	7	9	8
68. Did they try to bring the problem into the open so that it could be solved?	1	2	7	9	8
69. Were the police honest in what they said to you and in their reporting of their contact with you?	1	2	7	9	8
70. Did the police do anything that you thought was improper or dishonest?	1	2	7	9	8

71. Could the police do anything to try to reduce the chance of a similar problem in the future?

YES 1
NO .... 2 (SKIP TO Q73)
DON'T KNOW .... 9 (SKIP TO Q73)

72. Did they do what they could to try to prevent similar problems in the future?

YES 1
NO 2
DON'T KNOW 9

73. Did your contact with the police involve a dispute between you and other people?

YES 1
NO .... 2 (SKIP TO Q76)
DON'T KNOW .... 9 (SKIP TO Q76)

74. Did the police try to reduce anger among those involved?

YES 1
NO 2
DON'T KNOW 9

75. Did the methods used by the police . . .

favor one person over another 1
or were they equally fair to
everyone involved in the dispute? 2
DON'T KNOW 9

76. Do you know of any agency or organization that you could have complained to if you had felt that the police were unfair?

YES 1
NO 2
DON'T KNOW 9

77. How much of a chance or opportunity did the police give you to tell your side of the story before making any decisions about how to handle the situation? Did you have . . .

a great deal of opportunity, ... 1
some opportunity, ... 2
a little opportunity, or 3
not much opportunity at all? 4
DON'T KNOW 9

78. How much consideration did the police give to what you said when making their decisions about how to handle your situation? Did they give your views . . .

a great deal of consideration, ... 1
some consideration, ... 2
a little consideration, or 3
not much consideration at all? 4
DON'T KNOW 9

79. How much influence did you have over the decisions made by the police? Did you have . . .

a great deal of influence, ... 1
some influence, ... 2
a little influence, or 3
not much influence at all? 4
DON'T KNOW 9

80. Overall, how fair were the procedures used by the police to handle the situation when they stopped you? Were they . . .

    very fair, ... 1 (SKIP TO Q82)
    somewhat fair, ... 2
    somewhat unfair, or 3
    very unfair? 4
    DON'T KNOW .... 9 (SKIP TO Q82)

81. What about the way your contact was handled made you feel that it was unfair?

    _____

    _____

    _____

    _____

    _____

82. How hard did the police try to be fair to you? Did they try . . .

    very hard, ... 1
    quite hard, ... 2
    somewhat hard, or 3
    not hard at all? 4
    DON'T KNOW 9

83. Did the police treat you and handle their contact with you in the manner you expected they would if you were stopped by the police or did you receive better or worse treatment than you expected?

    EXPECTED 1
    BETTER THAN EXPECTED 2
    WORSE THAN EXPECTED 3
    DON'T KNOW 9

84. When you compare the way you were treated to the treatment people generally receive when they are stopped by the police for similar reasons, did you receive about the same treatment that others receive, or were you treated better or worse than others?

    THE SAME AS OTHERS .... 2 (SKIP TO Q87)
    BETTER THAN OTHERS .... 1 (SKIP TO Q87)
    WORSE THAN OTHERS 3
    DON'T KNOW .... 9 (SKIP TO Q87)

85. Do you think that you received worse treatement than others because of your race, sex, age, nationality or some other characteristic of you as a person?

    YES 1
    NO .... 2 (SKIP TO Q87)
    DON'T KNOW .... 9 (SKIP TO Q87)

86. What characteristic?

_____

_____

_____

_____

87. When you compare your treatment by the Chicago police to the treatment that you have received when you have had contact with the police in the past, would you say that you received about the same treatment as in the past, or that you were treated better or worse than in the past?

ABOUT THE SAME	2
BETTER	1
WORSE	3
NO PAST EXPERIENCE	4
DON'T KNOW	9

88. Overall, how fairly were you treated by the police? Were you treated . . .

very fairly,	1
somewhat fairly,	2
somewhat unfairly, or	3
very unfairly?	4
DON'T KNOW	9

89. How important was it to you whether or not you were treated well by the police? Was it . . .

very important,	1
quite important,	2
somewhat important, or	3
not important at all?	4
DON'T KNOW	9

90. How typical were the police officers you dealt with of Chicago police officers in general? Were they . . .

very typical,	1
quite typical,	2
somewhat typical, or	3
not typical at all?	4
DON'T KNOW	9

91. How much did your experience with the police tell you about how they would act if you were stopped by them in the future? Did it tell you . . .

a great deal,	1
something,	2
a little, or	3

not much at all? 4

DON'T KNOW 9

	Yes	No	DK
92. When you think about the experience, do you feel angry at the police?	1	2	9
93. Do you feel pleased with the police?	1	2	9
94. Do you feel frustrated with the police?	1	2	9

95. Do you know of any instances during the past year in which other members of your family or your neighbors or friends had contact with the Chicago police?

YES 1

NO .... 2 (SKIP TO Q99)

DON'T KNOW .... 9 (SKIP TO Q99)

96. When you compare the outcomes those people received from the police to the outcome you received, would you say that your outcome was about the same, better, or worse?

ABOUT THE SAME 2

BETTER 1

WORSE 3

DON'T KNOW 9

97. Would you say that the police treated you better, worse, or about the same way they treated these other people?

BETTER 1

WORSE 3

ABOUT THE SAME 2

DON'T KNOW 9

98. How similar are these people to you? Are they . . .

very similar, ... 1

quite similar, ... 2

somewhat similar, or 3

not similar at all? 4

DON'T KNOW 9

COURT

49. Briefly describe what happened.

_____

_____

_____

_____

_____

_____

_____
_____
_____
_____

50. How many months ago did this incident occur? _____

51. How serious was the problem about which you were in court? Was it . . .

very serious, ... 1
quite serious, ... 2
somewhat serious, or 3
not serious at all? 4
REFUSED 7
DON'T KNOW 9

52. I would like to ask you about the *outcome* of your case, that is what happened to you. Overall, how satisfied were you with the outcome of your case? Were you . . .

very satisfied, ... 1
somewhat satisfied, ... 2
somewhat dissatisfied, or 3
very dissatisfied? 4
REFUSED 7
DON'T KNOW 9

53. Did you have a choice concerning whether you would appear in court?

YES 1
NO 2
DON'T KNOW 9

53a. Were you represented by an attorney?

YES 1
NO 2
DON'T KNOW 9

53b. Were you the plaintiff or the defendant in the case? (THE PLAINTIFF IS THE PERSON WHO BEGINS THE SUIT BY MAKING A CLAIM AGAINST AN-OTHER PERSON. THAT OTHER PERSON IS THE DEFENDANT.)

PLAINTIFF 1
DEFENDANT 2
BOTH (COUNTERCLAIMS) 3
DON'T KNOW 9

53c. Do you know the final outcome of your case?

YES 1
NO .... 2 (SKIP TO Q64)
DON'T KNOW .... 9 (SKIP TO Q64)

53d. How was your case settled? Was there a guilty plea, a trial, an informal settlement, or was the case dismissed?

A GUILTY PLEA 1
A TRIAL 2
AN INFORMAL SETTLEMENT 3
CASE DISMISSED 4
CASE POSTPONED 5
OTHER (_____) 6
REFUSED 7
DON'T KNOW 9

53e. How did you feel about the outcome of your case? Were you . . .

very pleased, ... 1
pleased, ... 2
disappointed, or 3
very disappointed? 4
REFUSED 7
DON'T KNOW 9

53f. Were there things that the judge could have done to reach a better outcome in your case?

YES 1
NO 2
DON'T KNOW 9

53g. To what racial or ethnic group did the judge belong?

WHITE 1
MINORITY 3
DON'T KNOW 9
REFUSED 7

54. Was the outcome of your case what you thought that it would be before you went to court or was it better or worse than you expected?

EXPECTED 2
BETTER THAN EXPECTED 1
WORSE THAN EXPECTED 3
DON'T KNOW 9

55. When you compare the outcome of your case to the outcome people generally receive when they go to court for similar reasons, did you receive about the same outcome as others or did you receive a better or worse outcome than others usually receive?

THE SAME AS OTHERS .... 2 (SKIP TO Q58)
BETTER THAN OTHERS .... 1 (SKIP TO Q58)
WORSE THAN OTHERS 3
DON'T KNOW .... 9 (SKIP TO Q58)

56. Do you think that you received a worse outcome than others because of your race, sex, age, nationality or some other characteristic of you as a person?

YES 1

NO .... 2 (SKIP TO Q58)

DON'T KNOW .... 9 (SKIP TO Q58)

57. What characteristic?

_____

_____

_____

_____

58. When you compare the outcome of your case to the outcome you have received when you have been in court in the past, was the outcome about the same, better or worse than you have received in the past?

ABOUT THE SAME 2

BETTER 1

WORSE............................ 3

NO PAST EXPERIENCE.............. 4

DON'T KNOW 9

59. How fair was the outcome you received in court? Was it . . .

very fair, ... 1 (SKIP TO Q61)

somewhat fair, ... 2

somewhat unfair, or 3

very unfair? 4

DON'T KNOW .... 9 (SKIP TO Q61)

60. What about the outcome led you to feel it was unfair?

_____

_____

_____

_____

61. Did you feel that you received the outcome you deserved, a better outcome than you deserved, or a worse outcome than you deserved?

DESERVED OUTCOME 2

BETTER THAN DESERVED 1

WORSE THAN DESERVED 3

DON'T KNOW 9

62. How important was it to you whether you won or lost your case? Was it . . .

very important, ... 1

quite important, ... 2

somewhat important, or 3

not important at all? 4

DON'T KNOW 9

63. SKIP

64. I would also like to ask you about *the way you were treated* by the judge and other court officials, that is whether they were polite to you, listened to your side of the case, and handled your case in a fair way.

Overall, how satisfied were you with the manner in which you were treated by the judge? Were you . . .

very satisfied, ... 1
somewhat satisfied, ... 2
somewhat dissatisfied, or 3
very dissatisfied? 4
DON'T KNOW 9

	Yes	No	RF	DK	NA
65. Was the judge polite to you?	1	2	7	9	8
66. Did the judge show concern for your rights?	1	2	7	9	8
67. Did the judge get the information he needed to make good decisions about how to handle your case?	1	2	7	9	8
68. Did the judge try to bring the problem into the open so that it could be solved?	1	2	7	9	8

69. Did police officers or other government officials testify in your case?

YES 1
NO .... 2 (SKIP TO Q70)
DON'T KNOW .... 9 (SKIP TO Q70)

69a. Were they honest in what they said and in their reporting of their previous contact with you?

YES 1
NO 2
DON'T KNOW 9

70. Did the judge do anything that you thought was improper or dishonest?

YES 1
NO 2
DON'T KNOW 9

71. Could the judge do anything to try to reduce the chance of a similar problem in the future?

YES 1
NO .... 2 (SKIP TO Q73)
DON'T KNOW .... 9 (SKIP TO Q73)

72. Did the judge do what he could to try to prevent similar problems in the future?

    YES 1
    NO 2
    DON'T KNOW 9

73. Did your case involve a dispute between you and other people?

    YES 1
    NO .... 2 (SKIP TO Q76)
    DON'T KNOW .... 9 (SKIP TO Q76)

74. Did the judge try to reduce anger among those involved?

    YES 1
    NO 2
    DON'T KNOW 9

75. Did the methods used by the judge . . .

    favor one person over another, or 1
    were they equally fair to everyone
    involved in the dispute? 2
    DON'T KNOW 9

76. Do you know of any agency or organization that you could have complained to if you had felt that the judge was unfair?

    YES 1
    NO 2
    DON'T KNOW 9

77. How much of a chance or opportunity did the judge give you to tell your side of the story before making any decisions about how to handle your case? Did you have . . .

    a great deal of opportunity, ... 1
    some opportunity, ... 2
    a little opportunity, or 3
    not much opportunity at all? 4
    DON'T KNOW 9

78. How much consideration did the judge give to what you said when making decisions about how to handle your case? Were your views given . . .

    a great deal of consideration, ... 1
    some consideration, ... 2
    a little consideration, or 3
    not much consideration at all? 4
    DON'T KNOW 9

79. How much influence did you have over the decisions made by the judge? Did you have . . .

    a great deal of influence, ... 1

some influence, ... 2

a little influence, or 3

not much influence at all? 4

DON'T KNOW 9

80. Overall, how fair were the procedures used by the judge to handle your case? Were they . . .

very fair, ... 1 (SKIP TO Q82)

somewhat fair, ... 2

somewhat unfair, or 3

very unfair? 4

DON'T KNOW .... 9 (SKIP TO Q82)

81. What about the way your case was handled did you feel was unfair?

_____

_____

_____

_____

_____

82. How hard did the judge try to be fair to you? Did he try . . .

very hard, ... 1

quite hard, ... 2

somewhat hard, or 3

not hard at all? 4

REFUSED 7

DON'T KNOW 9

83. Did the judge treat you and handle your case in the manner that you expected he would before you went to court, or did you receive better or worse treatment than you expected?

EXPECTED 2

BETTER THAN EXPECTED 1

WORSE THAN EXPECTED 3

DON'T KNOW 9

84. When you compare the way you were treated in court to the treatment people generally receive when they go to court for similar reasons, did you receive about the same treatment as others, or did you receive better or worse treatment than others generally receive?

THE SAME AS OTHERS .... 1 (SKIP TO Q87)

BETTER THAN OTHERS .... 2 (SKIP TO Q87)

WORSE THAN OTHERS 3

DON'T KNOW .... 9 (SKIP TO Q87)

85. Do you think that the judge treated you worse than others because of your race, sex, age, nationality or some other characteristic of you as a person?

    YES 1

    NO .... 2 (SKIP TO Q87)

    DON'T KNOW .... 9 (SKIP TO Q87)

86. What characteristic?

    _____

    _____

    _____

    _____

87. When you compare the treatment you received in court to the treatment you have received when you have been in court in the past, was the treatment about the same, better, or worse than you have received in the past?

    ABOUT THE SAME 2

    BETTER 1

    WORSE 3

    NO PAST EXPERIENCE 4

    DON'T KNOW 9

88. Overall, how fairly were you treated by the judge? Were you treated . . .

    very fairly, ... 1

    somewhat fairly, ... 2

    somewhat unfairly, or 3

    very unfairly? 4

    DON'T KNOW 9

89. How important was it to you how well you were treated by the judge? Was it . . .

    very important, ... 1

    quite important, ... 2

    somewhat important, or 3

    not important at all? 4

    DON'T KNOW 9

90. How typical was the judge you dealt with of Chicago judges in general? Was he . . .

    very typical, ... 1

    quite typical, ... 2

    somewhat typical, or 3

    not typical at all? 4

    DON'T KNOW 9

91. How much did your experience with the judge tell you about how you would be treated if you went to court in the future? Did it tell you . . .

a great deal, ... 1
something, ... 2
a little, or 3
not much at all? 4
DON'T KNOW 9

	Yes	No	DK

92. When you think about the experience, do you feel angry
    at the judge?   1 .. 2 . 9

93. Do you feel pleased with the judge?   1 .. 2 . 9

94. Do you feel frustrated with the judge?   1 .. 2 . 9

95. Do you know of instances during the past year in which other members of your
    family or your neighbors or friends had contact with the Chicago courts?
                              YES 1
                              NO .... 2 (SKIP TO Q99)
                              DON'T KNOW .... 9 (SKIP TO Q99)

96. When you compare the outcomes those people received from the courts to the
    outcome you received, would you say that your outcome was about the same,
    better, or worse?
                              ABOUT THE SAME 2
                              BETTER 1
                              WORSE 3
                              DON'T KNOW 9

97. Would you say that the judge treated you better, worse, or about the same way he
    treated these other people?
                              BETTER 1
                              WORSE 3
                              ABOUT THE SAME 2
                              DON'T KNOW 9

98. How similar are these people to you? Are they . . .
                              very similar, ... 1
                              quite similar, ... 2
                              somewhat similar, or 3
                              not similar at all? 4
                              DON'T KNOW 9

Now I'd like to finish by asking you some background questions for statistical purposes.

99. Some people say that when it comes to politics they think of themselves as being
    liberal or conservative. Do you think of yourself in those terms?

```
                    YES ................. 1
                    NO ................. 2 (SKIP TO Q103)
                    REFUSED ........... 7 (SKIP TO Q104)
                    DON'T KNOW ....... 9 (SKIP TO Q104)
```

100. Would you consider yourself to be a liberal, a moderate or a conservative?

```
                    LIBERAL ........... 1
                    MODERATE ......... 2 (SKIP TO Q103)
                    CONSERVATIVE ...... 3 (SKIP TO Q102)
```

101. Are you slightly liberal, liberal, or extremely liberal?

```
        SLIGHTLY LIBERAL ................ 1 (SKIP TO Q104)
        LIBERAL ......................... 2 (SKIP TO Q104)
        EXTREMELY LIBERAL .............. 3 (SKIP TO Q104)
        DON'T KNOW ..................... 9 (SKIP TO Q104)
```

102. Are you slightly conservative, conservative, or extremely conservative?

```
        SLIGHTLY CONSERVATIVE .......... 1 (SKIP TO Q104)
        CONSERVATIVE ................... 2 (SKIP TO Q104)
        EXTREMELY CONSERVATIVE ........ 3 (SKIP TO Q104)
        DON'T KNOW ..................... 9 (SKIP TO Q104)
```

103. If you had to choose, would you call yourself a liberal, a conservative, or what?

```
        LIBERAL ........................................... 1
        CONSERVATIVE ..................................... 3
        MODERATE, MIDDLE OF THE ROAD,
        INDEPENDENT ...................................... 2
        OTHER (_____) ............................ 4
        REFUSED .......................................... 7
        DON'T KNOW ....................................... 9
```

104. In what year were you born? _____

105. I don't want to know your exact address, but I would like to know the area of Chicago that you live in. What is the zip code of the area of Chicago in which you live?

```
                    _____

                    REFUSED ................... 77777
                    DON'T KNOW ............... 99999
```

106. What is the name of the street that you live on?

```
_____ (RECORD EXACT SPELLING)
                    REFUSED ..................... 77
                    DON'T KNOW ................. 99
```

107. What street crosses it at the corner nearest your home?

————————————————————— (RECORD EXACT SPELLING)

REFUSED 77

DON'T KNOW 99

108. Was your total household income, from all sources, before taxes in 1983 . . .
(REPEAT UNTIL NO)

More than $10,000   NO 1

More than $15,000   NO 2

More than $20,000   NO 3

More than $30,000   NO 4

More than $50,000   NO 5

YES 6

DON'T KNOW 9

REFUSED 7

109. What is the highest grade or year of school that you have completed?

NONE 01

SOME GRADE SCHOOL 02

COMPLETED GRADE SCHOOL 03

SOME HIGH SCHOOL 04

COMPLETED HIGH SCHOOL 05

SOME COLLEGE, TECHNICAL SCHOOL 06

COLLEGE GRADUATE 07

GRADUATE SCHOOL/PROFESSIONAL

DEGREE 08

REFUSED 77

DON'T KNOW 99

110. What is your racial-ethnic background? Are you . . .

Asian, ... 1

Black, ... 2

Hispanic, ... 3

White, or 4

something else? (—————) 5

REFUSED 7

DON'T KNOW 9

111. Altogether, how many different telephone *numbers* are there in your household?

————————————————————————————

REFUSED 7

DON'T KNOW 9

	Yes	No	RF	DK	NA
112. Are you a police officer or court official?	1	2	7	9	8
113. Are you a lawyer?	1	2	7	9	8

114. Do you have friends or relatives that are
     police officers?   1 .. 2 . 7 .. 9 . 8
115. Do you have friends or relatives that are
     court officials or judges?   1 .. 2 . 7 .. 9 . 8

116. Thank you for completing the survey. We will be keeping track of changes in the
     quality of the police and courts over the next year. To understand how these
     changes affect you, we may need to talk to people again a year from now. May we
     call you back then?

                    YES 1
                    NO .... 2 (END INTERVIEW)

117. So that we can know who to ask for when we call back, may I have your name?
     1 . . . Yes ⟶ _____ (RECORD EXACT SPELLING/
                                    FIRST AND LAST NAME)
     2 . . . No ⟶ It is not necessary for me to have your full name. I just need
                    something that will help me to ask for you when I call back.
                    Could I have your initials, your first name, or something else
                    that would allow me to ask for you when I call back?

                    _____ (EXPLAIN WHAT THIS IS)

TIME ENDED: _____

   AM 1
   PM 2

1. HOW COOPERATIVE WAS THE RESPONDENT?
                    VERY COOPERATIVE 1
                    FAIRLY COOPERATIVE 2
                    NOT VERY COOPERATIVE 3

2. HOW INTERESTED WAS THE RESPONDENT IN THE INTERVIEW?
                    VERY INTERESTED 1
                    FAIRLY INTERESTED 2
                    NOT VERY INTERESTED 3

3. HOW ACCURATE DO YOU THINK THE INFORMATION GIVEN TO YOU WAS?
                    VERY ACCURATE 1
                    FAIRLY ACCURATE 2
                    NOT VERY ACCURATE 3

4. HOW GOOD WAS THE RESPONDENT'S ENGLISH?
                    VERY GOOD 1
                    FAIRLY GOOD 2
                    NOT VERY GOOD 3

OTHER COMMENTS:

Appendix B: Coefficient Alphas for Scales Used in the Analysis

	First Wave			Second Wave		
	Number of items	average r	alpha	Number of items	average r	alpha
All respondents						
Comply	6	.23	.64	6	.20	.60
Deterrence	6	.34	.76	6	.35	.76
Peers	6	.39	.79	6	.37	.78
Morality	6	.31	.73	6	.30	.72
Obligation	6	.18	.57	6	.38	.79
Support for Police	4	.51	.81	4	.59	.85
Support for Courts	4	.48	.79	4	.49	.79
Peformance of Police	14	.45	.92	14	.46	.92
Performance of Courts	10	.45	.89	10	.50	.91
Respondents with experience						
Distributive justice	2	.78	.88	2	.58	.73
Procedural justice	2	.81	.90	2	.78	.88

Appendix C: Frequency Data

A. Overall sample

1. Frequency of law-abiding behavior, first wave

		Frequency	Percentage
Disobey	1.00–1.50	2	0
	1.51–2.00	14	1
	2.01–2.50	50	4
	2.51–3.00	219	17
	3.01–3.50	414	30
Obey	3.51–4.00	678	50
Missing		198	

n = 1,575

Coefficient of skewness = .96, standard error = .07

2. Frequency of law-abiding behavior, second wave

		Frequency	Percentage
Disobey	2.00–2.50	3	0
	2.51–3.00	45	6
	3.01–3.50	73	10
	3.51–4.00	176	24
	4.01–4.50	203	28
Obey	4.51–5.00	226	31
Missing		78	

n = 804

Coefficient of skewness = .42, standard error = .18

3. Demographic characteristics and law breaking

	First wave		Second wave	
	zero-order correlations	beta weights	zero-order correlations	beta weights
Sex	.28***	.20***	.33***	.25***
Race	−.11***	−.08**	−.10**	−.03
Age	.38***	.34***	.41**	.33***

Education	−.26****	−.10**	−.31***	−.13***
Income	−.24***	−.07*	−.28***	−.08*
Conservatism	−.11***	−.07**	−.06*	−.04
R-squared		.24***		.29***
n		1,575		804

NOTE. High scores indicate being female, being white, being old, being well educated, having a high income, being conservative, and complying with the law.

4. Perceived obligation to obey the law, first wave

		Frequency	Percentage
High	1.00–1.50	922	64
	1.51–2.00	260	18
	2.01–2.50	133	9
	2.51–3.00	86	6
	3.01–3.50	18	1
Low	3.51–4.00	14	1
Missing		142	

n = 1,575
Coefficient of skewness = 1.11, standard error = 0.07

5. Support for legal authority, first wave

		Frequency	Percentage
High	1.00–1.50	47	4
	1.51–2.00	179	15
	2.01–2.50	381	32
	2.51–3.00	409	35
	3.01–3.50	135	11
Low	3.51–4.00	29	2
Missing		395	

n = 1,575
Coefficient of skewness = −0.07, standard error = 0.07

6. Legitimacy, first wave

	Frequency	Percentage
−3.0−−2.5	143	10
−2.5−−2.0	122	8
−2.0−−1.5	46	3

−1.5−−1.0	125	8
−1.0−−0.5	208	14
−0.5− 0.0	305	20
0.0− 0.5	269	18
0.5− 1.0	143	10
1.0− 1.5	83	6
1.5− 2.0	38	3
2.0− 2.5	9	1
2.5− 3.0	2	0
Missing	82	

n = 1,575

Coefficient of skewness = 0.34, standard error = 0.06

7. Demographic characteristics and legitimacy

	Obligation to obey		Support		Legitimacy	
	r	beta	r	beta	r	beta
Sex	−.05	−.03	.10***	.11***	−.05*	−.01
Race	.04	.06	−.14***	−.17***	−.03	−.04
Age	−.23***	−.21***	−.13***	−.08**	−.29***	−.26***
Education	.17***	.14***	.13***	.15***	.18***	.14***
Income	.02	−.10***	.02	.02	.07**	−.01
Conservatism	.15***	.12***	.13***	.09**	.07**	.03
R-squared		.09***		.07***		.10***

n = 1,575

NOTE. High scores indicate being female, being white, being old, being well educated, having a high income, and being conservative. Low scores indicate feeling obligated to obey, feeling supportive, and feeling that authorities are legitimate.

8. Evaluation of performance

	Frequency	Percentage
1.0–1.5	32	3
1.5–2.0	151	15
2.0–2.5	257	25
2.5–3.0	329	21
3.0–3.5	163	16
3.5–4.0	65	6
4.0–4.5	28	3
4.5–5.0	7	1
Missing	543	

n = 1,575

9. Demographic characteristics and evaluation of performance

	Police		Courts		Overall	
	r	beta	r	beta	r	beta
Sex	−.03	−.02	−.05	−.08**	−.06	−.07*
Race	.28***	.25***	.02	.07*	.16***	.18***
Age	.20***	.17***	.01	−.03	.09**	.05
Education	.01	−.04	−.10**	−.08*	−.05	−.07
Income	.10***	.06	−.10**	−.11**	−.05	−.05
Conservatism	−.10***	−.07*	−.06	−.05	−.08	−.06
R-squared		11%***		2%***		4%***

n = 1,575

NOTE. High scores indicate being female, being white, being old, being well educated, having a high income, and being conservative. High scores indicate positive evaluations.

B. Respondents with personal experience
1. Unfavorability of outcome in dealing with police and courts, first wave

	Called police	Stopped by police	Overall police	In court voluntarily	In court, not voluntarily	Overall court
Negative	15	17	16	7	23	13
	6	0	3	0	6	2
	11	1	7	5	0	3
	2	1	1	7	6	7
	11	16	13	20	11	18
	16	28	22	8	9	8
	14	25	19	42	31	38
Positive	25	13	19	11	14	12
n	303	202	505	95	47	147

n = 652

2. Unfavorability of outcome in dealing with police and courts, second wave

	Called police	Stopped by police	Overall police	In court voluntarily	In court, not voluntarily	Overall court
Negative	19	12	19	13	20	15
	4	0	4	8	0	5
	12	0	12	10	5	8

	3	0	2	3	5	3
	7	19	7	23	20	21
	24	25	24	8	0	7
	11	33	11	35	40	36
Positive	19	11	19	3	10	5
n	154	64	218	45	26	73

n = 291

3. Violations of expectancy (in percent)

	First wave		Second wave	
	Outcomes	Treatment	Outcomes	Treatment
Relative to the past				
Better	18	21	17	22
The same	55	54	64	58
Worse	10	11	11	11
No experience	15	15	8	8
Relative to others				
Better	28	22	25	23
The same	64	68	65	69
Worse	9	10	10	8
Relative to expectations				
Better	32	32	28	32
The same	43	46	49	49
Worse	25	22	23	19
Relative to the experiences of friends and family				
Better	32	38	24	20
The same	54	58	66	69
Worse	14	4	11	11

4. Relationship among relative judgments, first wave

	Outcomes				Treatment		
	Expectations of respondent	Experience of others	Experience of respondent	Experience of friends and family	Expectations of respondent	Experience of others	Experience of respondent
Outcomes							
Expectations of respondent							
Experience of others	.49***						
Experience of respondent	.43***	.42***					
Experience of friends and family	.20**	.26***	.25**				
Treatment							
Expectations of respondent	.47***	.31***	.34***	.08			
Experience of others	.42***	.62***	.38***	.34***	.34***		
Experience of respondent	.26***	.23***	.47***	.14	.21***	.24***	
Experience of friends and family	.15	.31***	.24***	.47***	.20**	.46***	.13

*p < .05; **p < .01; ***p < .001
NOTE. Entries are Pearson correlations.

5. Influence of judgments about relative outcome and treatment, first wave

| | Satisfaction | | | | Legitimacy |
	Outcome	Treatment	Affect	Evaluation	
Outcomes					
Expectations of respondent	.59***	.56***	.51***	.26***	.00
Experience of others	.38***	.37***	.35***	.14**	.02
Experience of respondent	.40***	.45***	.40***	.15**	.06
Experience of friends and family	.18**	.21**	.23***	.15	.10
Overall outcomes	.34***	.25***	.29***	.03	.09
Treatment					
Expectations of respondent	.40***	.44***	.41***	.22***	.06
Experience of others	.36***	.41***	.39***	.05	−.02
Experience of respondent	.22***	.24***	.23***	.00	.08
Experience of friends and family	.16	.13	.10	.15	.03
Overall treatment	.25***	.18***	.22***	.04	.06

*p < .05; **p < .01; ***p < .001

227

6. Relationships among judgments, first wave

	Level of outcome	Relative outcomes	Relative procedures	Distributive justice fair	Distributive justice deserved	Procedural justice fair	Procedural justice treatment
Level of outcome							
Relative outcomes	.42***						
Relative procedures	.32***	.47***					
Distributive justice							
fair	.48***	.56***	.38***				
deserved	.50***	.54	.33***	.78***			
Procedural justice							
fair	.43***	.51***	.44***	.73***	.48***		
treatment	.41***	.52***	.46***	.74***	.51***	.81***	
Evaluation	.28***	.26***	.22***	.30***	.12**	.45***	.44***
Obligation	-.02	-.02	.00	.03	-.07	.07	.13**
Support	.16***	.15**	.11**	.16***	.07	.13**	.32***

*p < .05; **p < .01; ***p < .001

7. Relationship among indices, second wave

	Level of outcome	Relative outcomes	Relative procedures	Distributive justice		Procedural justice	
				fair	deserved	fair	treatment
Level of outcome							
Relative outcomes	.43***						
Relative procedures	.25***	.52***					
Distributive justice							
fair	.44***	.60***	.59***				
deserved	.37***	.42***	.34***	.58***			
Procedural justice							
fair	.34***	.53***	.50***	.84***	.54***		
treatment	.31***	.51***	.51***	.75***	.48***	.78***	

*p < .05; **p < .01; ***p < .001

Notes

Chapter 1: Procedural Justice, Legitimacy, and Compliance

1. This possibility is what underlies Rawls's concept of being behind the veil of ignorance. If people are in a situation in which they cannot know what procedure is likely to benefit them, they can then judge fairness in abstract terms (Rawls 1971).
2. Because it is assumed that people use control over decisions to create favorable outcomes for themselves, the degree of decision control should be related to the favorability of outcome.

Chapter 2: Design of the Chicago Study

1. It was not always clear whether the person had a personal stake in the outcome (for example, when the person called the police to report an accident), so this distinction was not perfectly maintained. The goal, however, was to focus on those situations where a citizen had an experience with the police or courts over an issue that concerned the citizen personally.
2. A major problem in interpreting correlational studies is the possibility that the observed relationship between two variables is due to their relationship to some third, unobserved variable. For example, general attitudes toward the courts held before an incident might affect both the respondents' judgments about their experience and their evaluations of the courts after their experience. If this were true, judgments about experience would appear to influence evaluations after the experience of the courts, even if they really had no such effect. This methodological problem can be solved in two ways. First, a panel of respondents can be interviewed repeatedly, and the early interviews can then be used to assess directly the influence of prior attitudes on judgments about the experience, as well as on attitudes after the experience. Second, experiments can be conducted in which people are randomly assigned to have varying experiences; this eliminates the possibility of third variables. For a more detailed discussion of the benefits and costs of using correlational data in situations of this type see Lind and Tyler (1988).
3. Several versions of Bryant's approach are possible. The Chicago study used the version that was found by Czaja, Blair, and Sebestik (1982) to produce the random sample most representative of the population.
4. Response rate was calculated in the most conservative manner. Respondents who refused to be interviewed (or for whom the initial household contact refused to be

interviewed) were treated as nonrespondents, as were households where the telephone number was dialed six separate times without an answer, or where the respondents were willing to be interviewed only at times when the study could not accommodate them. Telephone numbers of businesses and numbers out of service were counted neither as respondents nor as nonrespondents.

5. The questionnaire used in the second wave contained questions about experience identical to those on the questionnaire used in the first. There was however one necessary change: in the first wave of interviews respondents were asked what happened when they called the police. Several respondents volunteered that nothing happened, because the emergency number was not answered. This unforeseen response was added to the questionnaire used in the second wave.

6. Although these respondents were excluded from the analysis discussed here, their responses were analyzed nonetheless. The separate analysis of these respondents showed that they reacted to their experiences in the same way as the smaller group of respondents studied (n = 652). As would be expected, the more superficial experiences of the excluded group had a weaker influence on their views about legal authorities.

7. Among the complete sample of respondents (n = 1,575), women respondents were less likely to be white (r = .10, p < .001), were older (r = .09, p < .001), had lower incomes (r = .26, p < .001), and were less well educated (r = .12, p < .001). Sex was unrelated to ideology (r = .03, n.s.). White and Asian respondents were older than black, Hispanic, and "other" respondents. They also had higher incomes (r = .32, p < .001) and were better educated (r = .28, p < .001). Finally, white and Asian respondents were marginally more conservative (r = .08, p < .05). Older respondents were poorer (r = .13, p < .001), less well educated (r = .21, p < .001), and more conservative (r = .08, p < .05). Respondents with high incomes were better educated (r = .47, p < .001), but income was unrelated to ideology (r = .01, n.s.). Finally, highly educated respondents were more liberal (r = .12, p < .001).

8. As was already outlined, a response rate can be calculated in various ways. The rate of 60% is conservative. It includes as refusals telephones that were never answered and people who were out of town or ill during the survey.

9. The problem of losing respondents was anticipated, and vigorous efforts were made during the study to interview a random sample of the original respondents. The demographics reported suggest that the panel is still biased despite these efforts, but that the bias is small.

10. Several demographic characteristics assessed during the first wave predicted the likelihood of being reinterviewed. These included race (r = .09, p < .001; white and Asian respondents were more likely to be reinterviewed), education (r = .10, p < .001; more highly educated respondents were more likely to be), and income (r = .12, p < .001; respondents with higher incomes were more likely to be). Age, sex, and ideology (liberal or conservative) did not predict the likelihood of being reinterviewed. Nor did any of the attitudes examined in the Chicago study, including perceived

obligation to obey the law; support for the police and courts; evaluations of the quality of the performance of the police and courts; beliefs that disobeying the law is morally wrong, that peers would disapprove of law breaking, and that law breakers are caught; or inclination to seek help from the police and courts in solving personal problems. Similarly, the likelihood of being reinterviewed was unrelated to self-reported frequency of law breaking.

Chapter 3: Legitimacy as a Theoretical Issue

1. The preoccupation of the authorities with securing public compliance with the law arises from a focus on maintaining existing institutions, and assumes that their maintenance is desirable. It is equally possible to believe that existing institutions are unjust and need to be changed; in such a case the focus will be on the conditions under which leaders' directives will not be obeyed. Such noncompliance would lead to instability in the system and ultimately to the possibility of forming new institutions.

2. It is important to remember that in this discussion the issue of noncompliance is seen from the perspective of the authorities. Sometimes widespread noncompliance with a law indicates that there is a conflict in values in a culture. In the case of laws governing drugs, sexual conduct, and the like, a segment of the public does not view the prohibited behavior as wrong. This raises the larger issue of why laws that deviate from the values of a substantial minority of the polity develop, and whether legal authorities should enforce them.

   Laws that are disobeyed because of conflicting values should be distinguished from laws like those requiring motorists to stop at a red light; the latter are more likely to be supported by members of society, even though people may violate them in their daily lives.

3. It is not inherent in law and legal regulations that they be regarded as restrictive. The positive social values that arise from regulation by social rules can be understood by the individual, who can then comply with the rules out of an enthusiastic commitment to their purposes. Such a perspective has been called postconventional by Kohlberg. In contrast, conventional views of the law focus on the obligation to obey, without attention to the purposes underlying the existence of laws. The conventional orientation characterizes the majority of American adults.

4. That formal authorities have positive benefits is hardly a new idea. Political theorists have long recognized the potential benefits of powerful authorities to society. Hobbes's *Leviathan* for example, was conceptualized as an all-powerful political official. Hobbes viewed such an autocratic figure as needed to regulate effectively the behavior of citizens in an organized group.

5. This discussion of theories of public choice is concerned only with people's judgments and behavior in the legal arena. It assumes that when people are making personal choices, such as what car to buy, they function instrumentally. Although it is not my

purpose to explore personal choices, it should be noted that the assumption that self-interest governs such choices has been questioned in recent research (see Kahneman, Knetsch, and Thaler 1986).

6. Although they do not draw their ideas from psychology, economic models are similar to psychological models of learning in their conception of utility. Such models also emphasize that behavior is guided by concerns about personal gain and loss. Economic models differ from many early learning models in emphasizing the influence of prospective judgments instead of the effect of experiences (Lea 1978). More recent learning models, however, incorporate the idea that past experience is used to predict the future, and that such predictions shape current behavioral choices. Models of this type are quite consistent with economic approaches. Therefore to use the perspective of public choice models is roughly equivalent to viewing behavior from the perspective of modern learning theory. For examples see the social learning theory of Bandura (1972) and theories of social exchange (Thibaut and Kelley 1959).

7. The Chicago study was based on the conclusion of the literature on deterrence that deterrence mechanisms influence behavior. It is important to note, however, that recent research has raised questions about whether such effects actually occur (see Paternoster et al. 1984).

8. Because rewards and punishments are external features of the environment they are directly observable, and it is possible to influence them directly. Attitudes, in contrast, are not directly observable and are less directly under the influence of the authorities. Authorities can never be sure whether behavior that accords with their directives flows from attitudes and will continue when the behavior is no longer observed. For this reason the authorities may feel that they must maintain social control and compel behavior through deterrence.

This perspective on behavior develops from a perspective on the determinants of behavior grounded in attribution theory (Heider 1958), according to which behavior is determined jointly by environmental factors and internal attitudes or dispositions. Internal attitudes are forces within the person that make the person want to behave in a particular way; environmental factors are forces that shape the rewards and costs associated with different types of behavior, and that determine behavior when they are sufficiently strong. For example, people will obey the law in the presence of a police officer so that they do not receive a ticket. Behavior in such situations says nothing about people's attitudes, which determine behavior only when the police officer has left.

9. One of the most frequently studied behavioral questions is the question of why people vote. This behavior is difficult to understand from the perspective of theories of subjective expected utility, because of the low probability that a single vote will influence the outcome of an election. The expected gains of voting are very small, whereas the act of voting has clear personal costs (Laver 1981; Mueller 1979).

10. According to some theories, regulation by strategies of social control is more than just inefficient and costly: it is insufficient to sustain a complex democratic society if it is the only means used to secure compliance (Aubert 1979; Bauer 1968; Hart 1961).

From this perspective at least some public compliance must occur voluntarily and not be linked to the ability of the authorities to produce rewards or deliver punishments. For example, Hart suggests that for legal authority to be effective, "at least some must voluntarily cooperate in the system and accept its rules" (Hart 1961, 198).

11. All the theories outlined assume that legitimacy is an important influence on compliance. Citizens who accept the legitimacy of rules and authorities are expected to follow them irrespective of their sense of personal self-interest. Because citizens have a reservoir of goodwill toward them, authorities have a cushion of discretion. They need not justify to their constituency each decision or rule, which enables them to act in the long-term interest of those they represent. In the legal arena, citizens will obey laws and follow court decisions because they accept the right of legal authorities to make rules that regulate their behavior.

It is also possible for a reservoir of "bad will" to be created by the authorities. This would reflect a belief that the authorities are biased against a person or a person's group and should not be trusted or given discretionary authority. Research on the American political system has found that in general people have at least some reservoir of goodwill toward legal and political authorities, even if they are marginal members of society (see Tyler, Casper, and Fisher 1988).

12. There is considerable evidence that trust in legal and political authorities has steadily declined since the Second World War (Caddell 1979; Shaver 1980). Although there is recent evidence that this trend may have lessened or even reversed (Miller 1983), general levels of trust continue to be low.

Further, the United States may be entering a period of scarcity and economic decline. During such a period conflict over resources will intensify and legal authorities will be called on to increase their regulatory efforts; legal authorities will therefore be most in need of legitimacy, because they will expect more compliance from citizens in times of scarcity, but will have fewer resources to secure compliance.

13. Although the connection between legitimacy and support inherently involves an assumption, this assumption is borne out by several studies. Engstrom (1970) studied 288 children in the fourth to eighth grades and found that whites who showed greater support for the police were more likely to feel an obligation to obey the law (Gamma = .30). Among blacks there was no relationship between support and obligation to obey. Engstrom and Giles (1972) studied 165 ninth-graders and found that those who viewed the procedures used to make legal decisions as more appropriate (that is, who supported the actions of legal officials) were significantly more likely to say that they felt obligated to obey the law, regardless of their personal feelings. But neither of these studies provides a strong test of the relationship between support and legitimacy. In addition, Engstrom raises the possibility of differences in the strength of this relationship among subgroups.

14. Research by Converse (1964) and others found that concerns about group membership may be important to citizens. This possibility has been noted in the earlier discussion of people's concerns with their social groups.

15. The importance of commitment to procedures has also been recognized in the legal

arena. The "process jurisprudence" movement, for example, emphasizes that procedures for decision making should be neutral and distinct from the particular decisions made by judges (Hart and Sacks 1958; Hart and Wechsler 1953; Wechsler
1959).

16. In a study that directly compared the cushioning effect of incumbent legitimacy with
    that of institutional legitimacy (Rasinski, Tyler, and Fridkin 1985), high levels of
    incumbent legitimacy were found to increase the degree to which evaluations of
    incumbents' performance were based on producing positive outcomes, and not to
    lessen the link of evaluation of government to performance. High levels of institutional
    legitimacy, on the other hand, significantly lessened the degree to which the evalua-
    tion of government was linked to performance. The results also showed that institu-
    tional legitimacy does not influence the degree to which evaluations of incumbents are
    based on performance.

17. In fact, specific system support does have a strong socialization residue, in the form of
    party identification. This basic political predisposition is regarded as influencing
    adult assessments of policy preference. Self-interest is then dictated by the extent to
    which such preferences are indeed fulfilled by leaders. The difference is that so-
    cialization structures the judgments of self-interest, rather than replace self-interest
    as a motivating construct.

18. The importance of socialization in developing norms has been emphasized both in
    theories of political and legal socialization (Easton and Dennis 1969) and in the study
    of moral development (Hoffman 1977). In both areas childhood and adolescence are
    important periods for the formation of norms.

19. Also related to judgments of self-interest is the question of how people choose the
    alternatives with which they compare the authorities they deal with, for it seems likely
    that people do not evaluate authorities or procedures in absolute terms. How these
    alternatives are conceived is beyond the scope of this book.

20. There is also an exception to the generally positive role of legitimacy in promoting
    compliance with the law found in the studies reviewed in table 3.1. Rodgers and Lewis
    (1974) found that legitimacy promoted general compliance with the law, but not
    compliance in several specific, hypothetical cases.

21. This is somewhat of an overstatement, for many of the studies reviewed examine
    hypothetical willingness to riot in particular circumstances. Still, the number of
    studies employing actual behavior is greater in the literature on rioting than in any of
    the other types of literature reviewed.

22. In making this calculation the study by Useem and Useem (1979) was omitted. (Their
    study is discussed later.) R-values were transformed into z-values, the average of the
    z-values was computed, and this value was transformed into an r-value.

23. The hypothesis that we would like to test is that a lack of legitimacy causes the legal
    and political systems to collapse. This hypothesis applies to the macro level. Aggre-
    gate studies indicate that societies with low levels of political support for government
    suffer from more riots and rebellions than other societies do (Levy 1981), but it is not

clear whether such societies can survive nonetheless. This book does not explore this issue.

Chapter 4: Measuring Legitimacy and Compliance

1. There are two reasons why people may say they do not break the law. First, they may have been asked about a period during which they in fact did not. Second, they may have reasons for wanting to misreport their behavior. Varying the time frame used in the survey question will influence only the first of these reasons.

2. It is important to recognize, however, that the correlation between self-report of different types of behavior is limited in magnitude by their skewed frequencies of response.

3. Compliance with the law is more likely among women than among men ($r = .28$, $p < .001$), whites and Asians ($r = .11$, $p < .001$), older respondents ($r = .38$, $p < .001$), highly educated respondents ($r = .26$, $p < .001$), respondents with high incomes ($r = .24$, $p < .001$), and liberals ($r = .11$, $p < .001$).

4. The issues of informal sanctions and moral disapproval by peers were confounded in the category peer disapproval. People could be concerned that their peers would sanction them by depriving them of the group's resources, or that their peers would merely think their behavior was wrong. These issues were confounded because the Chicago study did not focus on social influences of the group. The combined variable was therefore included to capture these influences. That it was not important for the purposes of the Chicago study to differentiate moral disapproval and informal sanction of course does not mean that this distinction is unimportant conceptually.

5. The measures of deterrence, peer approval, and personal morality used in the second wave were not presented, because they are essentially the same as the measures used in the first wave.

6. The items pertaining to obligation are correlated only weakly (mean $r = .18$). Unfortunately, the skewed distribution of the responses to the items leads the correlation between items to be artificially low, so that the correlation coefficient does not accurately reflect their association. In fact, the items are highly related, with 33 percent of the sample endorsing all six. This leads to a skewed distribution of obligation scores (see appendix C).

7. These revised items were also more strongly correlated (mean $r = .38$), producing a more normally distributed scale of obligation. Although more normally distributed, the scale is still skewed (coefficient of skewness = 0.14, standard error = 0.09).

8. For both the police and the courts, items within the support scales were highly intercorrelated (mean r for the police = .51; for the courts $r = .48$). In addition, those who supported the police also supported the courts ($r = .51$). A combined support scale has a normal distribution (see appendix C).

9. The correlation for obligation was $r = .22$, $p < .001$; for support $r = .11$, $p < .001$.

10. The distribution of the legitimacy scale is shown in appendix C.

11. Demographic variables explain 9 percent of the variance in perceived obligation to obey, 7 percent of the variance in support, and 10 percent of the variance in legitimacy.

12. Obligation to obey is related to personal morality (r = .21, p < .001), peer disapproval (r = .16, p < .001), and estimates of the likelihood of being caught (r = .13, p < .001). Support is related to personal morality (r = .12, p < .001), peer disapproval (r = .16, p < .001), and estimates of the likelihood of being caught (r = .12, p < .001). Legitimacy also is related to personal morality (r = .18, p < .001), peer disapproval (r = .17, p < .001), and estimates of the likelihood of being caught (r = .12, p < .001).

13. In the sample from the second wave 74 percent said they thought some people received better treatment than others from the police, and 70 percent said this about the courts. Only 19 percent said people like themselves were treated worse than others by the police, and only 19 percent said this about the courts.

14. For the fourteen items that applied to the police the average correlation was .45. In the case of the courts there was no distinction comparable to that between calling the police and being stopped by the police, so fewer items were used. For the ten items pertaining to the courts the mean correlation was also r = .45. The correlation between the two scales in the first wave's sample was r = .51. The correlation between performance evaluations and legitimacy in the first wave was r = .45, p < .001.

The scales measuring general assessments of performance for the police and courts included items pertaining to how well the authorities generally performed (an instrumental issue) and to whether they generally provided fair treatment and outcomes (normative issues). These general assessments of quality and fairness were uniformly found to be highly related, demonstrating that respondents found it difficult to differentiate between these two issues on an abstract level.

The inability of respondents to differentiate instrumental issues from normative issues when making general evaluations suggests that the strategy of focusing on recent personal experiences was sound. If general views alone were used, it would be difficult to distinguish instrumental reactions to legal authorities from normative ones.

Chapter 5: Does Legitimacy Contribute Independently to Compliance?

1. The Pearson correlation is r = .22, p < .001. One problem with the Pearson correlation is that the skewed distribution of the compliance index makes the correlation potentially unreliable. To correct this problem the PRELIS data-screening program was used to compute a normal score for the minimal value of the compliance scale (Joreskog and Sorbom 1986b). The correlation between legitimacy and compliance using this adjusted compliance scale is r = .24.

2. The figure of 5 percent is the same whether the correlation matrix uses the unadjusted

correlation of the variables to compliance, or a preprocessed compliance score of the type described in note 1 is used. In contrast, deterrence alone explains 8 percent of the variance in compliance, peer opinion 12 percent, and morality 18 percent. Performance evaluation explains none of the variance.

3. An examination of the standard errors around each of the ten means also reveals that variance in compliance is homogeneous from one level of legitimacy to another.

4. In addition to adjusting for reliability of measurement, the regression analysis used a correlation matrix that was preprocessed by PRELIS. The preprocessing allowed two types of adjustment to be made. First, the compliance measure from the first wave was adjusted for its skewed distribution (that is, treated as a censored variable; see Joreskog and Sorbom 1986b). The compliance measure from the second wave was not skewed, so no adjustment was made. Second, the PRELIS analysis allowed attitudinal scales to be treated as continuous variables; demographic indicators were treated as ordinal (see Joreskog and Sorbom 1986b). These adjustments were made in all the structural equations reported in later chapters.

5. Corrections for reliability of measurement were made with the LISREL program (Joreskog and Sorbom 1986a). Multiple regressions were run with the error matrix fixed at one minus the coefficient alpha value for each scale. Demographic characteristics were assumed to be measured with perfect reliability.

6. One way the regression analysis shown may distort the true influences on compliance is by masking the effects of deterrence and peer influence. Both factors have strong zero-order correlations with compliance, but each is also strongly related to the other and to personal morality. Once this joint association is removed only personal morality has a strong independent effect on compliance.

Use of the regression approach in this situation seems potentially inappropriate, for some of the independent variables share a conceptual similarity. The most obvious case is that of peer disapproval and personal morality. These two concepts are clearly related to each other; people no doubt draw much of their sense of what is right and wrong from their knowledge of peer disapproval. Similarly, whether people think they will be formally sanctioned for breaking the law is related to whether they think they will be informally sanctioned. To the extent that this is true, it does not make sense to treat these indicators as distinct: they should be thought of instead as making up one influence on compliance.

This methodological issue is important only if we care whether sanction and peer influence have effects. The manner in which the influence of these variables is conceptualized does not change the findings about legitimacy, which has an independent influence even when these factors are controlled for.

7. Although they do not influence compliance with the law, evaluations of performance have a strong influence on the likelihood that a person will seek help from the legal authorities. People were asked whether they would go to the police if their homes were burglarized or to report neighborhood problems, and whether they would go to court if they had a grievance against a business or a neighbor. Evaluations of performance were found to be the primary determinant of whether people said they would seek help

from one or the other. In contrast, the legitimacy of the authorities had only a minor influence.

8. This analysis is unlike the earlier examination of beta weights, terms which reflect the independent contribution of each term to an equation. Any joint variance (variance that can be explained by more than one term in the equation) is removed. In a usefulness analysis joint variance is included in the explanatory power of the first group of variables entered into the equation.

9. This analysis was performed using correlations adjusted by PRELIS.

10. One year after the first interview, 804 respondents were interviewed again. Legitimacy was again found to have a statistically significant influence on compliance in a reliability-adjusted equation (beta = .13, p < .01). Compliance was also found to be influenced by personal morality (beta = .32, p < .001), sex (beta = .25, p < .001), age (beta = .20, p < .001), and peer disapproval (beta = .09, p < .05). Without adjustments for reliability, legitimacy still had a significant influence (beta = .08, p < .05).

11. If judgments made at the first wave are used to predict the level of compliance reported during the second, legitimacy is found to have a significant effect on compliance (beta = .19, p < .001).

12. In the analysis, controls were introduced for the reliability of measurement of each variable, with demographic factors assumed to be perfectly measured. In addition, to simplify the causal model, four demographic variables that were insignificant in the initial regression analysis were omitted in the panel study. Those variables were race, education, income, and liberalism or conservatism. The more complex analysis was also performed with all demographic variables included. It is not reported, because the inclusion of these additional variables does not show that they have any significant influence, and does not change the influence of the variables already in the equation.

13. A panel study of compliance simultaneously examines the influence of the data from two waves (with corrections for reliability of measurement). According to panel analysis, legitimacy at the first wave influences compliance at the first wave (beta = .12, p < .05), and legitimacy at the second influences compliance at the second (beta = .12, p < .05).

14. The correlation for the feeling of obligation is r = .22 and for support r = .11.

15. The beta for obligation is .08, p < .001. The beta for support is .03 (n.s.).

16. The beta for support for the police is .04 (p < .05). The beta for support for the courts is .03 (n.s.).

17. A panel analysis shows that compliance at the first wave is influenced by obligation (beta = .32, p < .05), support for the police (beta = .23, p < .05), and support for the courts (beta = .23, p < .05). Compliance at the second wave is influenced by obligation (beta = .12, p < .05) and support for the police (beta = .15, p < .05).

18. Among those who thought the likelihood of being caught and punished for law breaking was high the correlation between legitimacy and compliance was .15; among those who thought it was low the correlation was .22. These two correlations are not significantly different in magnitude.

19. A correlation of r = .22 as opposed to one of r = .13 (z for the significance of the difference in magnitude between the two correlations is 2.89).

20. These variables are discussed in detail elsewhere in this book.

21. Respondents with recent personal experience (n = 652) were divided into subgroups five times, with each division made according to a different aspect of recent personal experience. Within each subgroup the correlation between legitimacy and compliance was calculated. The first dimension was the absolute favorability of the outcome. Among those with favorable outcomes, the correlation between legitimacy and compliance was .15; among those with unfavorable outcomes it was .10. These two correlations do not differ significantly in magnitude. Correlations of similar magnitude were also found when respondents were divided into subgroups based on relative favorability of outcome (favorable r = .22, unfavorable r = .20); relative favorability of treatment (favorable r = .18, unfavorable r = .14); and distributive fairness (fair r = .15, unfair r = .11). The only significant difference was with judgments of procedural justice (fair r = .25, unfair r = .11; z for differences in the magnitude of correlation coefficients is 1.75, p < .10).

22. The correlations are r = .26 for liberals and r = .13 for moderates (z for the significance of the difference between correlations is 2.25).

Chapter 6: What Do People Want from Legal Authorities?

1. The political science perspective on the sources of legitimacy and support, discussed in chapter 2, is similar to the one that concerns the basis of people's personal experiences with authorities, in that it also emphasizes the role of poor outcomes from the system in generating dissatisfaction and distrust. Two types of poor outcome have been suggested: the first occurs when leaders fail to deal effectively with societal problems (Citrin 1974; House and Mason 1975; Miller 1974; Wright 1981), the second when leaders enact policies contrary to the values of citizens (Wright 1981).

2. Psychological theories of expectancy developed out of models of learning theory, and as a result focused on violated expectations of outcome. It is also possible that people react to violations of their procedural expectations: they may become accustomed to particular ways of resolving problems and react with distress when their procedural expectations are violated. Although this suggestion is not advanced in the theories of expectation noted here, the influence of violations in procedural expectations is tested in the Chicago study.

3. According to theories of expectancy, people's reaction to their experiences can be shaped by violated expectations. It may be, however, that people translate such judgments of expectancy into judgments of violations in deservedness, by processing them through a normative framework. If this is the case, to move conceptually from theories of expectancy to judgments of distributive injustice is simply to follow a path that people take in their own reactions to events. But it is clearly possible to dis-

tinguish theoretically between violations of expectancy and feelings that one has not received what one deserves. Whether people actually make such a separation in their own thinking is an empirical question.

4. As has been noted, it is important to distinguish judgments of distributive fairness from violations of expectancy, which do not necessarily involve any judgment on a person's part that some standard of fairness is being violated. Direct comparisons of these two versions of outcome theory show that distributive injustice typically influences behavior (see Lawler 1977).

5. The literature reviewed here deals with legal and political authorities. There is also a literature on the evaluation of authorities in the workplace, as well as a large literature on the determinants of satisfaction in the workplace. These are reviewed in Lind and Tyler (1988).

6. Evaluations of the judge were influenced by absolute favorability of outcome (beta = .03, n.s.), relative favorability of outcome (beta = .27, p < .001), distributive justice (beta = .45, p < .001), and procedural justice (beta = .41, p < .001). Evaluations of the court were influenced by absolute favorability of outcome (beta = .02, n.s.), relative favorability of outcome (beta = .09, p < .05), distributive justice (beta = .12, n.s.), and procedural justice (beta = .38, p < .001).

7. Favorability of outcome would still influence satisfaction with outcome and evaluations of the judge and court if it influenced judgments of fairness. A causal model that allows for such influence finds that it indeed occurs. Absolute favorability of outcome influences judgments of both distributive fairness (beta = .19, p < .01) and procedural fairness (beta = .17, p < .05). Favorability of outcome relative to expectations also influences both distributive fairness (beta = .43, p < .001) and procedural fairness (beta = .17, p < .05). Favorability of outcome relative to others (general or specific) had no influence on judgments of fairness.

8. One potential difficulty of studying inputs into reactions on this general level is illustrated by the assessment of procedural justice. It may well be that many respondents were not very knowledgeable about the procedural justice of the Reagan administration's policymaking process, and it is therefore difficult to know the basis of their judgments. But most respondents did answer the question: however well informed or ill informed they may be, people are willing to express an opinion on matters of this kind.

9. Earlier it was noted that the respondents in the Chicago study did not differentiate favorability and fairness when asked general questions about the police and courts. This failure to differentiate did not occur in the study by Tyler, Rasinski, and McGraw (1985), which suggests that people have more highly developed frameworks for evaluating political issues than they do for evaluating legal authorities.

10. Evaluations of President Reagan were influenced by procedural justice (beta = .47, p < .001), political party (beta = .20, p < .001), ideology (beta = .16, p < .001), and sex (beta = .13, p < .01). Trust in the national government was influenced only by procedural justice (beta = .61, p < .001).

11. The literature on the effects of procedural justice on behavior has also explored such effects in work settings. For a discussion of this literature see Lind and Tyler (1988).

12. An indirect inference of the effects of procedural justice can be made, because the authors measure participation in the process of settlement. Studies of procedural fairness find that participation is usually highly correlated with judgments that the process was fair.

Chapter 7: Measuring the Psychological Variables

1. Although the Chicago study is more elaborate than past studies, it also suffers from a limited focus. In particular, no measures of absolute procedural favorability were included (corresponding to scales measuring favorability of outcome). Although this conceptual category is clear, it is not clear what questions would correspond to it— perhaps questions like "How favorable was the procedure to you?"

2. An analysis of the data collected in the Chicago study shows that the decision to focus on specific experiences was sound. Respondents were asked not only questions about their recent personal experiences, but also general questions about the police and courts. These questions also differentiated judgments of the quality of performance, fairness of outcome, and procedural fairness.

   People differentiate the various aspects of experience much less clearly on the general level. In other words, people are able to distinguish favorability of outcome and procedural fairness very clearly in the context of a specific experience. But if they are asked whether the police generally solve problems and whether they generally treat people fairly, the two judgments tend to be highly correlated. In the case of the police, favorability and fairness were correlated on average to the degree $r = .50$; for the courts the correlation was $r = .64$. It would therefore be difficult to distinguish between these various aspects of evaluation using data from the general level.

   It is interesting that people seem better able to distinguish among various aspects of how the police perform than among various aspects of how the courts do. This accords with other evidence that people seem more knowledgeable about the police than the courts, and may be due to the greater frequency with which people have personal experiences with the police.

3. It is also important that judgments about experience may be shaped by prior views about the law and legal authority. A panel design was therefore used, so that the extent and nature of the influence of prior views could be established.

4. Respondents may have felt that they appeared voluntarily, even if they were defendants, because they could have settled the case out of court in spite of not having done so.

5. The analysis of favorability of outcome can be replicated by using the 291 respondents who had experience during the period between the two waves of the study. The findings of the analysis are similar to those reported above; the only difference is that

voluntary and involuntary contacts in court do not differ in the favorability of their outcomes, as had been the case in the first wave. Given the smaller samples used in the second wave, the first offers a more stable estimate of favorability of outcome in different types of contact.

6. This approach was used because of the difficulty of determining the appropriate referent for comparison. This has been a general problem in research into relative deprivation.

7. Respondents in the second wave also rated the unfavorability of outcome of their contact with legal authorities according to the four reference standards outlined earlier: what they expected before the contact, what they received in the past, what they thought others generally received in similar cases, and what their friends, family, or neighbors received in the past.

  Unfavorability in relation to prior experiences was assessed by asking respondents to compare their recent outcomes with those they had experienced in the past. Sixty-four percent of respondents felt that their outcomes had been similar in the past, 17 percent that they had been better, and 11 percent that they had been worse; 8 percent had no past experience. In relation to the outcomes of other people "in similar situations," 65 percent of respondents said they received similar outcomes, 25 percent said they had better outcomes, and 10 percent said they had worse outcomes. In relation to expectations, 49 percent of respondents said they received the outcomes they expected, 28 percent said they had better outcomes than they expected, and 23 percent said they had worse outcomes than they expected. Finally, unfavorability was assessed in relation to the recent experiences of family, neighbors, or friends. Of those respondents with experience, 28 percent said they knew of experiences that others from this group had had with the police or courts during the preceding year. Sixty-six percent said their own outcome was similar, 24 percent said it was better, and 11 percent said it was worse.

8. It would have been helpful to have indicators of the absolute quality of the process, but it was unfortunately not clear how to conceptualize absolute dimensions of process.

9. Respondents in the second wave began by comparing their treatment with past experiences. Much as in the first wave, 58 percent said their treatment was the same as in the past, 22 percent said it was better, and 11 percent said it was worse; 8 percent had no experience.

  Respondents then rated their treatment in comparison with what other people in similar situations had received. Sixty-nine percent said that their treatment was similar to that received by others, 23 percent said it was better, and 8 percent said it was worse. When comparing their treatment with what they had expected, 49 percent of respondents said they were treated as they had expected they would be, 32 percent said they had been treated better, and 19 percent said they had been treated worse. Finally, respondents compared their treatment with that recently given to friends or family. Of those aware of other cases comparable with their own, 69 percent said their treatment was similar to that of others, 20 percent said that it was better, and 11 percent said that it was worse.

10. The difficulty is in how to combine the two questions. Should "too much" attention and "too little" be collapsed into one category, so that the scale has two points (the right amount of attention, and too much or too little attention)? Conceptually this is probably the purest way to proceed, but it may not be realistic. It is also possible to treat the scale as a continuum, with more attention than deserved being more positive than as much attention as deserved. To examine the potential implications of the two approaches, two scales were created—one folded and the other not. These two scales were then correlated to indicators of satisfaction with outcome and satisfaction with treatment. For the folded scale the correlations were .46 and .46. For the nonfolded version of the scale the correlations were .58 and .54. Because the nonfolded scale clearly was more strongly related to the subjective experiences of the respondents, it was used in the study.

The theoretical implication of this scaling decision is that people who received too much attention were treated as more satisfied than those who received as much as they deserved. This suggests that concerns about distributive justice are not symmetrical: those with an unfair advantage are not the same as those at an unfair disadvantage.

The same two questions used in the first wave were used to assess distributive fairness in the second. These included questions about the fairness of the outcome the respondent received (58 percent called it very fair, 23 percent somewhat fair, 8 percent somewhat unfair, and 10 percent very unfair) and about whether the authorities gave the case or problem the attention it deserved (62 percent said the right amount of attention was given, 13 percent said more attention was given than was deserved, and 25 percent said less attention was given than was deserved).

11. In the second wave procedural fairness was again assessed, by asking respondents "how fair" the procedures used by the police or courts were and "how fairly" the respondents were treated by the authorities. Most respondents said the procedures were fair (58 percent called them very fair, 27 percent somewhat fair, 6 percent somewhat unfair, and 10 percent very unfair) and that they were fairly treated (55 percent said very fairly, 29 percent somewhat fairly, 9 percent somewhat unfairly, and 8 percent very unfairly).

12. We can replicate these findings in the sample from the second by examining the influence of each judgment on the second wave's dependent variables. As in the first wave's sample, violations of expectation had the strongest relationship to the dependent variable.

13. Each judgment has high internal consistency ($r = .78$ for distributive justice, $r = .81$ for procedural justice). The two judgments are also related to each other (mean $r = .62$).

14. Each judgment has high internal consistency ($r = .58$ for distributive justice, $r = .78$ for procedural justice). The two judgments are also related to each other (mean $r = .66$).

15. As in the first wave of interviews, two types of dependent variable were assessed in the second: personal satisfaction and evaluations of legal authorities. Questions about satisfaction addressed citizens' personal satisfaction with their outcomes (50 percent

were very satisfied, 24 percent somewhat satisfied, 10 percent somewhat dissatisfied, and 17 percent very dissatisfied) and with their treatment (53 percent were very satisfied, 25 percent somewhat satisfied, 13 percent somewhat dissatisfied, and 9 percent very dissatisfied).

Respondents were also asked about the influence of their experience on their feelings toward the authorities with whom they dealt. They were asked whether they felt anger (21 percent said yes) or frustration (28 percent said yes), or were pleased with the authorities (62 percent said yes). Finally, questions were asked to elicit the degree to which respondents generalized about the type of authority they had dealt with, and rated the quality of performance of the police and courts and the legitimacy of legal authority. Each respondent was given the evaluation score for the authority (police or courts) with whom he or she had dealt.

Chapter 8: Does Experience Influence Legitimacy?

1. Reliability-adjusted regression techniques have been used to control for differences in the reliability of measurement associated with the various constructs in the regression equations. Why not do the same thing here? The problem is that the indices of relative judgments may not constitute alternative measures of relative judgments, because they are conceptually independent. There is no reason why a person need feel that an experience is better than one reference point simply because it is better than another. In other words, just because an experience is better than what happened to a person in the past does not mean that it should be better than the experience of others. It might therefore be inappropriate to use the relationship between indices of relative outcome or quality of treatment as an index of reliability. Reliability of measurement is also less of an issue in this analysis than it was in the earlier discussion of legitimacy, so reliability adjustments will not be made here.

2. Fairness judgments explained 21 percent of the variance in satisfaction with outcome beyond what could be explained by judgments unrelated to fairness (p < .001), whereas judgments unrelated to fairness explained 1 percent of the variance in satisfaction with outcome beyond what could be explained by fairness judgments (n.s.). In an equation including both types of judgment the most important factor was distributive justice (beta = .39, p < .001), followed by procedural justice (beta = .31, p < .001). Satisfaction with outcome was influenced also by relative outcome judgments (beta = .18, p < .001).

Fairness judgments explained 27 percent of the variance in satisfaction with treatment beyond what could be explained by judgments unrelated to fairness (p < .001), which in turn explained 1 percent of the variance in satisfaction with treatment beyond what could be explained by fairness judgments (n.s.). In an equation including both types of judgment the most important factor was procedural justice (beta = .55, p < .001), followed by distributive justice (beta = .18, p < .001). Satisfaction with outcome was also influenced by relative outcome judgments (beta = .13, p < .001).

Fairness judgments explained 22 percent of the variance in affect beyond what could be explained by judgments unrelated to fairness (p < .001), which in turn explained 1 percent of the variance in affect beyond what could be explained by fairness judgments (n.s.). In an equation including both types of judgment the most important factor was procedural justice (beta = .45, p < .001), followed by distributive justice (beta = .24, p < .001). Satisfaction with outcome was also influenced by relative outcome judgments (beta = .09, p < .01).

3. Fairness judgments explained 18 percent of the variance in performance evaluation beyond what could be explained by judgments unrelated to fairness (p < .001); judgments unrelated to fairness explained none of the variance in satisfaction with outcome beyond what could be explained by fairness judgments (n.s.). In an equation including both types of judgment the most important factor was procedural justice (beta = .41, p < .001), followed by distributive justice (beta = .22, p < .001). None of the outcome terms influenced evaluations of performance.

Fairness judgments explained 4 percent of the variance in legitimacy beyond what could be explained by judgments unrelated to fairness (p < .001); judgments unrelated to fairness explained none of the variance in legitimacy beyond what could be explained by fairness judgments (n.s.). In an equation including both types of judgment the most important factor was procedural justice (beta = .20, p < .01). Satisfaction with outcome was also influenced by relative outcome judgments (beta = −.18, p < .01).

4. One puzzling finding in note 3 is the negative influence that judgments of relative outcome have in the case of legitimacy. This effect is quite strong (beta = −.18), but is it real? An examination of the zero-order correlation between judgments of relative outcome level and legitimacy suggests not: the correlation is 0.00. On the other hand, the beta for procedural justice corresponds to a similarly high zero-order correlation (r = .19, p < .001). The strong negative beta found in this case is an artifact of the use of beta weights to measure independent contributions. When one factor (procedural justice) dominates the equation so strongly, spurious effects of this type can emerge.

5. An analysis of judgments based on experience can also be performed by using the interviews from the second wave. The results of such an analysis generally replicate the results already discussed. One exception is that the outcome measures have a much greater influence on satisfaction with outcome in the first wave than they do in the second.

6. Judgments of distributive fairness were influenced by absolute favorability of outcome (beta = .29, p < .05), outcome relative to expectations of outcome (beta = .57, p < .05), and procedure relative to procedural expectations (beta = .22, p < .05). Judgments of procedural fairness were influenced by absolute favorability of outcome (beta = .17, p < .05), outcome relative to expectations of outcome (beta = .37, p < .05), and procedure relative to procedural expectations (beta = .51, p < .05).

7. There are two possible explanations for this finding. First, those who are positively predisposed toward the authorities may interpret their experiences in a more favorable way—although it is possible that people with favorable predispositions actually have

more positive experiences. Their attitude may elicit more positive actions from police officers and judges. The Chicago study does not differentiate between these two perspectives on the effects that were found. What is clear is that prior views influence judgments about the experience.

8. In a survey of more than 2,000 federal employees, Alexander and Ruderman (1987) found that judgments of procedural justice were more important than judgments of distributive justice for a variety of organizational attitudes, including job satisfaction, evaluation of supervisors, organizational harmony, and trust in management. For one index—the behavorial intention to leave government and seek another job—distributive justice was more important than procedural justice.

9. The interpretation presented here suggests that prior views influence the interpretation of experience. Another possibility is that prior views influence the nature of experience: in other words, people with positive prior views may behave in a way that elicits fair procedures from the authorities with whom they deal. Because the interaction studied here was not directly observed, this possibility cannot be discounted.

10. An additional argument in favor of a procedural focus is that people find it more comfortable than a focus on outcome. In many situations a focus on outcome makes more salient the errors relating to outcome that are inherent in most procedures. For example, if people are trying to decide how much error is acceptable in trials, they are forced to recognize that any procedure will lead to some erroneous outcomes. It has recently been argued that people do not find such awareness of error as troubling as has commonly been believed (see MacCoun and Tyler 1988).

11. One should not assume that defendants will view plea bargaining as procedurally unfair (Casper, Tyler, and Fisher 1988; Landis and Goodstein 1986).

Chapter 9: The Psychology of Procedural Justice

1. In his discussion of procedural justice, Leventhal (1980) examines potential criteria against which a procedure might be evaluated. His discussion involves consideration of both objective aspects of fairness and determinants of the subjective feeling of being fairly treated. Only the latter issue is examined here: the Chicago study dealt with those aspects of a procedure that influence people's judgments of its fairness.

2. According to such theories equity promotes productivity but harms group feeling. Equality, on the other hand, enhances group feeling but hurts productivity.

Chapter 10: The Influence of Control

1. One potential problem with using self-reported data of the type collected in telephone interviews is that respondents may attempt to offer publicly defensible accounts of their experiences. To lessen the possibility of such effects in the Chicago study, respondents were not asked to explain the events that occurred during their experience. Instead, they were asked a series of questions about characteristics that their

experience might have had. Further, questions about the dependent variables of the analysis, evaluations of the police and courts, were asked before questions about the experience. Because questions about the experience were more specific and focused, they were less likely to be distorted, and it would have been difficult for respondents to extemporize during the interview a socially acceptable account of their actions.

2. When the dependent variable is procedural justice, beta = .45 (p < .001) for process control and .24 (p < .001) for decision control. When the dependent variable is evaluation, beta = .35 (p < .001) for process control and .13 (p < .001) for decision control. With support, both effects are equally strong (beta = .12, p < .01). Neither effect is significant in the case of obligation (beta = .07, n.s., for process control and beta = .04, n.s., for decision control).

3. Of the personal characteristics measured, the most suspect methodologically are the two measures of general views about how the police and courts treat citizens. Because all views are assessed at one time, it is possible that they are influenced by the experience the person has had, rather than reflect some general evaluation of the police or courts. Although plausible, this explanation is not supported by the data. The way citizens are treated in their own experience does not influence their views about whether the police generally treat citizens fairly (r = .05, n.s.).

4. Among those low in decision control, variations in process control influenced procedural justice (beta = .47, p < .001), performance evaluations (beta = .27, p < .001), and support for the authorities (beta = .19, p < .001).

5. When the outcome is important to the respondent the correlation of process control to procedural justice is r = .56, to evaluation r = .48, and to support r = .36. When the outcome is not important to the respondent the correlation of process control to procedural justice is r = .59, to evaluation r = .38, and to support r = .21. When the outcome is favorable to the respondent the correlation of process control to procedural justice is r = .48, to evaluation r = .32, and to support r = .18. When the outcome is favorable to the respondent the correlation of process control to procedural justice is r = .56, to evaluation r = .46, and to support r = .37.

6. Process control is related to decision control (r = .56, p < .001), impartiality (r = .34, p < .001), efforts to be fair (r = .58, p < .001), and consideration of views (r = .78, p < .001). Decision control is related to impartiality (r = .26, p < .001), efforts to be fair (r = .48, p < .001), and consideration of views (r = .64, p < .001). Impartiality is related to efforts to be fair (r = .46, p < .001) and consideration of views (r = .44, p < .001). And Finally, efforts to be fair are related to consideration of views (r = .65, p < .001).

7. The strongest influence on the relationship between background characteristics and judgments of process control and decision control is favorability of outcome. If the outcome is favorable, people believe that they have exercised decision control (r = .32), and that they have had process control (r = .24). Although clearly important, the influence of favorability of outcome is weaker than the overall influence of attitudinal factors.

8. Among all panel respondents with experience (n = 291), judgments of procedural justice were influenced by process control (beta = .46, p < .001), decision control

(beta = .20, p < .001), and expectations (beta = .10, p < .05). Satisfaction with treatment was influenced by process control (beta = .49, p < .001), decision control (beta = .17, p < .001), and expectations (beta = .12, p < .01). Affect was influenced by process control (beta = .37, p < .001), decision control (beta = .13, p < .01), and expectations (beta = .20, p < .001). Evaluations of performance were influenced by process control (beta = .13, p < .01), decision control (beta = .12, p < .05), and prior evaluations (beta = .50, p < .001). Support was not influenced by process control (beta = .07, n.s.), but it was influenced by decision control (beta = .10, p < .05) and prior support (beta = .53, p < .001).

Among those respondents who had an experience low in decision control (n = 134), procedural justice was influenced by process control (beta = .47, p < .001) and expectations (beta = .15, p < .05). Satisfaction with treatment was influenced by process control (beta = .55, p < .001), but not by expectations (beta = .12, n.s.). Affect was influenced by process control (beta = .44, p < .001) and expectations (beta = .20, p < .001). Evaluations were influenced by process control (beta = .15, p < .05) and prior evaluations (beta = .40, p < .001). Finally, support was influenced by process control (beta = .16, p < .05) and prior support (beta = .43, p < .001).

9. Among all panel respondents with experience (n = 291), prior evaluations and support influenced judgments of process control (R-squared = 3%, p < .001), consideration of views (R-squared = 4%, p < .001), and procedural justice (R-squared = 5%, p < .001), but not decision control (R-squared = 0%, n.s.). Among those respondents who had low decision control, prior evaluations and support influenced judgments of process control (R-squared = 5%, p < .05), consideration of views (R-squared = 7%, p < .01), and procedural justice (R-squared = 7%, p < .01), but not decision control (R-squared = 0%, n.s.).

10. It is important to note a potential methodological problem in analyzing the effect of prior attitudes on the interpretation of experiences. Prior attitudes can have an impact by influencing either the interpretation of experience or the experience itself. It may be that citizens with positive prior attitudes behave differently toward the police, and as a result have their views listened to and considered to a greater extent. If so, citizens will not be interpreting their experiences more positively: they will be creating more positive experiences. This possibility cannot be ruled out in the Chicago study, because the objective quality of the experience could not be measured. Some evidence against this interpretation surfaces when one selects only experiences over which the respondent had low decision control.

Chapter 11: Beyond Control

1. The way these judgments were examined is discussed in the earlier analysis of the effects of experience, where these same items were used to assess relative judgments of outcome and procedure. In this analysis only the items concerning outcome are used.

2. Leventhal defines ethicality as "compatibility with fundamental moral and ethical

values." There are of course many values that might be relevant to judgments of procedural justice. Here the focus is on two potentially important values: interpersonal norms governing relationships (such issues as politeness), and the more formal norms governing citizens' relationships to authorities (people's rights). One question that this raises is whether these two aspects of experience are really part of one construct. In this analysis they are treated as one owing to their high correlation (r = .59).

3. Favorability of outcome alone can explain 19 percent of the variance in procedural justice (p < .001) and 12 percent of the variance in judgments about the fairness of the authorities (p < .001). Favorability of outcome and violations of expectancy can explain 23 percent of the variance in procedural justice (p < .001) and 12 percent of the variance in judgments about the fairness of the authorities (p < .001). In contrast, the procedural justice criteria alone explain 69 percent of the variance in procedural justice (p < .001) and 24 percent of the variance in judgments about the fairness of the authorities (p < .001).

   Favorability of outcome and violations of expectancy explain 1 percent of the variance in procedural justice beyond what can be explained by the procedural justice criteria (n.s.) and 6 percent of the unique variance in judgments about the fairness of the authorities (p < .001). In contrast, the procedural justice criteria explain 47 percent of the variance beyond what can be explained by judgments on favorability of outcome and violations of expectancy (p < .001) and 18 percent of the variance in judgments about the fairness of the authorities (p < .001).

4. To load the dice in favor of the perspective based of favorability on outcome, judgments of consistency were treated not as indicators of procedural justice but as judgments of the favorability of outcome. It is also important to note that this analysis includes issues of neutrality and representation as noninstrumental influences. These elements of procedure are ambiguous and can be interpreted in either instrumental or noninstrumental terms. This analysis may therefore exaggerate noninstrumental influences to some degree.

5. It is important that in disputes the effects of being able to state one's case are typically confounded with another variable: that of hearing the other side's case. In most forums for resolving disputes all sides tell their stories, so each hears the other points of view. Many people come to the forum thinking that theirs is the only side to the dispute (see Conley and O'Barr 1988), so this is a significant opportunity for education. This education may contribute in turn to the value of stating one's case.

   It would be interesting to disentangle these two aspects of process control by studying one-sided process control and two-sided process control.

Chapter 13: The Psychology of Legitimacy

1. Further, evaluations of performance are irrelevant to compliance with the law. Everyday compliance is not related to how people evaluate the quality of the police and courts. Again, outcome measures are not the key to compliance.

2. The ease with which people embrace the group's identity is shown in the literature on social categorization (Tajfel 1981).
3. Part of the reason why people value participation may be that they exaggerate their control over group outcomes. People are predisposed to believe that they have control over outcomes, and given any evidence of influence they may exaggerate the extent to which they are influencing the third party (Langer 1983). It is important for this reason not to overstate the case: these effects do have aspects of decision control.

References

Abelson, R., Kinder, D. R., Peters, M. D., and Fiske, S. T. 1982. Affective and semantic components in political person perception. *Journal of Personality and Social Psychology* 42: 619–630.

Aberbach, J. D. 1969. Alienation and political behavior. *American Political Science Review* 62: 86–99.

Aberbach, J. D., and Walker, J. L. 1970. Political trust and racial ideology. *American Political Science Review* 64: 1199–1219.

Adler, J. W., Hensler, D. R., and Nelson, C. E. 1983. *Simple justice: How litigants fare in the Pittsburgh Court Arbitration Program*. Santa Monica: RAND.

Ajzen, I., and Fishbein, M. 1980. *Understanding attitudes and predicting social behavior*. Englewood Cliffs, N.J.: Prentice-Hall.

Alexander, S., and Ruderman, A. 1987. The role of procedural and distributive justice in organizational behavior. *Social Justice Research* 1: 177–198.

Andenaes, J. 1984. *Punishment and deterrence*. Ann Arbor: University of Michigan Press.

Anton, T. J. 1967. Roles and symbols in the determination of state expenditures. *Midwest Journal of Political Science* 11: 27–43.

Aubert, V. 1979. On methods of legal influence. In S. B. Burman and B. E. Harrell-Bond, eds., *The imposition of law*. New York: Academic Press.

Austin, W. G. 1979. Justice, freedom, and self-interest in intergroup conflict. In W. G. Austin and S. Worchel, eds., *The social psychology of intergroup relations*. Monterey, Calif.: Brooks/Cole.

Baker, R., Meyers, F. A., Jr., Corbett, A. M., and Rudoni, D. 1979. Evaluation of police services in medium-sized cities. *Law and Policy Quarterly* 1: 235–248.

Balch, G. 1974. Multiple indicators in survey research: The concept "sense of political efficacy." *Political Methodology* 1: 1–43.

Bandura, A. 1972. *Social learning theory*. Englewood Cliffs, N.J.: Prentice-Hall.

Barber, B. 1983. *The logic and limits of trust*. New Brunswick: Rutgers University Press.

Barrett-Howard, E., and Tyler, T. R. 1986. Procedural justice as a criterion in allocation decisions. *Journal of Personality and Social Psychology* 50: 296–304.

Barry, B., and Hardin, R. 1982. *Rational man and irrational society*. Beverly Hills: Sage.

Bauer, R. A. 1968. The study of policy formation: An introduction. In R. A. Bauer and K. J. Gergen, eds., *The study of policy formation*. New York: Free Press.

Bayley, D. H., and Mendelsohn, H. 1969. *Minorities and the police*. New York: Free Press.

Bellah, R. N., Madsen, R., Sullivan, W. M., Swidler, A., and Tipton, S. M. 1985. *Habits of the heart*. Berkeley: University of California Press.

Best, A., and Andreasen, A. R. 1977. Consumer response to unsatisfactory purchases. *Law and Society Review* 11: 701–742.

Bethea, R. M., Duran, E. S., and Boullion, T. L. 1985. *Statistical methods for engineers and scientists*. 2d ed. New York: Dekker.

Bies, R. J., and Moag, J. S. 1986. Interactional justice: Communication criteria of fairness. In R. J. Lewicki, B. H. Sheppard, and M. H. Bazerman, eds., *Research on negotiation in organizations*. Vol. 1. Greenwich, Conn.: JAI.

Bies, R. J., and Shapiro, D. L. 1987. Processual fairness judgments: The influence of causal accounts. *Social Justice Research* 1: 199–218.

Blasi, A. 1980. Bridging moral cognition and moral action. *Psychological Bulletin* 88: 1–45.

Blumstein, A., Cohen, J., and Nagin, D. 1978. *Deterrence and incapacitation: Estimating the effects of criminal sanctions on crime rates*. Washington: National Academy of Sciences.

Boulding, K. 1970. The impact of the draft on the legitimacy of the national state. In S. E. Deutsch and H. Howard, eds., *Where it's at: Radical perspectives in sociology*. New York: Harper and Row.

Boynton, G. R., Patterson, S. C., and Hedlund, R. 1968. The structure of public support for legislative institutions. *Midwest Journal of Political Science* 12: 163–180.

Brett, J. M. 1986. Procedural justice. In R. J. Lewicki, B. H. Sheppard, and M. H. Bazerman, eds., *Research on negotiation in organizations*. Greenwich, Conn.: JAI.

Brewer, M. B., and Kramer, R. 1986. Choice behavior in social dilemmas: Effects of social identity, group size, and decision framing. *Journal of Personality and Social Psychology* 50: 543–549.

Brown, D. W. 1974. Adolescent attitudes and lawful behavior. *Public Opinion Quarterly* 38: 98–106.

Bryant, B. E. 1975. Respondent selection in a time of changing household composition. *Journal of Marketing Research* 12: 129–135.

Caddell, P. H. 1979. Crisis of confidence: Trapped in a downward spiral. *Public Opinion* 5: 2–8.

Campbell, A. 1980. *The sense of well-being in America*. New York: McGraw-Hill.

Casper, J. 1972. *American criminal justice: The defendant's perspective*. Englewood Cliffs, N.J.: Prentice-Hall.

———. 1978. Having their day in court: Defendant evaluations of the fairness of their treatment. *Law and Society Review* 12: 237–251.

Casper, J., Tyler, T. R., and Fisher, B. 1988. Procedural justice among felony defendants. *Law and Society Review* 22: 483–507.

Citrin, J. 1974. Comment: The political relevance of trust in government. *American Political Science Review* 68: 973–988.

———. 1977. Political alienation as a social indicator: Attitudes and action. *Social Indicators Research* 4: 381–419.

Citrin, J., McClosky, H., Shanks, J. M., and Sniderman, P. M. 1975. Personal and political sources of political alienation. *British Journal of Political Science* 5: 1–31.

Cohen, A. K. 1966. *Deviance and control*. Englewood Cliffs, N.J.: Prentice-Hall.

Cohen, J., and Cohen, P. 1975. *Applied multiple regression/correlation analysis for the behavioral sciences*. Hillsdale, N.J.: Erlbaum.

Cohen, R. L. 1983. Participation as procedure: A critical examination of fair process and frustration effects in organizational settings. Paper presented at the Second Annual Conference on Justice and Law, Nags Head, N.C., June 12–18.

———. 1986. Power and justice in intergroup relations. In H. Bierhoff, J. Greenberg, and R. Cohen, eds., *Justice in intergroup relations*. New York: Plenum.

Colombotos, J. 1965. The effects of personal vs. telephone interviews on socially acceptable responses. *Public Opinion Quarterly* 29: 457–458.

Conley, J. 1988. Ethnographic perspectives on informal justice: What litigants want. Paper presented at the annual meeting of the Law and Society Association, Vail, Colo., June.

Conley, J., and O'Barr, W. 1988. Rules and relationships. Unpublished manuscript, School of Law, University of North Carolina, Chapel Hill.

Converse, P. 1964. The nature of belief systems in mass publics. In D. Apter, ed., *Ideology and discontent*. New York: Free Press.

Cornelius, G. W., Kanfer, R., and Lind, E. A. 1986. Evaluation fairness and work motivation. Unpublished manuscript, University of Illinois.

Craig, S. C. 1980. The mobilization of political discontent. *Political Behavior* 2: 189–209.

Craig, S. C., and Wald, K. D. 1985. Whose ox to gore? A comment on the relationship between political discontent and political violence. *Western Political Quarterly* 38: 652–662.

Crosby, F. 1976. A model of egotistical relative deprivation. *Psychological Review* 83: 85–113.

———. 1982. *Relative deprivation and working women*. New York: Oxford University Press.

Curran, B. 1977. *The legal needs of the public: The final report of a national survey*. Chicago: American Bar Foundation.

Czaja, R., Blair, J., and Sebestik, J. P. 1982. Respondent selection in a telephone survey: A comparison of three techniques. *Journal of Marketing Research* 19: 381–385.

Davies, J. C. 1962. Toward a theory of revolution. *American Sociological Review* 27: 5–19.

———. 1969. The J-curve of rising and declining satisfactions as a cause of some great revolutions and a contained rebellion. In H. D. Graham and T. R. Gurr, eds., *The History of Violence in America*. New York: Bantam.

De Carufel, A. 1981. The allocation and acquisition of resources in times of scarcity. In M. J. Lerner and S. C. Lerner, eds., *The justice motive in social behavior*. New York: Plenum.

Deutsch, M. 1982. Interdependence and psychological orientation. In V. J. Derlaga and J. Grzelak, eds., *Cooperation and helping behavior*. New York: Academic Press.

———. 1985. *Distributive justice*. New Haven and London: Yale University Press.

Dolbeare, K. M., and Hammond, P. E. 1970. Inertia in midway: Supreme Court decisions and local responses. *Journal of Legal Education* 23: 106–122.

Downs, A. 1957. *An Economic theory of democracy*. New York: Harper.

Easton, D. 1958. The perception of authority and political change. In C. J. Friedrich, ed., *Authority*. Cambridge: Harvard University Press.

———. 1965. *A systems analysis of political life*. Chicago: University of Chicago Press.

———. 1968. Political science. In D. L. Sills, ed., *International encyclopedia of the social sciences*. New York: Macmillan.

———. 1975. A reassessment of the concept of political support. *British Journal of Political Science* 5: 435–457.

Easton, D., and Dennis, J. 1969. *Children in the political system*. Chicago: University of Chicago Press.

Edelman, M. 1964. *The symbolic uses of politics*. Urbana: University of Illinois Press.

Eiser, J. R. 1976. Evaluation of choice-dilemma alternatives: Utility, morality, and social judgment. *British Journal of Social and Clinical Psychology* 15: 51–60.

Engstrom, R. L. 1970. Race and compliance: Differential political socialization. *Polity* 3: 101–111.

Engstrom, R. L., and Giles, M. W. 1972. Expectations and images: A note on diffuse support for legal institutions. *Law and Society Review* 6: 631–636.

Erickson, M. 1972. The changing relation between official and self-reported delinquency. *Journal of Criminal Law, Criminology, and Police Science* 2: 388–395.

Erickson, M., and Smith, W. B., Jr. 1974. On the relation between self-reported and actual deviance. *Humboldt Journal of Social Relations* 2: 106–113.

Farah, B. G., Barnes, S. H., and Heunks, F. 1979. Political dissatisfaction. In S. H. Barnes and M. Kaase, eds., *Political action: Mass participation in five western democracies*. Beverly Hills: Sage.

Farrington, P. 1973. Self-reports of deviant behavior: Predictive and stable? *Journal of Criminal Law and Criminology* 64: 99–110.

Felstiner, W. L. F., Abel, R. L., and Sarat, A. 1980–81. The emergence and transformation of disputes. *Law and Society Review* 15: 631–654.

Festinger, L. 1954. A theory of social comparison processes. *Human Relations* 7: 117–140.

Fetter, T. J. 1978. *State courts: A blueprint for the future*. Williamsburg, Va.: National Center for State Courts.

Fishbein, M., and Ajzen, I. 1975. *Belief, attitude, intention and behavior: An introduction to theory and research*. Reading, Mass.: Addison-Wesley.

Flacks, R. 1969. Protest or conform: Social psychological perspectives on legitimacy. *Journal of Applied Behavioral Science* 5: 127–149.

Flaming, K. H. 1968. Who "riots" and why? Black and white perspectives in Milwaukee. Milwaukee: Urban League.

Folger, R. 1977. Distributive and procedural justice: Combined impact of "voice" and peer opinions on responses to inequity. *Journal of Personality and Social Psychology* 35: 108–119.

———. 1986a. A referent cognitions theory of relative deprivation. In J. M. Olson, C. P. Hermann, and M. P. Zanna, eds., *Social comparison and relative deprivation: The Ontario symposium*. Vol. 4. Hillsdale, N.J.: Erlbaum.

———. 1986b. Rethinking equity theory: A referent cognitions model. In H. W. Bierhoff, R. L. Cohen, and J. Greenberg, eds., *Justice in social relations*. New York: Plenum.

Folger, R., and Greenberg, J. 1985. Procedural justice: An interpretive analysis of personnel systems. In K. Rowland and G. Ferris, eds., *Research in personnel and human resources management*. Vol. 3. Greenwich, Conn.: JAI.

Folger, R., Rosenfield, D., Grove, J., and Cochran, L. 1979. Effects of "voice" and peer opinions on responses to inequity. *Journal of Personality and Social Psychology* 37: 2253–2261.

French, J. R. P., Jr., and Raven, B. 1959. The bases of social power. In D. Cartwright, ed., *Studies in social power*. Ann Arbor: University of Michigan Press.

Fried, M. 1967. *The evolution of political society*. New York: Random House.

Friedland, N., Thibaut, J., and Walker, L. 1973. Some determinants of the violation of rules. *Journal of Applied Social Psychology* 3: 103–118.

Friedman, L. 1975. *The legal system: A social science perspective*. New York: Russell Sage.

Fry, W. R., and Chaney, G. 1981. Perceptions of procedural fairness as a function of distributive fairness. Paper presented at the annual meeting of the Midwestern Psychological Association, Detroit, May.

Fry, W. R., and Leventhal, G. S. 1979. Cross-situational procedural preferences: A comparison of allocation preferences and equity across different social settings. Paper presented at the annual meeting of the Southeastern Psychological Association, Washington, March.

Fuller, L. 1971. Human interaction and the law. In R. P. Wolff, ed., *The rule of law*. New York: Simon and Schuster.

Galegher, J., and Carroll, J. S. 1983. Voluntary sentencing guidelines: Prescription for justice or patent medicine? *Law and Human Behavior* 7: 361–400.

Gamson, W. A. 1968. *Power and discontent*. Homewood, Ill.: Dorsey.

Gerstein, R. 1970. The practice of fidelity to law. *Law and Society Review* 4: 479–493.

Gibbs, J. P. 1975. *Crime, punishment, and deterrence*. New York: Elsevier.

Gibson, H. B. 1967. Self-reported delinquency among schoolboys and their attitudes toward the police. *British Journal of Social and Clinical Psychology* 6: 168–173.

Gold, M. 1970. *Delinquent Behavior in an American city*. Englewood Cliffs, N.J.: Prentice-Hall.

Gottfredson, M. R., and Hindelang, M. J. 1977. A consideration of telescoping and memory decay biases in victimization surveys. *Journal of Criminal Justice* 5: 205–216.

Grasmick, H. G., and Green, D. E. 1980. Legal punishment, social disapproval, and internalization as inhibitors of illegal behavior. *Journal of Criminal Law and Criminology* 71: 325–335.

Greenberg, J. 1986a. Determinants of perceived fairness in performance appraisals. *Social Justice Research* 1: 219–234.

―――. 1986b. Reactions to procedural justice in payment distributions: Do the ends justify the means? *Journal of Applied Psychology* 72: 55–61.

―――. Looking fair vs. being fair. In B. M. Staw and L. L. Cummings, eds., *Research in Organizational Behavior*. Vol. 12. Greenwich, Conn.: JAI. In press.

Greenberg, J., and Folger, R. 1983. Procedural justice, participation, and the fair process effect in groups and organizations. In P. B. Paulus, ed., *Basic group processes*, 235–256. New York: Springer-Verlag.

Greenberg, J., and Tyler, T. R. 1987. Procedural justice in organizational settings. *Social Justice Research* 1: 127–142.

Groves, R. M., and Kahn, R. L. 1979. *Surveys by telephone: A national comparison with personal interviews*. New York: Academic Press.

Groves, R. M., Miller, P. V., and Cannell, C. F. 1981. *A methodological study of telephone and face-to-face interviewing*. Unpublished manuscript. Institute for Social Research, University of Michigan.

Gurr, T. R. 1970. *Why men rebel*. Princeton: Princeton University Press.

Gutek, B. 1978. On the accuracy of retrospective attitudinal data. *Public Opinion Quarterly* 42: 390–401.

Hart, H. L. A. 1961. *The concept of law*. Oxford: Oxford University Press.

Hart, H. M., and Sacks, A. M. 1958. *The legal process*. Unpublished manuscript, Harvard Law School.

Hart, H. M., and Wechsler, H. 1953. *The federal courts and the federal system*. Brooklyn: Foundation Press.

Heider, F. 1958. *The psychology of interpersonal relations*. New York: John Wiley & Sons.

Heinz, A. M. 1985. Procedure versus consequence: Experimental evidence of preferences for procedural and distributive justice. In S. Talarico, ed., *Courts and criminal justice: Emerging issues*. Beverly Hills: Sage.

Helson, H. 1964. *Adaptation-level theory*. New York: Harper and Row.

Hirschi, T., Hindelang, M. J., and Weis, J. G. 1980. The status of self-report measures. In M. W. Klein and K. S. Teilmann, eds., *Handbook of criminal justice evaluation*. Beverly Hills: Sage.

Hoffman, M. 1977. Moral internalization: Current theory and research. In L. Berkowitz, ed., *Advances in experimental social psychology*. Vol. 10. New York: Academic Press.

Hollander, E. 1978. *Leadership dynamics*. New York: Free Press.

————. 1980. Leadership and social exchange processes. In K. J. Gergen, M. S. Greenberg, and R. H. Willis, eds., *Social exchange: Advances in theory and research*. New York: Plenum.

Hollander, E., and Julian, J. W. 1970. Studies in leader legitimacy, influence, and innovation. In L. Berkowitz, ed., *Advances in Experimental Social Psychology*. Vol. 5: 33–70. New York: Academic Press.

Homans, G. 1961. *Social behavior: Its elementary forms*. London: Routledge and Kegan Paul.

Houlden, P. 1980. The impact of procedural modifications on evaluations of plea bargaining. *Law and Society Review* 15: 267–291.

Houlden, P., Latour, S., Walker, L., and Thibaut, J. 1978. Preference for modes of dispute resolution as a function of process and decision control. *Journal of Experimental Social Psychology* 14: 13–30.

House, J. S., and Mason, W. M. 1975. Political alienation in America, 1952–1968. *American Sociological Review* 40: 123–147.

Hyde, A. 1983. The concept of legitimation in the sociology of law. *Wisconsin Law Review*, 1983: 379–426.

Jacob, H. 1969. *Debtors in court: The consumption of government services*. Chicago: Rand McNally.

———. 1971. Black and white perceptions of justice in the city. *Law and Society Review* 6: 69–89.

———. 1980. Deterrent effects on formal and informal sanctions. In J. Brigham and D. W. Brown, eds., *Policy implementation*. Beverly Hills: Sage.

Jaros, D., and Roper, R. 1980. The U.S. Supreme Court: Myth, diffuse support, specific support, and legitimacy. *American Politics Quarterly* 8: 85–104.

Joreskog, K. G., and Sorbom, D. 1986a. *LISREL: Analysis of linear structural relationships by the method of maximum likelihood*. Uppsala, Sweden: University of Uppsala, Department of Statistics.

–––. 1986b. *PRELIS: A preprocessor for LISREL*. Mooresville, Ind.: Scientific Software.

Kahneman, D., Knetsch, J. L., and Thaler, R. 1986. Fairness as a constraint on profit seeking: Entitlements in the market. *American Economic Review* 76: 728–741.

Kanfer, R., Sawyer, J., Earley, P. C., and Lind, E. A. 1987. Fairness and participation in evaluation procedures. *Social Justice Research* 1: 235–249.

Katz, D., Gutek, B., Kahn, R. L., and Barton, E. 1975. *Bureaucratic encounters*. Ann Arbor: University of Michigan, Survey Research Center.

Kelley, H. H., and Thibaut, J. 1978. *Interpersonal relations: A theory of interdependence*. New York: John Wiley & Sons.

Kelling, G., Pate, T., Dieckman, D., and Brown, C. F. 1974. *The Kansas City preventive patrol experiment: A technical report*. Washington: Police Foundation.

Kelman, H. C. 1958. Compliance, identification, and internalization. *Journal of Conflict Resolution* 2: 51–60.

———. 1969. Patterns of personal involvement in the national system: A sociopsychological analysis of political legitimacy. In J. Rosenau, ed., *International politics and foreign policy*. Rev. ed. New York: Free Press.

Kelman, H. C., and Lawrence, L. H. 1972. Assignment of responsibility in the case of Lt. Calley: A preliminary report of a national survey. *Journal of Social Issues* 28: 177–212.

Kinder, D. R., and Sears, D. O. 1985. Public opinion and political action. In G. Lindzey and E. Aronson, eds., *The handbook of social psychology*. 3d ed. Vol. 2. New York: Random House.

Kramer, R. D., and Brewer, M. B. 1984. Effects of group identity on resource use in a simulated commons dilemma. *Journal of Personality and Social Psychology* 46: 1044–1057.

———. 1986. Social group identity and the emergence of cooperation in resource conservation dilemmas. In H. A. M. Wilke and D. M. Messick, eds., *Experimental social dilemmas*. Frankfurt am Main: Berne.

Krislov, S., Boyum, K., Clark, J. N., Schaefer, R. C., and White, S. O. 1972. *Compliance and the law*. Beverly Hills: Sage.

Kulik, J. A., Stein, K. B., and Sarbin, T. R. 1968. Disclosure of delinquent behavior under conditions of anonymity and nonanonymity. *Journal of Consulting and Clinical Psychology* 32: 506–509.

Kurtines, W. M. 1986. Moral behavior as rule governed behavior: Person and situation effects on moral decision making. *Journal of Personality and Social Psychology* 50: 784–791.

Ladinsky, J., and Susmilch, C. 1982. Community factors in the brokerage of consumer produce service problems. Unpublished manuscript, University of Wisconsin, Madison.

Landis, J. M., and Goodstein, L. I. 1986. When is justice fair? An integrated approach to the outcome versus procedure debate. *American Bar Foundation Research Journal*, 675–708.

Lane, R. E. 1988. Procedural goods in a democracy: How one is treated versus what one gets. *Social Justice Research* 2:177–192.

Langer, E. 1983. *The psychology of control*. Beverly Hills: Sage.

Lansing, J. B., Withey, S. B., and Wolfe, A. C. 1971. *Working papers on survey research in poverty areas*. Ann Arbor: University of Michigan, Institute for Social Research.

Laver, M. 1981. *The politics of private desires*. New York: Penguin.

Lawler, E., III. 1977. Satisfaction and behavior. In B. M. Staw, ed., *Psychological foundations of organizational behavior*. Santa Monica: Goodyear.

Lea, S. E. G. 1978. The psychology and economics of demand. *Psychological Bulletin* 85: 441–466.

Lehnen, R. G., and Skogan, W. G. 1981. *The national crime survey: Working papers*. Vol. 1. Washington: U.S. Department of Justice.

Lempert, R., and Sanders, J. 1986. *An invitation to law and social science*. New York: Longman.

Lerner, M. J. 1971. Justified self-interest and the responsibility for suffering. *Journal of Human Relations* 19: 550–559.

————. 1977. The justice motive: Some hypotheses as to its origins and forms. *Journal of Personality* 45: 1–52.

Leventhal, G. S. 1976. Fairness in social relationships. In J. Thibaut, J. T. Spense, and R. C. Carson, eds., *Contemporary topics in social psychology*. Morristown, N.J.: General Learning Press.

————. 1980. What should be done with equity theory? In K. J. Gergen, M. S. Greenberg, and R. H. Weiss, eds., *Social exchange: Advances in theory and research*, 27–55. New York: Plenum.

Levy, S. G. 1981. Political violence: A critical evaluation. In S. Long, ed., *The handbook of political behavior*. Vol. 2. New York: Plenum.

Lind, E. A. 1982. The psychology of courtroom procedure. In N. L. Kerr and R. M. Bray, eds., *The psychology of the courtroom*. New York: Academic Press.

Lind, E. A., Kurtz, S., Musante, L., Walker, L., and Thibaut, J. 1980. Procedure and outcome effects on reactions to adjudicated resolutions of conflicts of interest. *Journal of Personality and Social Psychology* 39: 643–653.

Lind, E. A., Lissak, R. E., and Conlon, A. E. 1983. Decision control and process control effects on procedural fairness judgments. *Journal of Applied Social Psychology* 4: 338–350.

Lind, E. A., and Tyler, T. R. 1988. *The social psychology of procedural justice*. New York: Plenum.

Lipset, S. M., and Schneider, W. 1983. *The confidence gap: Business, labor, and government in the public mind*. New York: Free Press.

Lissak, R. I., and Sheppard, B. H. 1983. Beyond fairness: The criterion problem in research on dispute resolution. *Basic and Applied Social Psychology* 13: 45–65.

McClosky, H., and Brill, A. 1983. *Dimensions of tolerance: What Americans believe about civil liberties*. New York: Russell Sage.

MacCoun, R. J., and Tyler, T. R. 1988. The basis of citizens' preferences for different forms of criminal jury. *Law and Human Behavior*, 12: 333–352.

McEwen, C., and Maiman, R. 1984. Mediation in small claims court: Achieving compliance through consent. *Law and Society Review* 18: 11–49.

———.1986. In search of legitimacy. *Law and Policy* 8: 257–274.

McPhail, C. 1971. Civil disorder participation: A critical examination of recent research. *American Sociological Review* 36: 1058–1073.

Martin, J. 1981. Relative deprivation: A theory of distributive justice for an era of shrinking resources. In L. L. Cummings and B. M. Staw, eds., *Research in organizational behavior*, Vol. 3. Greenwich, Conn.: JAI.

Martin, J., Scully, M., and Levitt, B. 1986. *Revolutionary visions of injustice: Damning the past, excusing the present, and neglecting the future*. Working paper 919, Graduate School of Business, Stanford University.

Mashaw, J. L. 1981. *Due process in the administrative state*. New Haven and London: Yale University Press.

Meier, R. F., and Johnson, W. T. 1977. Deterrence as social control: The legal and extralegal production of conformity. *American Sociological Review* 42: 292–304.

Merry, S. E. 1985. Concepts of law and justice among working-class Americans: Ideology as culture. *Legal Studies Forum* 9: 59–69.

———. 1986. Everyday understandings of law in working-class America. *American Ethnologist* 13: 253–270.

Merry, S. E., and Silbey, S. 1984. What do plaintiffs want? Reexamining the concept of dispute. *Justice System Journal* 9: 151–178.

Messick, D., and Brewer, M. 1983. Solving social dilemmas. In L. Wheeler and P. Shaver, eds., *Review of personality and social psychology*. Vol. 4. Beverly Hills: Sage.

Messick, D. M., Wilke, H., Brewer, M. B., Kramer, R. M., Zemke, P. E., and Lui, L. 1983. Individual adaptations and structural change as solutions to social dilemmas. *Journal of Personality and Social Psychology* 44: 294–309.

Michener, H. A., and Lawler, E., III. 1975. Endorsement of formal leaders: An integrative model. *Journal of Personality and Social Psychology* 31: 216–223.

Milgram, S. 1974. *Obedience to Authority*. New York: Harper and Row.

Miller, A. 1974. Political issues and trust in government: 1964–1970. *American Political Science Review* 68: 951–972.

————. 1979. The institutional focus of political distrust. Paper presented at the annual meeting of the American Political Science Association, Washington, September.

————. 1983. Is confidence rebounding? *Public opinion* 6: 16–20.

Miller, D. T. 1977. Personal deserving versus justice for others. *Journal of Experimental Social Psychology* 13: 1–13.

Moore, B. 1978. *Injustice: The social bases of obedience and revolt*. White Plains, N.Y.: Sharpe.

Morrissey v. *Brewer* 408 U.S. 471 (1972).

Mueller, D. 1979. *Public choice*. New York: Cambridge University Press.

Mueller, E. N. 1970a. Correlates and consequences of belief in the legitimacy of regime structures. *Midwest Journal of Political Science* 14: 392–412.

————. 1970b. The representation of citizens by political authorities: Consequences for regime support. *American Political Science Review* 64: 1149–1166.

————. 1972. A test of a partial theory of potential for political violence. *American Political Science Review* 66: 928–959.

————. 1977. Behavioral correlates of political support. *American Political Science Review* 71: 454–467.

————. 1979. *Aggressive political participation*. Princeton: Princeton University Press.

————. 1980. The psychology of political protest and violence. In T. R. Gurr, ed., *Handbook of political conflict*. New York: Free Press.

Muller, E. N., and Jukam, T. O. 1977. On the meaning of political support. *American Political Science Review* 71: 1561–1595.

Muller, E. N., Jukam, T. O., and Seligson, M. 1982. Diffuse political support and anti-system political behavior: A comparative analysis. *American Journal of Political Science* 26: 240–264.

Murphy, W. F., and Tanenhaus, J. 1969. Public opinion and the United States Supreme Court: A preliminary mapping of some prerequisites for court legitimization of regime changes. In J. B. Grossman and J. Tanenhaus, eds., *Frontiers in judicial research*. New York: John Wiley & Sons.

O'Barr, W. 1988. The ethnography of storytelling: An anthropological perspective on accounts in legal contexts. Paper presented at the annual meeting of the Law and Society Association, Vail, Colo., June.

O'Barr, W., and Conley, J. M. 1985. Litigant satisfaction versus legal adequacy in small claims court narratives. *Law and Society Review* 19: 661–702.

Okun, A. M. 1975. *Equality and efficiency: The big tradeoff*. Washington: Brookings Institution.

Olsen, M. E. 1968. Perceived legitimacy of social protest actions. *Social Problems* 15: 297–310.

Ophuls, W. 1977. *Ecology and the politics of scarcity*. San Francisco: Free Press.

Opotow, S. 1987. Modifying the scope of justice: An experimental examination. Paper presented at meeting of the American Psychological Association, New York, August.

Orbell, J. M., van de Kragt, A. J. C., and Dawes, R. M. 1988. Explaining discussion-induced cooperation. *Journal of Personality and Social Psychology* 54: 811–819.

Paige, J. M. 1971. Political orientation and riot participation. *American Sociological Review* 36: 810–820.

Parks, R. B. 1976. Police responses to victimization: Effects on citizen attitudes and perceptions. In W. G. Skogan, ed., *Sample surveys of the victims of crime*. Cambridge, Mass.: Ballinger.

Parsons, T. 1963. On the concept of influence. *Public Opinion Quarterly* 27: 63–82.

———. 1967. Some reflections on the place of force in social process. In T. Parsons, ed., *Sociological theory and modern society*. New York: Free Press.

Paternoster, R., Saltzman, L. E., Waldo, G. P., and Chiricos, T. G. 1984. Perceived risk and social control: Do sanctions really deter? *Law and Society Review* 17: 457–479.

Polk, K., and Ruby, C. H. 1978. *Respondent loss in the longitudinal study of deviant behavior*. San Francisco: National Council on Crime and Delinquency.

Pruitt, D. 1981. *Negotiation behavior*. New York: Academic Press.

Quinn, R. P., Gutek, B. A., and Walsh, J. T. 1980. Telephone interviewing: A reappraisal and a field experiment. *Basic and Applied Social Psychology* 1: 127–154.

Rasinski, K. A. 1987. What's fair is fair—or is it? Value differences underlying public views about social justice. *Journal of Personality and Social Psychology* 53: 201–211.

Rasinski, K. A., and Tyler, T. R. 1986. Social psychology and political behavior. In S. Long, ed., *Political behavior annual* 1: 103–128. Boulder: Westview.

———. 1987. Fairness and vote choice in the 1986 presidential election. *American Politics Quarterly* 16: 5–24.

Rasinski, K. A., Tyler, T. R., and Fridkin, K. 1985. Legitimacy and leadership endorsement. *Journal of Personality and Social Psychology* 49: 386–394.

Rawls, J. 1971. *A theory of justice*. Cambridge: Harvard University Press.

Reis, H. 1986. Levels of interest in the study of interpersonal justice. In H. W. Bierhoff, R. L. Cohen, and J. Greenberg, eds., *Justice in social relations*. New York: Plenum.

Reiss, A. J., Jr. 1978. Analytical studies of victimization by crime using the national crime survey panel. Washington: Law Enforcement Assistance Administration.

Rodgers, H. R., and Lewis, E. 1974. Political support and compliance attitudes. *American Politics Quarterly* 2: 61–77.

Rogers, T. F. 1976. Interviews by telephone and in person: Quality of responses and field performance. *Public Opinion Quarterly* 40: 51–65.

Rosenberg, M. 1979. *Conceiving the self*. New York: Basic Books.

Ross, H. L. 1981. *Deterring the drinking driver*. Lexington, Mass.: Lexington Books.

Samuelson, C. D., Messick, D. M., Rutte, C. D., and Wilke, H. 1984. Individual and structural solutions to resource dilemmas in two cultures. *Journal of Personality and Social Psychology* 47: 94–104.

Sanders, J., and Hamilton, L. 1987. Is there a "common law" of responsibility? *Law and Human Behavior* 11: 277–297.

Saphire, R. B. 1978. Specifying due process values. *University of Pennsylvania Law Review* 127: 111–195.

Sarat, A. 1975. Support for the legal system. *American Politics Quarterly* 3: 3–24.

————. 1977. Studying American legal culture: An assessment of survey evidence. *Law and Society Review* 11: 427–488.

Scheingold, S. A. 1974. *The politics of rights*. New Haven and London: Yale University Press.

Schneider, A. L. 1977. *The Portland forward records check of crime victims*. Washington: Law Enforcement Assistance Administration.

Schwartz, D. C. 1973. *Political alienation and political behavior*. Chicago: Aldine.

Schwartz, R. D. 1978. Moral order and sociology of law: Trends, problems, and prospects. *Annual Review of Sociology* 4: 577–601.

Schwartz, R. D., and Orleans, S. 1967. On legal sanctions. *University of Chicago Law Review* 34: 274–300.

Sears, D. O. 1983. The persistence of early political predispositions. In L. Wheeler and P. Shaver, eds., *Review of personality and social psychology*, Vol. 4. Beverly Hills: Sage.

Sears, D. O., Lau, R. R., Tyler, T. R., and Allen, H. M., Jr. 1980. Self-interest and symbolic politics in policy attitudes and Presidential voting. *American Political Science Review* 74: 670–684.

Sears, D. O., Tyler, T. R., Citrin, J., and Kinder, D. R. 1978. Political system support and public response to the energy crisis. *American Journal of Political Science* 22: 56–82.

Seligson, M. A. 1980. Trust, efficacy, and modes of political participation: A study of Costa Rican peasants. *British Journal of Political Science* 10: 75–98.

Shapiro, M. J. 1969. Rational political man: A synthesis of economic and social psychological perspectives. *American Political Science Review* 63: 1106–1119.

Shaver, P. 1980. The public distrust. *Psychology Today*, October.

Sheppard, B. H., and Lewicki, R. J. 1987. Toward general principles of managerial fairness. *Social Justice Research* 1: 161–176.

Sheppard, B. H., Saunders, D., and Minton, J. 1988. Procedural justice from the third-party perspective. *Journal of Personality and Social Psychology* 54: 629–637.

Silberman, M. 1976. Toward a theory of criminal deterrence. *American Sociological Review* 41: 442–461.

Skogan, W. G. 1975. Public policy and public evaluations of criminal justice system performance. In J. A. Gardiner and M. A. Mulkey, eds., *Crime and criminal justice: Issues in public policy analysis*. Lexington, Mass.: Lexington Books.

————. 1978. *The Center for Urban Affairs random digit dialing telephone survey*. Evanston, Ill.: Northwestern University.

Sullivan, J. L., Piereson, J., and Marcus, G. 1982. *Political tolerance and American democracy*. Chicago: University of Chicago Press.

Tajfel, H. 1981. *Human groups and social categories*. Cambridge: Cambridge University Press.

Tapp, J. L., and Kohlberg, L. 1977. Developing senses of law and legal justice. In J. L. Tapp and F. J. Levine, eds., *Law, justice and the individual in society*. New York: Holt, Rinehart, and Winston.

Thibaut, J., and Kelley, H. H. 1959. *The social psychology of groups*. New York: John Wiley & Sons.

Thibaut, J., and Faucheux, C. 1965. The development of contractual norms in a bargaining situation under two types of stress. *Journal of Experimental Social Psychology* 1: 89–102.

Thibaut, J., and Walker, L. 1975. *Procedural justice: A psychological analysis*. Hillsdale, N.J.: Erlbaum.

———. 1978. A theory of procedure. *California Law Review* 66: 541–566.

Tittle, C. R. 1980. *Sanction and social deviance: A question of deterrence*. New York: Praeger.

Troldahl, V. C., and Carter, R. E., Jr. 1964. Random selection of respondents within households in phone surveys. *Journal of Marketing Research* 1: 71–76.

Tuchfarber, A. J., and Klecka, W. R. 1976. *Random digit dialing: Lowering the cost of victimization surveys*. Washington: Police Foundation.

Tyler, T. R. 1984. The role of perceived injustice in defendant's evaluations of their courtroom experience. *Law and Society Review* 18: 51–74.

———. 1986a. When does procedural justice matter in organizational settings? In R. J. Lewicki, B. H. Sheppard, and M. Bazerman, eds., *Research on negotiation in organizations*. Vol. 1, pp. 7–23. Greenwich, Conn.: JAI.

———. 1986b. Justice and leadership endorsement. In R. R. Lau and D. O. Sears, eds., *Political cognition*, 257–278. Hillsdale, N.J.: Erlbaum.

———. 1986c. The psychology of leadership evaluation. In H. Bierhoff, J. Greenberg, and R. Cohen, eds., *Justice in intergroup relations*. New York: Plenum.

———. 1987a. Conditions leading to value-expressive effects in judgments of procedural justice: A test of four models. *Journal of Personality and Social Psychology* 52: 333–344.

———. 1987b. The psychology of dispute resolution: Implications for the mediation of disputes by third parties. *Negotiation Journal* 3: 367–374.

———. 1987c. Procedural justice: Future directions. *Social Justice Research* 1: 41–65.

———. 1987d. *Public views about the criminal justice system*. Washington: National Academy of Sciences.

———. 1988a. What is procedural justice? Criteria used by citizens to assess the fairness of legal procedures. *Law and Society Review* 22: 301–355.

———. 1989. The quality of dispute resolution processes and outcomes: Measurement problems and possibilities. *Denver University Law Review* 66: 419–436.

Tyler, T. R., and Bies, R. Interpersonal aspects of procedural justice. In J. S. Carroll, ed., *Advances in applied social psychology: Business settings*. In press.

Tyler, T. R., and Caine, A. 1981. The influence of outcomes and procedures on satisfaction with formal leaders. *Journal of Personality and Social Psychology* 41: 642–655.

Tyler, T. R., Casper, J. D., and Fisher, B. 1989. Maintaining allegiance toward political authorities: The role of prior attitudes and the use of fair procedures. *American Journal of Political Science* 33: 612–628.

Tyler, T. R., and Cook, F. L. 1984. The mass media and judgments of risk: Distinguishing impact on personal and societal level judgments. *Journal of Personality and Social Psychology* 47: 693–708.

Tyler, T. R., and Folger, R. 1980. Distributional and procedural aspects of satisfaction with citizen-police encounters. *Basic and Applied Social Psychology* 1: 281–292.

Tyler, T. R., and Lavrakas, P. 1986. Mass media effects: Distinguishing impact on personal and societal level judgments. In R. Perloff and S. Krauss, eds., *Mass communication effects and political information processing*, 141–156. Beverly Hills: Sage.

Tyler, T. R., and Lind, E. A. 1986. Procedural processes and legal institutions. Paper delivered at the International Conference on Social Justice in Human Relations, Leiden, Netherlands, July.

Tyler, T. R., and McGraw, K. 1986. Ideology and the interpretation of personal experience: Procedural justice and political quiescence. *Journal of Social Issues* 42: 115–128.

Tyler, T. R., Rasinski, K., and Griffin, E. 1986. Alternative images of the citizen: Implications for public policy. *American Psychologist* 41: 970–978.

Tyler, T. R., Rasinski, K., and McGraw, K. 1985. The influence of perceived injustice on the endorsement of political leaders. *Journal of Applied Social Psychology* 15: 700–725.

Tyler, T. R., Rasinski, K., and Spodick, N. 1985. The influence of voice on satisfaction with leaders: Exploring the meaning of process control. *Journal of Personality and Social Psychology* 48: 72–81.

Useem, B. 1982. Trust in government and the Boston anti-busing movement. *Western Politics Quarterly* 35: 81–91.

Useem, B., and Useem, M. 1979. Government legitimacy and political stability. *Social Forces* 57: 840–852.

Von Neumann, J., and Morgenstern, O. 1947. *Theory of games and economic behavior*. 2d ed. Princeton: Princeton University Press.

Wahlke, J. 1971. Policy demands and system support: The role of the represented. *British Journal of Political Science* 1: 271–290.

Walker, D., Richardson, R. J., Williams, O., Denyer, T., and McGaughey, S. 1972. Contact and support: An empirical assessment of public attitudes toward the police and the courts. *North Carolina Law Review* 51: 43–79.

Walker, L., and Lind, E. A. 1984. Psychological studies of procedural models. In G. M. Stephenson and J. H. Davis, eds., *Progress in applied social psychology*, Vol. 2. New York: John Wiley & Sons.

Walster, E., Walster, G., and Berscheid, E. 1978. *Equity: Theory and research*. Boston: Allyn and Bacon.

Wasby, S. 1970. *The impact of the United States Supreme Court*. Homewood, Ill.: Dorsey.

Weber, M. 1947. *The theory of social and economic organization*, trans. A. M. Henderson and T. Parsons. New York: Free Press.

Wechsler, H. 1959. Toward neutral principles of constitutional law. *Harvard Law Review* 73: 1–35.

Westbrook, S. D. 1980. Sociopolitical alienation and military efficiency. *Armed Forces and Society* 6: 170–189.

Wish, M., Deutsch, M., and Kaplan, S. J. 1976. Perceived dimensions of interpersonal relations. *Journal of Personality and Social Psychology* 33: 409–420.

Wish, M., and Kaplan, S. J. 1977. Toward an implicit theory of interpersonal communication. *Sociometry* 40: 234–246.

Wood, A. L. 1974. *Deviant behavior and control strategies*. Lexington, Mass.: Lexington Books.

Worchel, P., Hester, P. G., and Kopala, P. S. 1974. Collective protest and legitimacy of authority. *Journal of Conflict Resolution* 18: 37–54.

Wright, J. D. 1976. *The dissent of the governed: Alienation and democracy in America*. New York: Academic Press.

———. 1981. Political disaffection. In S. Long, ed., *Handbook of political behavior*. New York: Plenum.

Wrong, D. 1980. *Power: Its forms, bases and uses*. New York: Harper and Row.

Zimring, F. E., and Hawkins, G. J. 1973. *Deterrence: The legal threat in crime control*. Chicago: University of Chicago Press.

Index

Adaptation level theory, 72

Affective attachments, and diffuse support, 177

Authorities: effect of experience on evaluations of, 5, 50–56, 72, 80–81, 86–87, 94, 140; public support of, 26–27; perspective on morality of, 26–27; personal morality of, 66; fairness of, 138–40, 149; instrumental perspective on fairness of, 138–39; Leventhal's criteria of ethicality and, 138–39, 152; effect of prior views on evaluations of, 143–46; motivations of, 151–52; self-esteem and, 152–53; consistency of, 153–54; abuses by, 155; norms and, 165–66; citizens' interactions with, 175

Bargainer's dilemma, 170–71

Behavior, instrumental perspective on, 20–21

Bias, 119

Calls to police, in study sample, 87–88

Chicago study: design of, 6, 8–15; characteristics of sample, 12–15; other studies versus, 85–86

Compliance: normative perspective on, 3–4, 21–22, 24–25, 161; effect of morality on, 4, 44–45; political psychology perspective on, 8; sociological perspective on, 8; local government and, 9–10; public choice perspective on, 21–22, 71–72; legitimacy and, 30–32, 38–39, 58–64, 170–72; specific versus general levels of, 30–31; normative concerns about, 36–39, 57, 64–65; self-reporting of, 40–41; demographic correlates of, 42; deterrence and, 42–44, 64–65; social factors and, 42–45; peer disapproval and, 44; effect of quality of service on, 50–56; effect of experience on, 63–64, 87, 102–04, 105, 108; procedural justice and, 82–83; distributive justice perspective on, 103–04, 108; theories of, 161

Consistency: Leventhal's theory of procedural justice and, 118–19, 135; of authorities, 153–54

Control theory: instrumental perspective on, 6–7, 116, 125, 146–48; procedural justice and, 115, 126–30, 137–38; in Chicago study, 125–26; value-expression in, 125, 133–34; perspective on experience of, 126; results of Chicago study and, 133–34. *See also* Procedural justice; Process control

Courts, 72, 89, 109–10; procedural justice and, 142

Decision control, 116–17, 147

Decision making, 117–18, 128–29, 175

Deterrence: instrumental perspective on, 3; drunk driving and, 22–23; attitudes on, 42–44; compliance and, 42–44, 64–65; normative commitment and, 64–65

Diffuse support, 176–77

Disputes, 122, 142–43

Distributive justice, 5–6; in psychology, 73; procedural justice versus, 78–80; perspective on compliance of, 103–04, 108; trade-offs and, 120–21

Drunk driving, 22–23

Economic perspective on compliance, 22

Ethical attitudes, two-stage model of, 6